This collection of essays examines the relations between European and Islamic thought and culture from the late eighteenth to the twentieth century. The long first essay is concerned with the development of ideas about Islam in European thought and scholarship, showing in particular how the views of nineteenth-century thinkers and scholars reflected the dominant philosophical and historical ideas of their age. Subsequent chapters are devoted to individual writers who played an important part in forming and communicating an image of Islamic history and civilization: Louis Massignon, H. A. R. Gibb, Marshall Hodgson and Jacques Berque, together with the scholar–soldier T. E. Lawrence. The final three essays look at the subject from the other side, and deal with some of the reactions of the Islamic world to the powerful new ideas of European civilization, including the first modern Arabic encyclopaedia and the first translation of Homer.

ISLAM IN EUROPEAN THOUGHT

ISLAM IN
EUROPEAN THOUGHT

ALBERT HOURANI

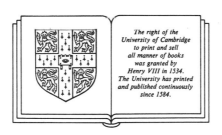

The right of the
University of Cambridge
to print and sell
all manner of books
was granted by
Henry VIII in 1534.
The University has printed
and published continuously
since 1584.

CAMBRIDGE UNIVERSITY PRESS

CAMBRIDGE

NEW YORK   PORT CHESTER   MELBOURNE   SYDNEY

Published by the Press Syndicate of the University of Cambridge
The Pitt Building, Trumpington Street, Cambridge CB2 1RP
40 West 20th Street, New York, NY 10011, USA
10 Stamford Road, Oakleigh, Melbourne 3166, Australia

First Published 1991

**Printed in Great Britain at the
University Press, Cambridge**

British Library cataloguing in publication data
Hourani, Albert 1915–
Islam in European thought and other essays.
1. Europe. Cultural relations with Islamic countries,
history 2. Islamic countries. Cultural relations with
Europe, history
I. Title
303.4824017671

Library of Congress cataloguing in publication data
Hourani, Albert Habib.
Islam in European thought and other essays/Albert Hourani.
p.   cm.
Includes bibliographical references and index.
ISBN   0521–39213–6
1. Middle East – Study and teaching – Europe – History. 2. Middle
East – Relations – Europe. 3. Europe – Relations – Middle East.
4. Europe – Intellectual life – Miscellanea. I. Title.
DS61.9.E85H68   1991
303.4′825604–dc20   90–37704   CIP

ISBN 0 521 39213 6 hardback

To André Raymond
in friendship and admiration

CONTENTS

⸎

ACKNOWLEDGEMENTS

THESE essays were written at different times and for various purposes. There is, therefore, inevitably some overlap between them, and there may be some inconsistencies, since my ideas may have changed between writing one and another of them; I have not tried to remove these. I have been tempted to try to bring them up to date, in particular where stated or implied predictions have proved to be unfounded, or when I have changed my mind about certain statements. I have resisted the temptation, although sometimes I have corrected small errors and added references to relevant books or articles published since an essay was written.

'Islam in European thought' is based on lectures given first as the F. D. Maurice Lectures at King's College, London, in 1986, and then in another form as the Tanner Lectures at Clare Hall in 1989. The lectures were published in *Tanner Lectures on Human Values*, vol. XI. (University of Utah Press, Salt Lake City, Utah, 1990), pp. 223–87. 'Wednesday afternoons remembered' was published in *Fi sirat Jamal* (University of Khartoum Press, 1988), pp. 127–40. 'Marshall Hodgson and the venture of Islam' was published in the *Journal of Near Eastern Studies*, 37, i (January 1978), pp. 53–62. 'Islamic History, Middle Eastern history, modern history' was delivered as a lecture at the seventh Giorgio Levi Della Vida Conference at the University of California, Los Angeles, in 1979, and published in M. Kerr, ed., *Islamic Studies: A Tradition and its Problems* (Undena Publications, Malibu, Calif. 1980), pp. 5–26. 'T. E. Lawrence and Louis Massignon' was published in the *Times Literary Supplement* (8 July 1983), pp. 733–4. 'In search of a new Andalusia: Jacques Berque and the Arabs' was published in C. Hourani, ed., *The Arab Cultural Scene: Literary Review Supplement* (Namara Press, London, 1982), pp. 7–11. 'Culture and change: the Middle East in the eighteenth century' was published as the introduction to part 3 of T. Naff and R. Owen, eds., *Studies in Eighteenth Century Islamic History* (Southern Illinois University Press, Carbondale, Ill. 1977), pp. 253–76 and 397–9. 'Bustani's encyclopaedia' was published in the *Journal of Islamic Studies*, 1 (1990), pp. 111–19, and in French translation as 'L'encyclopédie de Bustani' in *Rivages et déserts: hommage à Jacques Berque* (Sindbad, Paris, 1989), pp. 197–208. 'Sulaiman al-Bustani and the *Iliad*' is to be published by the American University of Beirut Press in a volume of essays in memory of Malcolm Kerr.

I am grateful to the owners of the copyright of the various essays for giving me permission to publish them in this book: The Tanner Lectures, the University of Khartoum Press, the University of Chicago Press, the Regents of the University of California, *The Times Literary Supplement*, Namara Press, Southern Illinois University Press, *The Journal of Islamic Studies* and the American University of Beirut Press.

I must also thank the Department of the History and Philosophy of Religion of King's College, London, for inviting me to give the F. D. Maurice Lectures; the President and Fellows of Clare Hall, Cambridge, for inviting me to give the Tanner Lectures; and the Gustave E. von Grunebaum Center for Near Eastern Studies at the University of California, Los Angeles, and the then Director of the Center, the late Malcolm Kerr, for inviting me to the Levi Della Vida Conference and awarding me the Giorgio Levi Della Vida Medal. I am most grateful, too, to friends and colleagues who provided information, corrections and ideas for one or other of the essays: Kevin Reinhart for some important comments on the first essay and David Abulafia for giving valuable information for it; Kenneth Brown for allowing me to use his translation of a passage from one of Jacques Berque's works; and Butrus Abu Manneh for valuable criticism and corrections of the essays on the two Bustanis.

I should also like to thank Gail Vernazza, who typed the first essay, and Elizabeth Bullock, who typed most of the others with unfailing care and accuracy; Joanne S. Ainsworth, for her skilful editing of The Tanner Lectures; and Katharina Brett who arranged for the publication of the book by the Cambridge University Press. I am most grateful to Margaret Jean Acland who copy-edited the book in the most careful and accurate way, and saved me from innumerable errors and inconsistencies, and to Barbara Hird, who compiled the index so professionally.

INTRODUCTION

THESE essays reflect an interest of long standing in the ways in which intellectual traditions grow: the process by which ideas accumulate and are handed on from one generation to another, changing, developing and acquiring authority as they do so. My years as a teacher of Middle Eastern history at Oxford have given me a special concern with two examples of this process. One of them is the formation in Europe of a certain view of Islam and the culture associated with it: a view derived from an increasing knowledge of what Muslims believe and what they have done in history, and also from changing ideas in Europe about religion and history. The second concern is with the development of the scholarly tradition known loosely as 'orientalism': the elaboration of techniques for identifying, editing and interpreting written texts, and the transmission of them from one generation to another, by a chain – a *silsila*, to give it its Arabic term – of teachers and students.

These two processes have been closely connected with each other: scholars do not work in abstraction, their minds are formed by the culture of their age and previous ages, and they bring to the task of interpreting what they have extracted from their sources principles of selection, emphasis and arrangement derived from the ideas and convictions their lives have taught them.

The first and longest essay in this book attempts to trace the relationship between these two processes: to show the roots of the European tradition of Islamic studies in ideas about God, man, history and society which lie at the heart of European thought. In particular, it tries to show how the study of Islam, when it emerged as a separate discipline in the nineteenth century, was given its direction by certain ideas which were current at the time: ideas about cultural history, the nature and development of religions, the ways in which holy books should be understood and the relationships between languages. I have tried to trace the two most important chains of Islamic scholarship, those which began in Paris and Leiden in the seventeenth century. By the second half of the nineteenth century Islamic scholarship had developed an organization – methods of teaching, publication and communication – and acquired a self-perpetuating authority which has continued to exist until today.

I have paid special attention to Ignaz Goldziher, because he seems to me to have a central position in the history I am tracing: he was heir to both the great *silsilas*, with a mind moulded by the dominant ideas of his age (and also by his own Jewish tradition). Two of Goldziher's writings in particular, that on the origins and growth of the Hadith (The Traditions of the Prophet) and that on the development of Islamic theology and law, have created a kind of orthodoxy which has retained its power until our own time.

I do not myself belong to any of the great *silsilas*. I came to Middle Eastern history by another route, and I taught it at a university which has been rather marginal in the history of Islamic studies on the whole, even though the teaching of Arabic in Oxford goes back to the seventeenth century. I was fortunate, however, to have colleagues trained in the central tradition – among those who have died, I think of H. A. R. Gibb, Richard Walzer, Samuel Stern, Joseph Schacht and Robin Zaehner – and I was at Oxford at a time when attempts were being made to give new strength to 'oriental studies' in Britain, with financial help from the government. The most important figure in this process was H. A. R. Gibb, for as long as he remained in Oxford as Laudian Professor of Arabic. I have written about him at greater length elsewhere,[1] and in the second essay I try to place him in the context of the growth of Islamic studies in Britain. (This essay is also a tribute to one of the first of my graduate students, Jamal Muhammad Ahmed, a gifted writer, and for a time Minister of Foreign Affairs in the Sudan.)

Like all the 'orientalists' of his generation, Gibb was called upon to teach over too wide a range: language, literature and history. He thought of himself as being first of all a historian, and one of the problems of his life in Oxford was that of trying to persuade historians to pay more attention to the history of regions

---

[1] 'H. A. R. Gibb: the vocation of an orientalist' in *Europe and the Middle East* (London, 1980), pp. 104–34.

lying beyond Europe, and to give it what he thought should be its rightful place in the curriculum of study. Among the reasons for which he finally left Oxford for Harvard was his belief (a well-founded one) that history departments in America would be more receptive to the idea of world history, and that students of good quality whose minds had been formed as historians could be persuaded to devote themselves to the study of the world of Islam.

As a historian, Gibb was concerned both to use the sources in order to discover what had happened in Islamic history (as in his studies of the life of Saladin), and to give a broad interpretation of the development of those societies in which Islam was the dominant religion; his essay, 'An interpretation of Islamic history',[2] is a seminal work. An American historian, who was not Gibb's student but felt the influence of his ideas, was Marshall Hodgson, whose book *The Venture of Islam* is the subject of my third essay. Every word in the title and subtitle is significant, carefully chosen and deserving of reflection: 'venture', 'Islam', 'conscience', 'history' and 'world society'. I wrote this essay as a review when the book first appeared, and greeted it with enthusiasm as the most important and original attempt to provide the categories through which Islamic history can be understood within the context of the history of the whole Oikoumene, that is to say, the world of settled agriculture, cities and high culture. I still find it a remarkable and exciting book, and should now add to it another work of broad synthesis, the work of one of Gibb's students in his Harvard period: Ira Lapidus's *History of Islamic Societies.*[3]

It is an underlying assumption of Hodgson's book, and also of Lapidus's, that, within the general history of the Oikoumene, there is such a thing as 'Islamic history': that is to say, there are certain characteristics of structure and development which have been common to societies where Islam has been the dominant religion. Gibb shared this assumption, although none of them would have thought that 'Islam' provided the key to everything which happened in 'Islamic' societies, still less that the history of these societies consists of recurrent cycles of similar phenomena. All three are fully aware that the history of any 'Islamic' society, in a specific time and place, is different from those of others. My

[2] S. J. Shaw and W. R. Polk, eds., *Studies on the Civilization of Islam* (London, 1962), pp. 3-33.
[3] (Cambridge, 1988).

own interest as a historian has lain mainly in those countries which lie around the eastern end of the Mediterranean and which can be called, in a loose sense, the Near or Middle East, and mainly in the last two centuries. It has been a matter of concern to to me to decide whether, and to what extent, the fact that Islam is the dominant religion of Egypt, Syria or Turkey will help us to understand its history in modern times. I had the opportunity to discuss this question at a conference held at the University of California in Los Angeles in 1979, and the result is the fourth essay; in it I put forward three alternative (or overlapping) principles of explanation, and come to the conclusion that the concept of 'Islamic history' does help us to explain certain aspects of modern Middle Eastern history. There is a clear hint in the conclusion to the essay that I suspected this to be no longer true of the period which began roughly at the end of the First World War: no more than other observers did I anticipate that the 1980s would be a period of what is loosely called 'the resurgence of Islam'.

In this essay and others, however, I show that I was aware of the ground from which the 'resurgence of Islam' would come: the changing consciousness of the 'Other', of that Arabic-speaking, mainly Muslim world, about which European scholars and historians, and I myself among them, have written. There had been a time when it could be treated as a passive body to be dissected, but travel, the experience of imperial rule, and the revolt against it, and the revival of indigenous traditions of thought and writing have made it impossible to think of the 'Orient' in this way. Scholarship is now carried on by some kind of collaboration between those trained in the western tradition and those who, in addition to that training, bring something from their own tradition of Islamic thought and belief. Nobody can now write with meaning about the world of Islam if he does not bring to it some sense of a living relationship with those of whom he writes. The fifth essay considers two men, different in many ways but similar in others, whose lives touched each other for a brief moment, and whose writings are marked by a vivid sense of the need to stretch out across the gulf created by power, enmity, and difference. The idea of being in a false position haunts T. E. Lawrence's *Seven Pillars of Wisdom*: when he asks leave to go away after the occupation of Damascus, it is because 'only for me was the event sorrowful and the phrase meaningless'.[4] Louis Massignon too repudiated 'our secular rage to understand, to conquer, to possess'.

The lives and personalities of Lawrence and Massignon have perplexed me for years. *Seven Pillars of Wisdom*, read when it was first published for general circulation in 1935, moved me deeply and was perhaps one of those half-recognized forces which gave direction to my own work as a historian; later, for thirteen years I was to look out of my bedroom window onto the bungalow in the garden of his parents' house in Polstead Road where he had lived when young. Massignon I met sometimes, and the memory of his face and conversation has remained in my imagination. I learnt much about him from friends and colleagues, and here too the spirit of place was important; I have had vivid thoughts of him whenever I have gone to the Greek Catholic church in Garden City, Cairo, restored by the care of his friend Mary Kahil. His thoughts about Islam and its relations with Christianity have provided themes for more than one of these essays.

Massignon's work had a profound influence on French scholars of his own and the next generations, and this can be seen in the writings of Jacques Berque, although the system of thought which underlies them is very different. My essay on Berque is both a tribute to a long friendship and an expression of gratitude for what I have learnt from him. Berque's books bear the imprint of the long experience of French rule and settlement in North Africa. Brought up in Algeria, imbibing the Arabic language along with his native French from an early age, with many years of residence and visits as an official and a scholar, Berque has taught us to distinguish the different rhythms of history: that which foreign rulers have tried to impose upon the Arab Muslim countries they have ruled, and that which those peoples have produced from within themselves. The title of one of his books, *Intérieurs du Maghreb*, indicates the dominant intention of his work: he looks beyond the rulers, and beyond the coastal cities of mixed population, to the towns and villages of the inland plateaux and valleys. His writings are also the expression of an act of faith: that, in spite of all that has happened, a human mutation has taken place; a synthesis of Latin and Arabic culture, of the traditions of the two sides of the Mediterranean, has come into existence and will continue to exist.

I have added to these essays three more which look at the

[4] *Seven Pillars of Wisdom* (London, 1935), p. 652.

stirrings in the consciousness of the 'Other', the attempts to find a new voice in the world. The first of them studies the last moment when it is still possible to speak of a self-sufficient world of Islamic culture. Although the political and economic conditions of self-sufficiency were ceasing to exist by the end of the eighteenth century, an educated Muslim could still look out upon the world with confidence in the strength and survival of the cultural tradition which he had received from the *silsila* of his teachers and ancestors.

Half a century later, this was no longer true. The expansion of European trade, military power and political influence led to attempts, first by indigenous and then by foreign rulers, to introduce new methods of administration, new legal codes and schools of a new kind. Knowledge of French and other European languages, and of the world which they opened, brought new questions and ideas. These stirrings of the mind took place above all in the ports and other cities where men and women of different religions and nationalities lived side by side, and where the traffic of ideas as well as goods could most easily and profitably take place. One of the most important of these cities was Beirut. In the last two essays, I write of two members of the Bustani family, Lebanese Christians whose minds were formed in Beirut and who played an important part in the attempt to understand the new world: Butrus, who edited the first Arabic encyclopaedia and helped to develop the modern style of clear expository Arabic prose; and Sulaiman, who extended the frontiers of Arabic poetic sensibility by translating the *Iliad* of Homer. Both these essays are tributes to friends. The first was written for a volume of essays in honour of Jacques Berque, and the second for a volume in memory of Malcolm Kerr, assassinated in 1984 in Beirut, where he was President of the American University: he was a friend of long standing, and it was he who had invited me to the conference at Los Angeles from which the fourth of these essays grew.

I

ISLAM IN EUROPEAN THOUGHT

I

FROM the time it first appeared, the religion of Islam was a problem for Christian Europe. Those who believed in it were the enemy on the frontier. In the seventh and eighth centuries armies fighting in the name of the first Muslim empire, the Caliphate, expanded into the heart of the Christian world. They occupied provinces of the Byzantine empire in Syria, the Holy Land and Egypt, and spread westwards into North Africa, Spain and Sicily; and the conquest was not only a military one, it was followed in course of time by conversions to Islam on a large scale. Between the eleventh and thirteenth centuries there was a Christian counter attack, successful for a time in the Holy Land, where a Latin kingdom of Jerusalem was created, and more permanently in Spain. The last Muslim kingdom in Spain was brought to an end in 1492, but by that time there was a further Muslim expansion elsewhere, by dynasties drawn from the Turkish peoples: the Saljuqs advanced into Anatolia, and later the Ottomans extinguished what was left of the Byzantine empire and occupied its capital, Constantinople, and expanded into eastern and central Europe. As late as the seventeenth century they were able to occupy the island of Crete and to threaten Vienna.

The relationship between Muslims and European Christians, however, was not simply one of holy war, of crusade and *jihad*. There was trade across the Mediterranean, and the balance of it changed in course of time; from the eleventh and twelfth centuries onwards the Italian ports expanded their trade, and, in the fifteenth and sixteenth centuries, ships from the ports of northern Europe began to appear in the Mediterranean and the Indian Ocean. There was also an exchange of ideas, and here the traffic moved mainly from the lands of Islam to those of Christendom: Arabic works of philosophy, science and medicine were translated into Latin, and until the sixteenth century the writings of the great medical scientist Ibn Sina were used in European medical schools.

Separated by conflict but held together by ties of different kinds, Christians and Muslims presented a religious and intellectual challenge to each other. What could each religion make of the claims of the other? For Muslim thinkers, the status of Christianity was clear. Jesus was one of the line of authentic prophets which had culminated in Muhammad, the 'Seal of the Prophets', and his authentic message was essentially the same as that of Muhammad. Christians had misunderstood their faith, however: they thought of their prophet as a god, and believed he had been crucified. The usual Muslim explanation for this was that they had 'corrupted' their scriptures, either by tampering with the text, or by misunderstanding its meaning. Properly understood, Muslim thinkers maintained, the Christian scriptures did not support Christian claims that Jesus was divine, and a passage of the Qur'an made clear that he had not been crucified but had somehow been taken up into heaven. Again, Christians did not accept the authenticity of the revelation given to Muhammad, but a proper interpretation of the Bible would show that it had foretold the coming of Muhammad.

For Christians, the matter was more difficult. They knew that Muslims believed in one God, who might be regarded, in His nature and operations, as being the God whom Christians worshipped, but they could not easily accept that Muhammad was an authentic prophet. The event to which Old Testament prophecy had pointed, the coming of Christ, had already taken place; what need was there for further prophets? The teaching of Muhammad, moreover, was a denial of the central doctrines of Christianity: the Incarnation and Crucifixion, and therefore also the Trinity and the Atonement. Could the Qur'an be regarded in any sense as the word of God? To the few Christians who knew anything about it, the Qur'an seemed to contain distorted echoes of biblical stories and themes.

With few exceptions, Christians in Europe who thought about Islam, during the first thousand or so years of the confrontation, did so in a state of ignorance. The Qur'an was indeed available in Latin translation from the twelfth century onwards; the first translation was made under the direction of Peter the Venerable, Abbot of Cluny. Some Arabic philosophical works were well known in translation, those which carried on the tradition of Greek thought. There was very limited knowledge, however, of those works of theology, law and spirituality in which what had been given in the Qur'an was articulated into a system of thought and practice. There were a few exceptions: in the thirteenth century, some of the Dominican houses in Spain were centres of Islamic studies, but even these declined in later centuries. On the Muslim side, rather more was known, and indeed had to be known. Christians continued to live in some Muslim countries, and particularly in Spain, Egypt and Syria, and many of them lived through the medium of the Arabic language. Knowledge of what they believed and practised was therefore available, and it was necessary for administrative and political purposes. The extent of the knowledge should not be exaggerated, however: its limits are shown in such works as al-Ghazali's refutation of the doctrine of the divinity of Christ.[1]

Looking at Islam with a mixture of fear, bewilderment and uneasy recognition of a kind of spiritual kinship, Christians could see it in more than one light. Occasionally the spiritual kinship was acknowledged. There is extant, for example, a letter written by Pope Gregory VII to a Muslim prince in Algeria, al-Nasir, in 1076. In it he says:

> there is a charity which we owe to each other more than to other peoples, because we recognize and confess one sole God, although in different ways, and we praise and worship Him every day as creator and ruler of the world.[2]

There has been some discussion of this letter among scholars, and it seems that its significance should not be overstated. It has been suggested that there were practical reasons for the warm and friendly tone in which Gregory wrote: the need to protect the shrinking Christian communities of North Africa, the common opposition of the Papacy and al-Nasir to another Muslim ruler in North Africa, and perhaps the desire of merchants in Rome to have a share in the growing trade of the port of Bougie (Bijaya), in al-Nasir's domains. In other letters, written to Christians, Gregory wrote of Muslims and Islam in harsher ways. Nevertheless, the terms in which the letter is written show that there was

---

[1] al-Radd al-jamil li ilahiyat 'Isa bi sarih al-injil, ed. and trans. R. Chidiac, Réfutation excellente de la divinité de Jesus-Christ d'après les Evangiles (Paris, 1969).

[2] Text in J. P. Migne, ed., Patrologia Latina, vol. CXLVIII (Paris, 1853), pp. 450–2.

some awareness at the time that Muslims were not pagans, and this is the more surprising because it was written just before the beginning of the greatest episode of hostility, the Crusades.[3]

A more commonly held view was that which saw Islam as an offshoot or heresy of Christianity. This was the view of the first Christian theologian to consider it seriously, St John of Damascus (c. 675–749). He had himself been an official in the administration of the Umayyad caliph in Damascus, and knew Arabic. He includes Islam in a section of his work on Christian heresies: it believes in God, but denies certain of the essential truths of Christianity, and because of this denial even the truths which it accepts are devoid of meaning. The most widely held belief, however, was that which lay at the other end of the spectrum: Islam is a false religion, Allah is not God, Muhammad was not a prophet; Islam was invented by men whose motives and character were to be deplored, and propagated by the sword.[4]

2

Whatever European Christians thought of Islam, they could not deny that it was an important factor in human history, and one which needed to be explained. Awareness of the world of Islam increased in early modern times, between the sixteenth and eighteenth centuries, and in some ways its nature changed. The military challenge from the Ottoman empire had ceased to exist by the eighteenth century, as the balance of military strength shifted. Improvements in navigation made possible the exploration of the world by European ships and an expansion of European trade in the Mediterranean and the Indian Ocean, and there were the beginnings of European settlement. To the Italian trading communities, which had long existed in the ports of the eastern Mediterranean, there were added others: Aleppo, one of the main centres of Near Eastern trade, had several communities,

---

[3] Discussion in R. Lopez, 'Le facteur économique dans la politique africaine des Papes', *Revue historique*, 198 (1947), pp. 178–88; C. Courtois, 'Grégoire VII et l'Afrique du nord', *Revue historique*, 195 (1945), pp. 97–122, 193–226; J. Henninger, 'Sur la contribution des missionaries à la connaissance de l'islam, surtout pendant le moyen age', *Neue Zeitschrift für Missionswissenschaft*, 9 (1953), pp. 161–85; B. Z. Keder, *European Approaches towards the Muslims* (Princeton, N. J. 1984), pp. 56–7. I owe my understanding of this episode to the kindness of Dr David Abulafia.

[4] St John of Damascus, 'De Haeresibus' in Migne, *Patrologia Graeca*, vol. XCIV (Paris, 1860), pp. 764–74; English trans., D. J. Sahas, *John of Damascus on Islam* (Leiden, 1972), pp. 132–41.

including a number of English merchants (it is twice mentioned by Shakespeare, in *Othello* and *Macbeth*).[5] Portuguese, Dutch, French and English merchants also settled in some of the Indian ports. A new kind of political relationship began to appear: European states had ambassadors and consuls in the Ottoman domains, although the Ottoman sultan did not have his own permanent embassies in Europe until the time of the Napoleonic wars. Treaties and alliances were discussed: the French and Ottomans made an agreement against the Habsburgs, and the British and others tried to establish relations with the Safavid Shahs of Iran.

As relations grew closer, intellectual awareness also expanded. The direct importance of Islam to scholars and thinkers diminished: the religious controversies of Europe in the time of the Reformation and Counter-Reformation revolved around a new set of problems, and the development of European science and medicine made what had been written in Arabic less important. In some ways, however, Islam was still relevant to the religious concerns of the age. Although comparative philology did not yet exist as a scientific discipline, it was generally recognized that Arabic had a close relationship with the languages of the Bible, Hebrew and Aramaic, and study of it might throw light on them; knowledge too of the Near Eastern environment in which the events recorded in the Bible had taken place might help to explain them. Among educated people, travel, commerce and literature brought some awareness of the phenomenon, majestic and puzzling, of Islamic civilization, stretching from the Atlantic to the Pacific, with Arabic as its *lingua franca,* the most universal language which had ever existed. This awareness was expressed by Dr Johnson:

There are two objects of curiosity – the Christian world, and the Mahometan world. All the rest may be considered as barbarous.[6]

How far did such changes have an effect upon attitudes towards Islam? The spectrum of possible attitudes still existed. At one extreme, there was total rejection of Islam as a religion. Thus Pascal entitled the seventeenth of his *Pensées* 'against Muhammad'. Christ is everything, he asserted, which Muhammad is not.

---

[5] *Macbeth,* Act I, Scene 5; *Othello,* Act V, Scene 2.
[6] G. Birkbeck Hill, ed., *Boswell's Life of Johnson,* revised edn, L. F. Powell, vol. IV (Oxford, 1934), p. 199.

Muhammad is without authority, his coming was not foretold, he worked no miracles, he revealed no mysteries: 'Any man could do what Muhammad has done; no man could do what Jesus has done'. Muhammad took the path of human success; Jesus Christ died for humanity.[7]

Such themes continued to be repeated, but as time went on there might be a significant change of emphasis: there was less denigration of Muhammad as a man, and greater recognition of his human qualities and extraordinary achievements. Thus Joseph White, Professor of Arabic at Oxford, took as his subject for the Bampton Lectures in 1784 'a comparison of Islam and Christianity by their origins, evidence and effects'.[8] He does not accept that the appearance of Islam was in any sense a miraculous event, or that it has played any part in the providential design for mankind. It is a purely natural religion, supported by borrowings from the Jewish and Christian scriptures. Its success too can be explained in natural terms, by the corruption of the Christian Church of the times on the one hand, and the personality of the Prophet on the other. Far from being the 'monster of ignorance and vice' depicted by Christian authors, Muhammad was, so White claims:

an extraordinary character [of] splendid talents and profound artifice ... endowed with a greatness of mind which could brave the storms of adversity [by] ... the sheer force of a bold and fertile genius.[9]

To explain such a change in emphasis and judgement, it is necessary to look at the growth in knowledge of Islam, and also at certain changes towards religion as such. Joseph White and his contemporaries could draw upon 200 years of European scholarship. The first systematic study of Islam and its history in western Europe goes back to the late sixteenth century. In 1587 regular teaching of Arabic began at the Collège de France in Paris; the first two professors were medical doctors, and that is significant of one of the ways in which knowledge of Arabic was important at the time; the third was a Maronite priest from Lebanon, and that too is significant in another way, as showing the first collaboration between European and indigenous scholars.[10] Soon afterwards, in

[7] Pensées, no. 17.
[8] Sermons Preached before the University of Oxford, in the Year 1784, at the Lecture founded by the Rev. John Bampton, 2nd edn (London, 1785).
[9] Ibid., pp. 165f.
[10] P. Casanova, L'enseignement de l'arabe au collège de France (Paris, 1910).

1613, a chair of Arabic was created at the University of Leiden in the Netherlands, and the first holder of it was a famous scholar, Thomas Erpenius. In England, a chair was created at Cambridge in 1632 and one at Oxford in 1634. From this time there began a serious and sustained study of Arabic sources, from which the human figure of Muhammad emerged more clearly.

To follow this development in England only, it is necessary to begin with the first holder of the chair at Oxford, Edward Pococke (1604–91). He spent two lengthy periods in the Near East, first at Aleppo as chaplain to the English merchants, and then at Istanbul. In both places he collected manuscripts or had them copied for him. One of the works which emerged from his study of them was his *Specimen Historiae Arabum*, the introduction to which shows the extent of scholarly knowledge in his time: it includes Arabic genealogies, information about the religion of Arabia before Islam, a description of the basic tenets of Islam and a translation of one of the creeds, that of al-Ghazali.[11] At the turn of the century, George Sale (c. 1697–1736) made the first accurate English translation of the Qur'an, itself owing much to a recent Latin version, that of Lodovico Marracci. Here too the introduction is important; it poses the question of God's purpose in the coming of Muhammad. He was not, so Sale believed, immediately inspired by God, but God used his human inclination and interests for His own ends: 'to be a scourge to the Christian Church for not living answerably to that most holy religion which they had received'.[12] This was only possible because of Muhammad's remarkable qualities: his conviction that he had been sent to restore the true religion, his enthusiasm (in the eighteenth-century sense of strong feelings not fully restrained within the bounds of reason), his piercing and sagacious intelligence, good judgement, cheerful temper, and agreeable and polite manners.

In the same generation Simon Ockley (1678–1720) published a *History of the Saracens* in which a similar picture of Muhammad appears. He was not an inspired prophet, but a man of remarkable achievements, who not only preserved the knowledge and wisdom of earlier times, but brought about a moral reform. The Arabs restored to Europe

---

11 *Specimen Historiae Arabum*, new edn (Oxford, 1806).
12 G. Sale, *The Koran* (London, 1734), 'Preliminary discourse', p. 38.

Things of Universal Necessity, the Fear of God, the Regulation of our Appetites, prudent Oeconomy, Decency and Sobriety of Behaviour.[13]

Along with the increase of knowledge there went a change in ways of looking at religion, and indeed in the meaning of the word 'religion' itself. As Wilfred Cantwell Smith has shown in his book, *The Meaning and End of Religion*, the modern use of the term appears in the sixteenth and seventeenth centuries. In earlier times it had meant simply forms of worship, but now it came to mean any system of beliefs and practices constructed by human beings. If the word is used in this way, then there can be different religions, all of them worthy of rational study and consideration.[14]

This awakening of curiosity in the varieties of the religious spirit is clear, for example, in the life of Robert Boyle (1627–91), a well-known 'natural philosopher' and one of the founders of the Royal Society. In his autobiography, Boyle describes a spiritual crisis in his early life. During the Grand Tour he visited a Carthusian monastery near Grenoble, and there he was overcome by 'such strange and hideous thoughts, and such distracting doubts of some of the fundamentals of Christianity' that he was tempted to kill himself, until 'at last it pleased God … to restore unto him the withdrawn sense of His favour'.[15] From this crisis he derived a beneficial lesson: 'to be seriously inquisitive of the truth of the very fundamentals of Christianity, and to hear what both Turks and Jews, and the chief sects of Christians could alledge for their several opinions'.[16] It was only on the basis of such an inquiry, he thought, that his own beliefs could be firmly grounded. In his will, he provided for a series of lectures, to be delivered annually, in order to prove the Christian religion against 'Atheists, Theists, Pagans, Jews and Mahometans'.[17]

When Christianity was seen in this light, in its relations with other religions, and when all of them were viewed as systems of belief and practice articulated by human beings, more than one conclusion could be drawn. It was possible to regard Christianity as being different, in its origins and beliefs, from all others, but it was also possible to see all of them as the products of human

---

[13] *The History of the Saracens*, 2nd edn (London, 1718), vol. II, p. ii.

[14] *The Meaning and End of Religion* (London, 1964).

[15] 'An account of Philaretus, during his minority' in *Works of the Hon. Robert Boyle* (London, 1744), vol. I, p. 12.

[16] Ibid.

[17] L. T. More, *The Life and Works of the Hon. Robert Boyle* (London, 1944), p. 132.

minds and feelings, and Christianity was not necessarily unique, or necessarily the best of them.

In some writers of the eighteenth century, indeed, there was a tendency to use the career and mission of Muhammad as an oblique way of criticizing Christianity, at least in the form in which the churches had taught it. Muhammad could be shown as an example of the excesses of enthusiasm and ambition, and his followers as examples too of human credulity; alternatively, he could be seen as preaching a religion which was more rational, or nearer to a purely natural faith, than Christianity.

This was the view of some of the French thinkers of the eighteenth century, and we can hear an echo of it in Napoleon's statements about Islam. In the Arabic proclamation issued when he landed in Egypt in 1798, he assured the Egyptians that the French 'worship God far more than the Mamluks do, and respect the Prophet and the glorious Qur'an ... the French are true Muslims'.[18] No doubt there was something in this of political propaganda, but there was also an admiration for the achievements of Muhammad (a subject to which Napoleon returned in later life), and a certain view of religion: there is a God or Supreme Being, whose existence can be apprehended by reason, but whose nature and mode of operation have been distorted by specific religions; these religions can be arranged on a scale, according to the extent to which their teachings approach the truth to which reason can lead us.

Such an idea could be formulated in many ways, ranging from genuine rational conviction to almost complete scepticism or agnosticism. Edmund Gibbon lay near to the point of scepticism, but to him Muhammad appeared in as favourable a light as any religious leader could. Chapter 50 of *The Decline and Fall of the Roman Empire* is devoted to Muhammad and the rise of Islam. It is a work of remarkable learning, based on wide reading in works of European scholarship and also in the works of such travellers of Chardin, Volney and Niebuhr. Gibbon has an opinion about Muhammad which is clearly formulated, and favourable up to a point. Muhammad, he believes, had 'an original and superior genius', formed in solitude, as it must be: 'conversation enriches the understanding, but solitude is the school of genius'. The

---

[18] 'Abd al-Rahman al-Jabarti, *'Aja'ib al-athar fi'l-tarajim wa'l-akhbar* (Cairo, AH 1322/1904–5), vol. III, p. 4.

product of that solitude was the Qur'an, 'a glorious testimony to the unity of God'. It expressed the idea of

an infinite and eternal being, without form or place, without issue or similitude, present to our most secret thoughts, existing by the necessity of his own nature, and deriving from himself all moral and intellectual perfection.

This is, Gibbon adds, 'a creed too sublime, perhaps, for our present faculties'; for this reason there are dangers in it, and Muhammad was not immune from them:

The unity of God is an idea most congenial to nature and reason; and a slight conversation with the Jews and Christians would teach him to despise and detest the idolatry of Mecca ... the energy of a mind incessantly bent on the same object would convert a general obligation into a particular call; the warm suggestions of the understanding would be felt as the inspirations of Heaven ... how the conscience may slumber in a mixed and middle state between self-illusion and voluntary fraud.

As Muhammad grew more successful, Gibbon thinks, his motives may have changed:

Charity may believe that the original motives of Mahomet were those of pure and genuine benevolence; but ... the injustice of Mecca and the choice of Medina transformed the citizen into a prince, the humble preacher into the leader of armies ... a politician may suspect that he secretly smiled ... at the enthusiasm of his youth and the credulity of his proselytes.[19]

(We find here what was to become a familiar theme of European scholarship, the difference between the Muhammad of Mecca and of Medina.)

3

By the beginning of the nineteenth century, Europeans who thought about Islam could take up two kinds of attitude towards it (of course, with many variations in both of them). They could see Islam as the enemy and rival of Christianity, using some Christian truths for its own purposes, or else as one of the forms which human reason and feeling have taken in their attempt to know and define the nature of God and the universe. Common to both these attitudes was acceptance of the fact that Muhammad and his followers had played an important part in the history of the world. By this time, moreover, it was more difficult not to take up an

---

[19] E. Gibbon, *The Decline and Fall of the Roman Empire*, chapter 50.

attitude of some kind towards Islam, as towards the other religions of the world, because of the changing relations between Europe and the peoples of Asia and Africa among whom religions other than Christianity were predominant. Trade was expanding as new methods of manufacture were invented and adopted, and new means of communication were developed: the steamship, railway and telegraph. The expansion of Europe brought back new knowledge of the world outside, and also created new responsibilities: British, French and Dutch rule was extended over ports and their hinterlands in the countries around the Mediterranean Sea and the Indian Ocean, and Russian rule expanded southwards towards the Black Sea and eastwards into Asia.

In this century, therefore, there was a renewal of thought about Islam. It took many forms, which differed to some extent according to the experiences of the various European nations. In Britain, and among British people in the empire, an incentive was given to the idea of opposition between Christianity and Islam by the new religious spirit of Evangelicalism. the idea that salvation lay only in the consciousness of sin and acceptance of the gospel of Christ, and that one who knows himself to be saved has a duty to confront others with this truth. Such a confrontation was now possible on a larger scale than before, because of the growth of organized missionary activities, and because the expanding empire, and the Indian empire in particular, provided a field both of great opportunity and of responsibility.

In general, the attitude of missionaries who had been touched by the Evangelical spirit was one of hostility towards Islam, and acceptance of the duty to try to convert Muslims. Thomas Valpy French (1825–91), Principal of St John's College at Agra and later Bishop of Lahore, can serve as an example. Early in his work of mission he came to believe that 'Christianity and Muhamma-danism are as distinct as earth and heaven, and could not possibly be true together'.[20] Later in life he resigned his post as bishop because he thought it his duty to preach the gospel in Arabia, in the heart of the world of Islam; he died on his way there, at Muscat.

In some instances the confrontation was direct, and we have records of at least two of them. The first was a controversy in writing between Henry Martyn (1781–1812), a famous mission-

---

[20] H. Birks, *Life and Correspondence of Thomas Valpy French* (London, 1895), vol. I, p. 69.

ary in India, and two Iranian Shiʻi divines, during Martyn's visit to Shiraz in 1811. The main points at issue were questions which had always been central in polemics between Muslims and Christians. Is the Qur'an a miracle? Martyn denied it, and the *mulla*s expressed the orthodox view that the Qur'an is unique and inimitable, and this is a proof of its divine origin. Was the coming of Muhammad foretold in the Bible? Here too the *mulla*s gave the orthodox view: it was foretold, but the text of the Bible had been corrupted or misinterpreted by the Church. Were the moral qualities of Muhammad and his followers such as to permit the belief that Islam was of divine origin? Here the discussion revolved around familiar themes: the plurality of the Prophet's wives, and the spread of Islam by force of arms.[21]

A public controversy of a more direct kind was held in Agra in 1854, between Karl Pfander, a German missionary in the service of the Church Missionary Society, and a Muslim divine, Shaikh Rahmatullah al-Kairanawi. Pfander had been brought up in a tradition of German pietism not dissimilar to Evangelicalism. Encouraged by some Evangelical officials of the East India Company, he followed an active policy of preaching and writing, published a long book on sin and salvation, and was challenged to a public debate by Shaikh Rahmatullah. The main argument revolved around the question whether the Christian scriptures had been altered so as to conceal the evidence for the future coming of the Prophet Muhammad. The debate was inconclusive because Pfander withdrew after the second session, but it is clear from the reports that he did not get the better of the exchanges; Rahmatullah had some knowledge of the new German science of biblical criticism, which he had derived from an Indian Muslim doctor who knew English well, and he used this to put the question of the authenticity and authority of the Bible in a new light.[22]

It was not only the missionaries who were imbued with the new Evangelical spirit. Many of the British officials in India were also touched by it. One of them, William Muir (1819–1905), was present at the debate at Agra. A few years earlier, he had written an article, 'The Muhammadan controversy', which showed that

---

[21] For Martyn, see S. Lee, *Controversial Tracts on Christianity and Mohammedanism* (Cambridge, 1894).

[22] A. Powell, 'Mawlana Rahmat Allah Kairanawi and Muslim-Christian controversy in India in the mid-19th century', *Journal of the Royal Asiatic Society* (1976), pp. 42–63.

total opposition to Islam which was characteristic of the Evangelicals. Islam, he said, was

> the only undisguised and formidable antagonist of Christianity ... an active and powerful enemy ... It is just because Muhammadanism acknowledges the divine original, and has borrowed so many of the weapons of Christianity, that it is so dangerous an adversary.[23]

In later life, after Muir's Indian career came to an end, he became Principal of Edinburgh University and wrote a famous *Life of Muhammad*, which was to remain for many years the standard English book on the subject. It conveys much the same message as the earlier article. Muhammad was a mixture of good and bad qualities, with the bad coming to predominate in his later life. It is a delusion to suppose that Islam is a kind of Christianity, or can be an Evangelical preparation for it:

> There is in it just so much truth, truth borrowed from previous Relevations yet cast in another mould, as to divert attention from the need for more.[24]

Outside the ranks of Evangelical Christians, it may be that the other range of attitudes was becoming more widespread: those derived from the idea that Islam is, within its limits, an authentic expression of the human need to believe in a God, and one which has values of its own. Such an idea was expressed, in a rather confused form, in a work which was to have a great and lasting influence in the English-speaking world: Thomas Carlyle's lecture on 'The hero as prophet' in *On Heroes, Hero-Worship and the Heroic in History*, published in 1841. Carlyle accepts Muhammad as a prophet, according to his own definition of prophecy: 'a silent great soul: one of those who cannot but be in earnest'. He was alive to 'the great mystery of existence ... the unspeakable fact, "Here am I"'. In some sense he was inspired:

> Such light had come, as it could, to illuminate the darkness of this wild Arabian soul. As confused, dazzling splendour as of life and Heaven ... he called it revelation and the Angel Gabriel; who of us may yet know what to call it?[25]

One of those who listened to Carlyle's lectures was F. D. Maurice, a leading theologian of the Church of England, and one who aroused controversy and some bewilderment in his own time

---

[23] *The Mohammedan Controversy* (Edinburgh, 1897), pp. 1–63.
[24] *The Life of Mohammed*, revised edn (Edinburgh, 1912), p. 522.
[25] *On Heroes, Hero-Worship and the Heroic in History*: lecture 2, 'The hero as prophet'.

and later: John Stuart Mill, who was not in sympathy with his ideas, said of him, 'there was more intellectual power wasted in Maurice than in any other of my contemporaries'.[26] In a letter, Maurice praised the charity of Carlyle's view of Muhammad, but disagreed with his idea of religion. Carlyle, he said,

regards the world as without a centre and [Christian doctrine] as only one of the mythical ventures in which certain actions ... have wrapt themselves up.[27]

Maurice's own views of other religions were given a few years later in his book, *The Religions of the World and Their Relations with Christianity*. These were lectures given in the series founded by Robert Boyle. They were delivered in 1845–6, when Maurice was professor of literature and history at King's College, London, and soon to become professor of theology there; this was some years before the controversy which was to lead to his dismissal from his chair. In the lectures, Maurice addressed himself to problems raised, as he believed, by the circumstances of his time and place. England was becoming a colonizing country; there was a responsibility of preaching the gospel to non-Christians, and this involved knowing what their religions were and how Christianity stood in relation to them. This in turn raised another question. What is Christianity? Is it simply one among the religions of the world, or does it have a privileged position which marks it out from them, and gives it a truth which they do not possess? Maurice declares himself to be conscious of 'a tremendous change in the feelings of men towards religious systems'. Disturbing questions are being asked:

Might not particular soils be adapted to particular religions? ... Might not a better day be at hand, in which all religions alike should be found to have done their work of partial good, of greater evil, and when something much more comprehensive and satisfactory should supersede them?

The great political revolution of the late eighteenth century had given rise to the accusation that religions were maintained in the interests of politicians or priests, and this accusation was made as much against Christianity as against other religions, or even more. It was necessary therefore to ask what religion really is.[28]

For Maurice, the essence of religion was 'the faith in men's

[26] *Autobiography* (London, 1873), p. 153.
[27] F. Maurice, *The Life of Frederick Denison Maurice* (London, 1884), vol. I, p. 282.
[28] *The Religions of the World and Their Relations with Christianity* (London, 1847), pp. 3ff.

hearts'. He meant by this something specific: faith for him was not simply a human quality, an essential part of the constitution of a human being, it was derived from 'the revelation of God to man, not [simply] any pious or religious sentiments which men may have concerning God'. This revelation has a content: that God exists and has revealed His will for human beings, that His will is a loving will, that it has revealed itself progressively in history, and this progress has been completed in a person, the perfect image of God, 'a uniting and reconciling spirit, which raises [men] above the broken forms and shadows of earth'.[29]

Maurice looks at each of the higher religions in the light of this principle. When he comes to Islam, first of all he considers five false or inadequate explanations of its success. It cannot be explained simply by the force of its arms: where did that force come from, if not from the strength and nature of the faith of Muslims? It was not the result of human credulity, for this could not explain why Islam has survived and flourished so vigorously. It cannot be said that the whole content of Islam was taken from the Old and New Testaments: Muhammad must at least have been inspired by them, they 'must have taken possession of him'. The personality of Muhammad, the strength of his conviction and exaltation, cannot by itself be the sole reason; it must also be shown why this personality has had such a great and lasting effect upon mankind, and this is the more difficult to explain because the religion which he preached is one which condemns all worship of human beings.

Is there another explanation? Can the success of Islam be seen as a judgement of God upon guilty nations: the Christian peoples of the East who had lost the Christian virtues and were sunk in the worship of images, religious ceremonies and philosophical theories, and the pagans who had not known Christianity or had known it but rejected it? In putting forward this suggestion Maurice may have been echoing the thought expressed in a book which he had read: Charles Forster's *Mahometanism Unveiled* (1822), a bizarre work at best (Forster's grandson, the novelist E. M. Forster, went further, and said his books 'are worthless'[30]). The argument of the book is that Muhammad was the antagonist of Christ, but his life nevertheless had a providential purpose: by fighting against idolatry, Judaism and Christian heresies, Islam could 'shape the course of things indirectly' towards Christianity,

29 Ibid, p. 151.   30 *Marianne Thornton* (London, 1956), pp. 145, 163.

and so was 'essential to the recovery and ultimate perfection of the pure belief'.[31]

Maurice thought there was some truth in this theory: Islam had indeed brought back into the world 'the sense of a divine almighty Will, to which all human wills should bow', the assertion of a being not dependent on ourselves, the ground of man's being. It shares with Christianity certain essential truths: that there is one God who makes His will known to mankind, that His speech is recorded in a Book to which we can safely look as an authority, and that all who accept this truth form a body or community called by God to the work of preaching this truth. Thus Islam has served a useful purpose in the world by calling men back to knowledge to these truths, and in this sense Muhammad can be said to have had a vocation from God. His witness saved the Church:

> The Middle Ages turn more upon [Muhammad] ... than I had at all imagined till I came to think more of them. There would have been no belief in Christ if there had not been that broad firm assertion of an absolute God.[32]

This 'Muhammadan witness' had something lacking in it, however. In Maurice's view, the God of Islam is sheer will: not 'a great moral being who deigns to raise His creatures out of their degradation, and reveals to them what He is and why He has created them'. Considered in isolation, will can easily become a dead fate and lead to indifference or despair. For Muhammad, history carries 'no hope of a progress', and the religion which began with him is like all the religions of the world except Christianity:

> broken, divided, superstitious schemes for propitiating an unwilling and ungracious Being, because they have not been able to perceive the uniting point, because they have been obliged to *create* it, somewhere in the natural or the spiritual world.[33]

4

Maurice's book is a sign of the development of the idea of religions as human attempts to articulate something which comes from outside the human world, 'the faith in men's hearts'. Seen in this perspective, the Qur'an and the life of the Prophet could be

---

[31] C. Forster, *Mahometanism Unveiled* (London, 1829), vol. I, p. 108, vol. II, p. 351.
[32] Maurice, *Life*, p. 239.   [33] Ibid, p. 230; Maurice, *Religions*, pp. 10ff, 135ff.

regarded as being at worst a distortion of ideas taken from other religions, and at best a valid but limited testimony to the truth. Without going further back, it is possible to trace this way of looking at religion to the thought of Immanuel Kant (1724–1804). In a late work, *Religion within the Limits of Reason Alone*, Kant distinguished 'true religion' from 'ecclesiastical faiths'. 'True religion', he said, contains two elements: the moral law, an intuition made articulate by practical reason, and a certain way of seeing that law, as a divine command; the existence of God is seen as the necessary presupposition of the moral imperative. 'Ecclesiastical faiths', for their part, are based on belief in a revealed scripture, and they should be judged by whether or not they conform to 'true religion'. Among them Christianity has a unique position, for it is the faith which most fully expresses 'true religion', and holds out to mankind the supreme human exemplar of the moral ideal, but it is possible for other faiths embodied in scriptures to express 'true religion', at least in part.[34]

Such a line of thought was carried further by a thinker of the next generation, Friedrich Schleiermacher (1768–1834), and he had something explicit to say about Islam. In his *Addresses on Religion* (1799),[35] he suggested that the basis of all religion is human feeling, but perhaps 'feeling' is too weak a word to express what he means; one exponent of this thought has defined it as 'a mode of objective apprehension ... a species of an awareness of spiritual things'.[36] More specifically, it is the apprehension of being absolutely dependent, or – in other terms – of having a certain relationship with God (whom he also calls 'the World Spirit'). This is a universal feeling, present in all human beings. It is anterior to knowing and doing, but human beings try to articulate it in ideas and express it in actions, and these attempts have given rise to different religious communities, each founded by a 'hero of religion', and each having its own distinctive articulation of religious feeling in theology and practice. Such communities differ from each other in the emphasis which they lay upon one or other aspect of the relationship between God and

---

[34] *Die Religion innerhalb der Grenzen der blossenn Vernunft* in W. Weischedel, ed., *Werke*, vol. IV (Berlin, 1984), pp. 654–879; English trans., *Religion within the Limits of Reason Alone* (New York, 1934).

[35] *Über die Religion: Reden an die Gebilden unter ihren Verchtern* in *Kritische Gesamtausgabe*, part I, vol. II (Berlin, 1984), pp. 185–326; English trans., R. Crouter, *On Religion* (Cambridge, 1939).

[36] H. R. Mackintosh, *Types of Modern Theology* (London, 1937), pp. 31ff.

man, and the fullness with which they express the feeling of dependence which is the ground of all of them.

It is possible, therefore, to construct a scale of religions. In a later work, Schleiermacher makes a distinction between those which accept the idea of dependence upon a single Supreme Being and those which do not. Among the monotheistic religions, there are three great ones, Judaism, Christianity, and Islam, or it might be better to say there are two, since Judaism is in the process of extinction. Christianity and Islam are 'still contending for the mastery of the human race'.[37] In looking at this contest, Schleiermacher writes as a Christian who believes his faith is undoubtedly superior. Through Christ, he believes, the idea of dependence is expressed with a 'glorious clarity', and to it is added the further idea that all that is finite needs a higher mediator to be brought into accord with God. All religions are corrupt, however, even Christianity; this is unavoidable, when the Infinite descends into the sphere of time and submits to the influence of finite minds. No man or community possesses the whole of religion, but all have something of truth in them:

This excludes the idea that the Christian religion should adopt, in regard to other forms of piety, the attitude of the true towards the false ... error does not exist and for itself, but always together with some truth, 'and we have never fully understood it until we have discovered its connection with truth.[38]

Such ideas were a stimulus to the examination of those historical factors which had shaped the development of different religions and given them their share of the truth and their limitations. For most writers of early centuries, and even for many such as Maurice in the nineteenth century, Islam meant the Qur'an, the Prophet Muhammad and the early conquests of the Muslims. There was little sense of a culture, a body of ideas, practices and institutions which had grown over time and was still living. During the first half of the nineteenth century, however, a different view of it would emerge as the idea developed that all beliefs, cultures and institutions are shaped by the flow of history. To look at different cultures and societies, and at the religions which had played a major part in forming them, and to place them all within the framework of a general view of this history of

[37] Friedrich Schleiermacher, *Der Christliche Glaube* in *Sämtliche Werke*, 2nd edn (Berlin, 1842), part I, vol. III, p. 47; English trans., *The Christian Faith* (Edinburgh, 1928), p. 37.
[38] Ibid., p. 42; English trans., p. 33.

mankind, was the purpose of another German thinker of the same generation, J. G. Herder (1744–1803). In his *Reflections on the Philosophy of the History of Mankind*, he stated that the basic units of mankind were peoples or nations, formed within a particular physical environment by a gradually evolving way of life which expressed itself in customs and beliefs. Each of these peoples is distinguished by its language, and everything in its life is connected with everything else: 'all the works of God have their stability in themselves, and in their beautiful consistency'. These separate peoples cannot be reduced to each other or even, beyond a certain point, compared with each other. Herder was writing at the beginning of the period of European expansion, and he rejected the impossible attempt of

a united Europe to erect itself into a despot and compel all the nations of the world to be happy in her way . . . is not a proud thought of this kind treason against the majesty of nature?[39]

The purpose of history is not that one people should impose itself on others, but rather the attainment of a balance and harmony between them.

In this context, what should be said of Islam, or rather of the Arabs, for Islam in Herder's view was an expression of the Arabian spirit? The Arabs, he believed, 'from remotest times have fostered sublime conceptions'. They were 'for the most part solitary, romantic men'. (This was a time when a certain conception of the Arab of the desert as a noble figure began to appear in European writing, notably in the work of a Dutch traveller, Carsten Niebuhr, who saw the Beduin as having preserved the natural goodness of mankind: 'liberty, independence and simplicity'.) In Herder's view, Muhammad brought to birth what was already latent in Arabia, with the help of such Christian and Jewish ideas as he knew. The movement which he began showed the strengths and weaknesses which are typical of such movements. It was created and upheld by the virtues of the desert, courage and fidelity; it raised men out of their worship of the powers of nature and made them worshippers of the one God, and it raised them also from a savage state to 'a middle degree of civilization'. When the virtues of the desert grew weak, the Arabian civilization ceased to grow further, but it left something

---

[39] *Ideen zur Philosophie der Geschichte der Menschheit* (Riga and Leipzig, 1784–91), vol .II, p. 206; vol. III, p. 365; English trans., *Reflections on the Philosophy of the History of Mankind* (Chicago, 1968), pp. 78, 116.

behind it: the Arabic language, 'their noblest legacy', not the inheritance of the Arabs only, but a bond of intercourse between nations such as had never before existed.[40] (Herder was writing at a time when Arabic was still the *lingua franca* of a great part of the civilized world.)

A generation later, another attempt to give meaning to the whole of human history was made by G. W. F. Hegel (1770–1831). In his *Lectures on the Philosophy of History*, given at the University of Berlin in the 1820s, his basic category is not dissimilar to Herder's; it is that of a specific spirit which creates and animates a society and culture. The relations between the different spirits are not seen in the same way, however. For Herder, they are related by tensions and conflicts which may finally be resolved into harmony and balance; for Hegel, all are manifestations or phases of the one universal Spirit, and they are arranged on a temporal scale. All that exists in the world can be seen in a line of historical development, which carries its own meaning and end inside itself. History is 'the exhibition of the Spirit in the process of working out that which it is potentially'; the end of the process will be Freedom, defined as the full realization of the essence of human beings in art, thought and political life. The means through which the Spirit realizes itself are the passions and interests of individual human beings. Human history therefore consists of different phases, in each of which the universal Spirit manifests itself in a particular communal or national spirit or will. This spirit is dominant in its age, but it has its limits, and it is by negation of these that a new spirit arises in another people; once this has happened, the role of the national spirit which expressed the previous phase is finished.

Where do the Muslims or Arabs stand in this process? They played an essential part in it, for theirs was the human society in which the Spirit was embodied in one of the phases of its development. Their role was to assert

the principle of pure unity: nothing else exists – nothing can become fixed – the worship of the One remains the only bond by which the whole is capable of unity.

The acceptance and assertion of this principle by Muslims produced men of great moral elevation, having 'all the virtues that appertain to magnanimity and valour'. The very strength of the

[40] Ibid., vol. II, pp. 151–2; vol. IV, pp. 239–67; English trans., pp. 336–54.

principle contained its own limitations, however. The triumph of the Arabs was the triumph of enthusiasm, carrying forward the idea of universality, but on that basis nothing is firm. Once the enthusiasm died nothing was left:

Islam has long vanished from the stage of history, and has retreated into oriental ease and repose.[41]

5

In such systems of thought Islam played at most a secondary part, but in the next two generations both Islam and the Arabic language were to become directly relevant to certain central concerns of European scholarly thought. A new kind of study developed, that of languages in their relations to each other. It had been obvious for a long time that certain languages were similar to each other: the languages derived from Latin, or Hebrew, Syriac and Arabic. Towards the end of the eighteenth century, however, a new theory was put forward. In 1786 Sir William Jones (1746–94), a distinguished British student of things oriental, then resident in Calcutta as a judge under the East India Company, pointed out that there were similarities of vocabulary and structure between Sanskrit, some European languages, and perhaps Old Persian as well. He may not have been the first to notice this, but his idea was taken up, particularly by German scholars such as Franz Bopp (1791–1876). As the relationships among what came to be called the 'Indo-European' or 'Aryan' languages were studied, it became clear not only that they were similar, but that there were principles on the basis of which one language, or one form of a language, might have developed out of another, and that a number of similar languages might have a common origin. This theory could be applied not only to the Indo-European languages but to others as well; Hebrew, Syriac, Arabic and others could be regarded as forming the 'family' of Semitic languages.

Thus there developed the science of comparative philology, now absorbed into linguistics, at least in English-speaking countries, but one of the seminal sciences of the nineteenth century, because it was more than a study of the structure and history of

---

[41] G. W. F. Hegel, *Vorlesungen über die Philosophie der Geschichte* in *Sämtliche Werke*, vol. XI (Stutgart, 1928), pp. 453–9; English trans., *Lectures on the Philosophy of History* (London, 1857), pp. 369–74.

languages. At least in German and French, the term 'philology' referred to the study not only of languages but of what has been written in them: the texts which are a legacy of the past, and in particular those which express a collective view of the universe and man's place in it. Herder had emphasized that humanity is divided into nations, each of which sees itself and the universe through the medium of a specific language; this idea was taken up by Wilhelm von Humboldt (1767–1837) and others, and became a commonplace of thought in the age of romanticism.

One important offshoot of the study of comparative philology was the science or pseudo-science of comparative mythology, developed by F. Max Müller (1823–1900) and others. The basis of this was the idea that the most ancient literary products of a people – its folk-tales and religious writings – would reveal, if studied by strict linguistic analysis, its essential mentality and its inner history: that process by which higher religion and rational thought had developed out of stories and myths. Thus the comparative study of languages, properly conceived and pursued, could be a study of peoples with their specific mentalities, a kind of natural history of mankind. To some philologists, this study appeared as a liberating force: by showing that religious texts were a primitive way of expressing truth through myths, it could free the mind to express them rationally.

This system of ideas was to have a profound and far-reaching effect upon several fields of study. It was one of the impulses for the creation of the science of anthropology: the study of certain societies which still existed but stood at a lower stage of the development through which more advanced societies had passed. It also gave rise to a certain view of cultural history, and one which not all philologists accepted. Such a view was expressed with force by Ernest Renan (1823–92), one of the seminal figures in the formation of European ideas about Islam.

Renan's autobiography, *Souvenirs d'enfance et de jeunesse*, conveys a sense of his personality.[42] It shows how he lost his inherited Catholic faith at the seminary of St Sulpice in Paris, but retained a basic seriousness in his search for truth. The method by which this search should be conducted, he believed, was that of philology. He even spoke of the 'religion of philology', the faith that a precise study of texts in their historical context could reveal the essential

42 In *Oeuvres complètes*, vol. II (Paris, 1948), pp. 711–931; English trans., *Recollections of my Youth* (London, 1929).

nature of a people, and of humanity: 'the union of philology and philosophy, or erudition and thought, should be the nature of intellectual activity in our time'.[43]

His life was devoted to this activity. He wrote about the philology of the Semitic languages, the history of the Jews and the origins of Christianity, and published also a study of the Islamic philosopher Ibn Rushd (Averroes). Such studies, he believed, led to an important conclusion: that there is a natural course of development of human communities. They can pass through three stages of cultural growth: the first is that of religious literature and myths, of 'mankind projecting itself on to a world of its own imagining', the second that of science, and the third, into which mankind will move in the future, will be that of a synthesis between science and a 'religious' sense of oneness with nature.[44]

Different peoples, so Renan believed, have different abilities to move along this path. The nature of a language determines the culture which can be expressed in it, and peoples are therefore capable of producing cultures at various levels. There is a hierarchy of peoples, languages and cultures. At the lowest level are peoples who have no collective memory, that is to say, no culture. Above them are the first civilized races, the Chinese and others, who can rise to a certain height and no further. Above them again are the two 'great and noble races', the Semites and Aryans. The higher civilizations have grown out of the interaction between them, but they have made unequal contributions to them.[45]

The Semitic spirit has produced monotheism, and Christianity and Islam have conquered the world, but it can produce nothing else – no myths, therefore no higher literature or art, because of

the terrible simplicity of the Semitic spirit, closing the human brain to every subtle idea, to every fine sentiment, to all rational research, in order to confront it with an eternal tautology: God is God.[46]

It has therefore prevented the growth of science. In a lecture on 'Islam and science', Renan repeated this thesis in other terms:

---

[43] E. Renan, *L'avenir de la science* in *Oeuvres complètes*, vol. III (Paris, 1949), p. 836.
[44] H. Wardman, *Ernest Renan: A Critical Biography* (London, 1964), pp. 46–7.
[45] E. Renan, *Historie générale et système comparé des langues sémitiques* in *Oeuvres complètes*, vol. VIII (Paris, 1948), pp. 585ff.
[46] E. Renan, 'De la part des peuples sémitiques dans l'histoire de la civilisation' in *Oeuvres complètes*, vol. II (Paris, 1948), p. 333.

Everyone who has been in the Orient or in Africa will have been struck by the kind of iron circle in which the believer's head is enclosed, making him absolutely closed to science, and incapable of opening himself to anything new.[47]

It is the Aryan spirit which had created everything else: political life in the real sense, art, literature – the Semitic peoples have nothing of it, apart from some poetry – above all science and philosophy. In these matters, 'we are entirely Greek'; even the so-called Arabic sciences were a continuation of Greek sciences, carried on not by Arabs but by Persians and converted Greeks, that is to say, by Aryans. Christianity too in its developed form is the work of Europeans. The future of humanity therefore lies with the peoples of Europe, but there is a necessary condition of this: the destruction of the Semitic element in civilization, and of the theocratic power of Islam.[48]

This was a strong attack, and there is a metaphorical element in it: Renan was thinking not only of the world of Islam but of the Roman Catholic Church and the spirituality of St Sulpice. His theories provoked a strong response. Jamal al-Din al-Afghani (1839–97), a Muslim writer and politician who believed in the possibility of a renewal of Islam, wrote a reply to the lecture on 'Islam and science',[49] and a young Hungarian Jewish scholar, Ignaz Goldziher (1850–1921), responded to Renan's theories about myths: in his book, *Mythology among the Hebrews*, he argued that the ancient Hebrews had in fact been capable of creating myths, and some of them were embedded in the scriptures, which could indeed only be understood if they were interpreted in the light of the new disciplines of philology and mythology.[50]

A line of scholarly endeavour closely connected with philology was biblical criticism: that is to say, the study of the texts of the Old and New Testaments by precise linguistic analysis, in order to ascertain when and by whom they were written, how they are related to each other, and what is the historical reality which they

[47] E. Renan, 'L'islamisme et la science' in *Oeuvres complètes*, vol. I (Paris, 1942), p. 946.

[48] Renan, 'De la part' in *Oeuvres complètes*, pp. 332–3.

[49] Djemaleddin al-Afghani, 'L'islamisme et la science', *Journal des Débats* (18–19 May 1883) reprinted in A. M. Goichon, *La réfutation des matérialistes* (Paris, 1942), pp. 174–89; English trans., N. Keddie, *An Islamic Response to Imperialism* (Berkeley, Calif., 1968), pp. 181–7.

[50] *Der Mythos bei den Hebräeern und seine geschichtliche Entwickelung* (Leipzig, 1876); English trans., R. Martineau, *Mythology among the Hebrews and its Historical Development* (London, 1877).

reflect, whether directly or indirectly. This line of investigation was to lead to results which were to be important for the study of Islam. So far as the Old Testament was concerned, the conclusions of the 'higher criticism' were given definitive expression by Julius Wellhausen (1844–1918) in his *History of Israel*, published in 1878. Out of an earlier Mosaic religion, he argued, there had emerged Judaism, an ethical monotheism preached by prophets; law and ritual came later.[51] Similarly, a study of the New Testament was believed to show that the 'historical Jesus' came first, and only later did the doctrines and institutions which are called 'Christianity' evolve.

Such theories could be taken to provide a model for the historical development of all religions: first of all there was a holy man or prophet, a 'hero of religion', to use Schleiermacher's term; only later was a religious system articulated, in doctrines, laws, practices and institutions. Such ideas had an obvious relevance to the history of Islam. Seen in this light, indeed, Islam might be of particular importance for the student of religion. Muhammad was the most recent in time of the 'heroes of religion', those claiming to be prophets and accepted by their followers as such; he had appeared in a period for which historical documentation was plentiful, and his life, actions and sayings were fully recorded in the *Hadith* (the Traditions of the Prophet) and the *Sira* (the traditional biography of him). Thus the methods refined by biblical scholars could be used to throw light upon the origin and development of Islam, and this in its turn might help to explain the way in which other religions more distant in origin and not so fully documented had grown up.

Such concerns can be seen in the work of Wellhausen himself. Together with his studies of Judaism he wrote about early Islamic history. He believed that knowledge of pre-Islamic Arabia and the formation of Islam could help to explain the way in which the Hebrews entered history. The prophet or religious hero came first, and so in his Islamic studies he laid emphasis on the life and personality of Muhammad, founder and leader of a community.[52] In the event, however, this line of thought was to have a result which had not perhaps been expected. The 'full light of history' in

---

[51] *Prolegomena zür Geschichte Israels* (Berlin, 1883); English trans., J. S. Black, *Prolegomena to the History of Israel* (Edinburgh, 1885).
[52] *Reste arabischer Heidentumes* (Berlin, 1887); *Prolegomena zür ältesten Geschichte des Islams* (Berlin, 1899).

which Muhammad appeared to have lived turned out not to be a full light at all. By the end of the nineteenth century, some scholars were casting doubt upon the *Hadith* as an authentic record of what the Prophet had said and done, although it could still be regarded as valuable in another way.

6

The growth of knowledge of the world outside Europe, the expansion of intellectual curiosity about all things in earth and heaven, the stimulus given by the speculations of philosophers and the inquiries of philologists and biblical scholars: all these led to the development of a specific tradition of Islamic studies, the slow accumulation of knowledge and understanding based on a study of written texts, and to some extent also on direct observation of a living reality. This scholarly work, beginning in the seventeenth century and carried on through the eighteenth and nineteenth centuries until today, is perhaps of more lasting importance than the theoretical formulations which gave it an impetus and direction.

It took a long time for Islamic studies to become a separate discipline; in many universities they were an appendage to Hebrew and biblical studies, and in some they still live together in uneasy cohabitation, and in danger of being isolated from the mainstreams of academic life. These studies were carried on, until recent times, by a small number of individuals. In the universities of Europe, two of the chairs of Arabic created in early modern times were of paramount importance: that of Leiden, where the tradition which had begun with Erpenius was carried on, and that of the Collège de France in Paris, where an unbroken line of teachers included some famous scholars. A further impetus was given to Islamic studies in France by the creation of the Ecole des Langues Orientales Vivantes at the end of the eighteenth century. The French tradition was enriched by Silvestre de Sacy (1758–1838), in some ways the founder of modern Islamic and Arabic studies.

In a weak tradition, maintained and transmitted by a small number of scholars scattered in different places, personal contacts are of particular importance; the tradition is handed on orally as much as by writing. The discoveries and ideas of scholars in Leiden and Paris were passed on by a kind of apostolic succession,

and scholars formed a chain of witnesses (a *silsila*, to use the
Arabic term). The influence of Leiden and Paris was particularly
strong in the German-speaking countries, which were to become
the centre of Islamic studies in Europe, because of a combination
of the special knowledge and skills which German students
learned from the older Dutch and French traditions with the ideas
about religion, history and language which were being generated
in Germany at the time. Perhaps the most important figures in the
flowering of German scholarship, not only because of their own
work but because of the students whose minds they formed, were
H. Fleischer (1801–88), a pupil of Silvestre de Sacy, who taught at
Leipzig for many years, and T. Nöldeke (1836–1930), who made
an important visit to Leiden in his early years and then taught at
Strasbourg.[53]

The tradition of Islamic studies was weaker and less central in
the English universities, perhaps for reasons connected with their
decline in the eighteenth century. At Cambridge, the revival of
interest began in the later nineteenth century, when W. Wright
(1830–89) was appointed professor of Arabic in 1879 after studying at Leiden; with him, Cambridge entered the main European
tradition, and he was followed by a number of distinguished
scholars, W. Robertson Smith (1846–94), R. A. Nicholson (1868–
1945) and E. G. Browne (1862–1926). At Oxford, the line of
professors who followed Pococke, the first holder of the chair of
Arabic, was undistinguished. A new era of distinction did not
begin until the appointment of D. S. Margoliouth (1858–1940) in
1889; he was extremely learned, but self-taught as an Arabic and
Islamic scholar, and did not have that close contact with older
scholars in the field which is important in forming the judgement;
in his mind there was a streak of fantasy, or perhaps of irony,
which led him sometimes to propose untenable theories. It was
only with his successor, H. A. R. Gibb (1895–1971) that Oxford
entered the mainstream, and it was not until the middle years of
the twentieth century that Islamic studies began to acquire a firm
institutional basis in Great Britain, because of the foundation of
the School of Oriental and African Studies, and the recommendations of a succession of official committees.

What was missing in British and other universities was partly
replaced by the experience of travel and residence in the world
of Islam. A remarkable observer of things Arab and Islamic,

[53] J. Fück, *Die arabischen Studien in Europe* (Leipzig, 1955).

E. W. Lane (1801–76), lived for many years in Cairo: his lexicon is still the fullest and most accurate dictionary of the early classical language, and his *Manners and Customs of the Modern Egyptians*, a vivid and detailed description of the lives of the inhabitants of Cairo, gives its reader a sense – missing in much of the scholarly work of the time– of a Muslim urban society and civilization still living and changing.[54] In the same way, J. von Hammer-Purgstall (1774–1856) spent some years as an official of the Austrian embassy in Istanbul, and, after he returned to Vienna, published works on Ottoman history and on Arabic, Turkish and Persian poetry which had an influence on Goethe and other German writers of his time.

Officials of the expanding empires – British, French, Dutch and Russian – had ample opportunities to learn oriental languages and observe the life of the countries where they served, and some of them became scholars. The tradition of the gentleman-scholar was particularly strong in the British empire in India, where the line which began with Sir William Jones was continued by many officials and army officers. There was a practical reason for this: in the earlier period at least, much of the administration and negotiations with indigenous rulers was carried on through the medium of Persian, the language of high culture in the Moghul empire and some of its successor-states. There was, also, however, a genuine stirring of intellectual curiosity and the imagination.

As the nineteenth century advanced, the work of individual scholars, scattered and isolated as they were, was made easier by the creation of an international system for the exchange of ideas and information. Scientific societies were established: the Asiatic Society of Bengal in 1786, the Royal Asiatic Society in London in 1823, the Societé Asiatique in Paris in 1822, the Deutsche Morgenlandische Gesellschaft in 1845; each of them published a journal. In 1873 the first of a series of international congresses of orientalists was held. There was also a network of correspondence between scholars. The need to overcome the loneliness of the isolated researcher explains the advice which one of them, Ignaz Goldziher, gave to a young correspondent: always answer letters and attend the congresses of orientalists.[55]

---

[54] *An Account of the Manners and Customs of the Modern Egyptians* (London, 1836).
[55] R. Simon, *Ignac Goldziher: His Life and Scholarship as Reflected in his Works and Correspondence* (Budapest/Leiden, 1986), p. 16.

7

The small group of rather isolated scholars had to do too many things, and it is not surprising that they did not do all of them equally well. Their basic tasks were to study and teach Arabic and other languages of Islamic culture, and to provide the means to understand what had been written in them. They produced grammars such as those of Silvestre de Sacy and William Wright, and dictionaries, for example, E. W. Lane's *Arabic–English Lexicon* and the Turkish and English lexicon of J. W. Redhouse. They catalogued manuscripts in the great European libraries and edited some of the most important works of theology, law, history and literature. Some of the editions were collective works of scholars in different countries: the history of al-Tabari was edited by M. J. de Goeje (1836–1909) and others, and Ibn Sa'd's biographical dictionary by E. Sachau (1845–1930) and others. (Even now, however, only a small proportion of the extant documents of Islamic civilization have been published, and fewer still in satisfactory scholarly editions.) In some instances, translations were based upon the editions, and brought new themes and images into European culture. *The Thousand and One Nights* had been well known since A. Galland (1646–1715) published his French translation, but now Ibn Khaldun's *Prolegomena* to his great history became known through W. M. de Slane's French translation, based on the edition of E. Quatremère (1782–1852); the *Shah-nameh* of Firdawsi, the national epic of Iran, was edited and translated into French by J. Mohl (1800–76); and early Arabic poetry was rendered into German by F. Rückert (1788–1866) and into English by C. J. Lyall (1845–1920). A number of scholarly travellers brought back knowledge of the topography and monuments of the Arabian lands where Islam had arisen: C. M. Doughty (1843–1926) in *Travels in Arabia Deserta*, and A. Musil (1868–1944) in a series of books based on wide travel in Syria, Mesopotamia and northern Arabia.[56]

---

[56] A. I. S. de Sacy, *Grammaire arabe*, 2 vols. (Paris, 1810); W. Wright, *Grammar of the Arabic Language*, 2 vols. (London, 1859–62); E. W. Lane, *An Arabic-English Lexicon*, 8 parts (London, 1863–93); J. W. Redhouse, *A Turkish and English Lexicon* (Constantinople, 1890); M. J. de Goeje *et al.*, trans., *Annales . . . al-Tabari: Tarikh al-rusul wa'l-muluk*, 15 vols. (Leiden, 1879–1901): Muhammad ibn Sa'd, *Kitab al tabaqat al-kabir*, trans. E. Sachau *et al.*, 9 vols. (Leiden, 1904–21): E. Quatremère, ed., *Prolegomènes d'Ibn Khaldoun*, 3 vols. (Paris, 1858), French trans. W. M. de Slane, *Prologomènes historiques d'Ibn Khaldun*, 3 vols. (Paris, 1862–8); Firdawsi, *Shah-nameh*, ed. J. Mohl, 7 vols. (Paris, 1838–78); French trans., J. Mohl, *Le livre des rois*, 7 vols.

If the great scholars of the nineteenth century had done nothing except this they would deserve well of their successors. A few of them, however, did try to go further, and insert what they had discovered into a broader framework, and it was natural that they should construct it out of the ideas which were current in their time. On the whole this was a secondary field of study which did not generate its own ideas, or at least did not produce ideas which could fertilize other fields.

The most important of the seminal ideas of the nineteenth century, for those who were working in this field, was that of a culture which was developed by the cumulative efforts of human beings over time and had a unique nature which was expressed in all its aspects. Perhaps the first systematic attempt to look at the history of Islam in this perspective was made by Alfred von Kremer (1828–89). An Austrian, he studied at the Oriental Academy in Vienna, where Hammer-Purgstall had taught earlier, and then entered the consular service of the Austrian empire and served for some thirty years in Alexandria, Cairo, Beirut and elsewhere. Among other works he wrote a history of civilization under the caliphs, published in two volumes in 1875–77. His guiding ideas were taken from Herder, Hegel and other German thinkers, and supported by vast knowledge; he was perhaps the first western historian to have been influenced by the writings of Ibn Khaldun (1332–1406), the great Arab historian and thinker about history, on whom he wrote a book. The basic category of his thought was that of a culture or civilization as the total expression of the spirit of a people. That spirit, he believed, manifested itself in two principal ways: in the state, a social phenomenon of which the rise and decline were governed by laws, and in the religious ideas which moulded the life of the family and the community. These two factors were closely linked with each other: the nature and fate of a society and civilization were determined by its leading ideas.[57]

Perhaps the most important figure in the formation of a European scholarly image of Islam, in its development and nature as a religious and cultural system, was Ignaz Goldziher. A

(Paris, 1876–8); F. Rückert, trans., *Hamasa oder die ältesten arabischen Volkslieder*, 2 vols. (Stuttgart, 1846); C. J. Lyall, *Translations of Ancient Arabian Poetry* (London, 1885); C. M. Doughty, *Travels in Arabia Deserta*, 2 vols. (Cambridge, 1888).

[57] Alfred von Kremer, *Culturgeschichte des Orients unter den Chalifen*, 2 vols. (Vienna, 1975–7); English trans., S. Khuda Bakhas, *The Orient under the Caliphs* (Calcutta, 1920).

Hungarian Jew, brought up mainly in Budapest, he has left us a record of his early life and a diary of his later years, which throw much light on the formation of his mind.[58] He had a modern secular education at the University of Budapest, and he seems to have been deeply influenced by the ferment of ideas in the Hungary of the time.[59] By the 'Compromise' of 1867, Hungary had been given virtual independence within the Austrian empire, which became a dual monarchy. Its first government was in favour of the emancipation of the Jews, and the idea was current of a cultural unity which would transcend differences of race and religion. Because of the patronage of the Minister of Education, Eötvös, the young Goldziher was given a scholarship to study abroad. He spent some time at Leiden and two years at Leipzig studying with Fleischer, the student of Silvestre de Sacy. It was here that he inserted himself in the main tradition of Islamic studies. Fleischer was his real teacher; when he died, Goldziher tells us:

I felt as if part of my own life was ended. As long as the teacher lived, one thought of oneself as his student.[60]

Through his studies during these years, Goldziher became aware of modern German thought and scholarship. He read Hegel's philosophy, works of biblical criticism and Protestant theology, philology and the penumbra of ideas which surrounded it; this reading set in motion the train of thought which led to his first book, *Mythology among the Hebrews*.

He also had another kind of education, however, a traditional Jewish one. He had a deep knowledge of Hebrew and the Talmud, and the nature and future of Judaism were to remain a central concern; by 1867, he tells us, 'Judaism was the pulse-beat of my life'. His Judaism, however, was not that of the traditional scholars. He accepted the ideas of the new science of biblical criticism, as they came to German-speaking Jewish communities through such writings as those of Abraham Geiger (1810–74). Authentic Judaism, according to this school of thought, was essentially the monotheism of the prophets; law and ritual came later, and were the products of particular times and places. This idea had implications for religious practice, but also for scholarship. Religious texts should be studied in their historical context,

---

[58] *Tagebuch* (Leiden, 1978).   [59] Simon, *Goldziher*, pp. 11–76.
[60] *Tagebuch*, p. 116.

and could be used in two different ways: to throw light on the events and persons of which they claimed to record the history, but also – and indeed primarily – to throw light on the age in which they had been produced.

In his early twenties a third influence was added to those of his two educations. He was given the opportunity to go to the Near East, and in 1873–4 he spent several months in Beirut, Damascus and Cairo. Beirut made little impact upon him, and he was not impressed by the American missionaries and their converts, but his weeks in Damascus were of lasting importance in his life. They gave him his first opportunity 'to enter the Muslim republic of thought'. He met scholars and divines, and he later described this time as 'the loveliest part of my life'.[61] In Cairo also he met scholars, including the reformer Jamal al-Din al-Afghani, and he obtained permission to attend lessons at the Azhar, the great centre of traditional Islamic learning; he was probably the first European scholar to do so.

This visit clearly left a permanent mark upon him. It gave him an awareness of Islam as a living community which was never to leave him, although he only returned once more to Egypt for a very short visit. It taught him the importance of jurisprudence and law in the thought-world of Islam. Above all, Islam appeared to him to be that towards which other religions should strive: a pure monotheism, an uncontaminated response to the call of God to the human heart: 'the only religion in which superstition and heathen elements were forbidden not by rationalism but by orthodox teaching'.[62] In these months, he tells us,

my way of thought was thoroughly turned towards Islam, and so was my sympathy ... I was not lying when I said that I believed in the prophetic missions of Muhammad ... My religion was henceforth the universal religion of the prophets.[63]

Islam, as he perceived it during these months, provided a touchstone by which he could judge the other monotheistic religions. He wished to do what he could to call Judaism back to what he believed to be its truth. To judge by his diary, he had a certain aversion to Christianity, at least as he saw it in the Holy Land; but he had a habit of writing bitter things which may not have expressed his real beliefs.

[61] Ibid., p. 58. For Goldziher's diary during his visit to the Near East, see R. Patai, *Ignaz Goldziher and his Oriental Diary* (Detroit, 1987).
[62] *Tagebuch*, p. 59.   [63] Ibid., p. 71.

He seems to have had the ambition to write a general comparative book on human cultures, but was prevented from doing so by pressure of work. By the time he returned to Budapest after his years of study and travel, the liberal atmosphere of Hungary had become clouded; Eötvös was dead and the government had changed. He was not given a substantive post in the university until 1904, and he earned his living as secretary of the Jewish community of Budapest. His diaries are full of complaints about the dull, menial work he had to do, and the way in which the rich Jews who controlled the community treated him. There is a mystery here. He was offered chairs at Prague, Heidelberg and elsewhere, and was approached about the chair at Cambridge in 1894. He need not have stayed in Budapest, and it is not clear why he did so; it may have been because of family obligations, but it may also have been because of a sense of loyalty to Hungary, and the idea that every man must have his place in the world, and this was his.

In the event he did not write his general book, but his detailed work on Islam is perhaps more important than that would have been. Such time as he had for scholarship he gave to the precise study of a wide range of Islamic religious and legal texts in their historical context. In what is perhaps the most famous and seminal of his writings, he applied the critical method he had learned in Germany to one of the basic texts of Islam, the *Hadith* or Traditions of the Prophet. He looked at it not as a sacred text which had come down unchanged from the time of the Prophet and his Companions, but as a body of writings produced by a process of gradual accumulation over many generations. It is not, therefore, to be accepted without question as a record of what Muhammad said and did, but is primarily of value as throwing light upon the religious and political controversies of the first centuries of Islamic history. This insight has had a profound effect upon all later studies of Islamic theology and law.[64]

Goldziher's comprehensive view of the way in which Islam had developed as a religious system was given expression in a series of lectures, written in 1907 to be given in the United States but never in fact delivered, and later published: *Introduction to Islamic Theology and Law*.[65] They show his attempt to fit the phenomena of Islam

[64] I. Goldziher, 'Über die Entwickelung des Hadith' In *Muhammedanische Studien*, vol. II (Halle, 1890), pp. 1–274; English trans., C. R. Barber and S. M. Stern, *Muslim Studies*, vol. II (London, 1971), pp. 17–251.
[65] *Vorlesungen über den Islam* (Heidelberg, 1910); English trans., A. and R. Hamori, *Introduction to Islamic Theology and Law* (Princeton, N. J., 1981).

into a framework derived from the German speculative thought of the nineteenth century. Its starting-point is Schleiermacher's theory of religion: the basis of all religions is the feeling of dependence, but in each of them it takes a special form which determines its character and development. In Islam the form which it takes is that of submission, which is the literal meaning of the word 'Islam' itself: man must submit his will to unbounded omnipotence. This was the insight formulated by the Prophet Muhammad; he may have taken his ideas from elsewhere, but he made them into something original and new by the force of passionate conviction. From that moment what we now know as Islam gradually developed. It was given its direction by the insights of the Prophet, but drew into itself elements from the religious systems of the civilizations incorporated into the universal world of Islam: Judaism, Christianity, Zoroastrianism and late classical antiquity.

Thus Goldziher saw the development of Islam as being broadly similar to that of other prophetic religions, as viewed by the scholars and theologians of his time: first came the prophet, then the prophetic revelation was fixed in a holy writ, then the theologians tried to explain and defend it and the legal scholars to draw out its practical implications. During this process, however, the lures and hazards of the world lay all around. For Muslims the Word of God, the Qur'an, revealed His will for mankind, and the elaboration of the *shari'a*, the 'holy law' or system of ideal morality, was therefore an essential and central part of the process by which Islam was articulated into a system, but it had its dangers: it could stifle the desire for holiness which lies at the heart of all religions. (No doubt Goldziher was thinking of Rabbinical Judaism as well as Islam.) Mysticism (Sufism) was a necessary counterbalance to this: a reassertion of the desire and need for holiness, for a personal relationship with God. Goldziher was one of the first scholars to see the importance of Sufism in the ethical system of Islam. He knew, however, that here too the tares of the world could spring up; Sufism had been a channel through which primordial beliefs had come into Islam. Nevertheless they could not destroy the sense of submission and all that flows from it:

A life lived in the spirit of Islam can be an ethically impeccable life, demanding compassion for God's creatures, honesty in one's dealings, love, loyalty, the suppression of selfish impulses,[66]

---

[66] Ibid., p. 16; English trans., p. 18.

The spirit of Islam, Goldziher believed, was still alive; his book is not simply a record of something which had existed in the past, it shows a concern for the present and future.

8

In Goldziher's work there is a sense of Islam as a living reality, changing over time but with its changes controlled, at least up to a point, by a vision of what 'a life lived in the spirit of Islam' should be: creating and maintaining a balance between the law, the articulation of God's word into precepts for action, and mysticism, the expression of the desire for holiness; drawing into itself ideas from the older civilizations engulfed in it; sustained by the learned elites of the great Islamic cities; and still living and growing. This is far from the view held a century earlier, of Islam as created by a man, sustained by the enthusiasm of a nomadic people, and ceasing to be of importance in world history once the first impulse had died out.

Rather similar ideas were carried in a different direction by another scholar of Goldziher's generation, C. Snouck Hurgronje (1857–1936), in whom the tradition of the school of Leiden may be said to have reached its peak. After his studies at Leiden there came two significant episodes in his life. The first was a year of residence at Mecca in 1884–5, as a seeker after understanding of Islam. The product of this was his book, *Mekka*, an account of the Pilgrimage and also a description of life in the holy city. Based as it is on his own observations, it is critical of certain western stereotypes of Muslim society. The Muslim conception of slavery, for example, is very different from that derived from the practices of European settlers in America; 'the Christian world', he declares, 'takes towards Islam an attitude of misunderstanding and falsehood'.[67] Similarly, the Muslim family is not what it is commonly supposed to be: segregation of women is less complete, monogamy is more common, women sometimes marry several times. Perhaps most important as showing the direction of his later work are his remarks about Islamic law:

It is a mistake to suppose that the so-called Moslem law has ever really dominated culture or has remained in intimate contact with the needs of society.[68]

---

[67] *Mekka*, 2 vols. (The Hague, 1888–9); partial English trans., J. N. Monahan, *Mekka in the Latter Part of the 19th Century* (Leiden/London, 1931), p. 19.
[68] Ibid., pp. 83f.

It is important not as law but as an ideal system of social morality, an influence on practice and a court of appeal 'when times are out of joint'. More important than the strict letter of the law, as an influence on the lives of the people of Mecca, is the teaching of the Sufi brotherhoods in regard to practice, moral discipline and meditation leading towards a sense of the presence of God. Among the educated, the teaching of the brotherhoods is not regarded as a substitute for religious learning, but as a means of giving value to obedience to the law; among the uneducated, it lays emphasis on the performance of religious duties and gives expression to human feelings while keeping control over them.[69]

After Snouck Hurgronje's sojourn in Mecca there came a long period of residence in the Dutch East Indies, from 1899 to 1906, as adviser to the colonial government on Muslim policy. This experience reinforced what he had learnt in Mecca, that Islam was a living and changing reality: what Muslims mean by it is constantly changing because of the particular circumstances of times and places. Even the theoretical formulations of lawyers and mystics have changed over time, and this process began very early, when 'the sober monotheism' of Muhammad was adapted to 'the religious ideals of western Asia and Egypt, both permeated with Hellenistic thought.'[70] If non-Muslims wish to understand Islam, they must study it in its historical reality, without judgements of value about what it ought to be.

The concept of Islam, however it is defined, is not adequate by itself, so Hurgronje believes, to explain all the phenomena of what are called 'Muslim societies'. They should be seen as 'fields of force'[71] resulting from the interaction between a certain norm derived from the teaching of Islam and the specific nature of a particular society, created by a long cumulative historical experience within its physical environment. This idea had practical implications. As adviser to the government, Hurgronje took it for granted that European rule would continue indefinitely, but believed it should be conducted in a way which was compatible with the natural evolution of the Muslim societies of Indonesia: modern education and the social process would lead to changes tending towards the evolution of a secular and rational civili-

[69] Ibid., pp. 170f.
[70] C. Snouck Hurgronje, *Selected Works*, ed. G. H. Bousquet and J. Schacht (Leiden, 1957), p. 76.
[71] J. Waardenburg, *L'islam dans le miroir de l'occident* (Paris, 1960), p. 97.

zation, and to this Islamic law would have nothing to contribute.[72]

The sense of Islam as something more than words in texts, as something living in individual Muslims, was new in European studies. It was expressed more fully, and in a very individual way, by a scholar of the next generation, who acknowledged his debt to previous masters, and to Goldziher in particular. Louis Massignon (1883–1962) was important because of his impact upon one of the two mainstreams of European scholarship, that of Paris, but also for the force and originality with which he posed certain questions to Christian thinkers who looked at Islam. To explain his ideas, it is best to begin where he himself began, in various fragments of autobiography and spiritual confession which are scattered through his writings. After early studies in Paris and visits to North Africa, he had a period of further study in Cairo, and from there went on an archaeological mission to Iraq. According to his own account, in May 1908 he was arrested by the Ottoman authorities, accused of being a spy, imprisoned, and threatened with death. He tried to commit suicide 'by sacred horror of myself', and became aware of unseen presences interceding for him, and had some kind of vision of God – the 'visitation of the Stranger'. This was followed by a sense of pardon and release:

sudden recollection, my eyes closed before an inner fire, which judges me and burns my heart, certainty of a pure Presence, unspeakable, creative, suspending my condemnation at the prayers of invisible beings, visitors to my prison, whose names strike my thought.[73]

For the first time he was able to pray, and his first prayer was in Arabic. He was released and brought back to health by the intercession of a family of Arab Muslim scholars in Baghdad.

Massignon's narrative of these events raises questions of more than one kind. First of all, what really happened on that day in May 1908? It is impossible to say for certain, but doubts have been expressed about his version. In the circumstances of the Ottoman empire at that time, a French citizen wandering in the countryside might well have been arrested by the local authorities, but would scarcely have been condemned to death. The French consular records of the time mention only an attack of

---

[72] Ibid., pp. 245ff.
[73] L. Massignon, 'La visitation de l'étranger' in *Parole donnée* (Paris, 1962), p. 71.

fever, caused possibly by sunstroke.[74] What seems likely is that Massignon had some kind of breakdown of health, leading to a moment of disordered consciousness, which precipitated a moral and spiritual crisis, in which he turned away from what he regarded as the moral confusion of his earlier life ('by sacred horror of myself'). It is less important to ask what happened, however, than to look for the meaning which he himself gave to the crisis. It produced or reinforced in him a certain view of history, and a certain view of Islam.

Massignon stood in conscious opposition to the kind of historical approach which was common in the nineteenth century: the view, that is to say, which saw history as having a meaning inside itself, moving by its own inner dynamism towards a goal which it could achieve in this world, and one which thought of great collectivities – nations or races or classes – as the carriers of this movement. For Massignon, the meaning of history was to be found rather in the working of the grace of God in individual souls, crossing all barriers between human communities – even religious communities – and its end was a goal which lay beyond the limits of the perishable world. The process revealed itself above all in the lives of certain individuals who had been touched by grace in some special way and had responded to it fully, by being witnesses to the presence of God and, if need be, by martyrdom. Such witnesses could offer their sufferings for those of others. There is here an influence from the French Catholic thought of the later nineteenth century. By some thinkers the Christian idea of vicarious suffering was developed into a doctrine of 'substitution', of suffering offered not for all mankind but for specific purposes, and not only for the sufferings of others but for their sins. Massignon may have learnt this idea from the novelist J. K. Huysmans (1848–1907) whom he had known in his early youth.[75]

In Massignon's view, there is a perpetual line of such substitutes, and their influence can extend beyond their deaths. The thought may have been in his mind that he had it in him to become one of this chain of witnesses, by prayer, intercession or even martyrdom. He did not speak with pride of a special

[74] G. Harpigny, *Islam et christianisme selon Louis Massignon* (Louvain-la-Neuve, 1981), p. 57; D. Massignon, 'La voyage en Mesopotamie et la conversion de Louis Massignon en 1908', *Islamochristiana*, 14 (1988), pp. 127–99.
[75] R. Griffiths, *The Reactionary Revolution* (London, 1966), pp. 149ff.

vocation, however, rather with a sense of unworthiness. He sometimes wrote of himself as having been an 'outlaw', and those who met him were conscious of some struggle inside him between conflicting forces.

He also had a certain, very individual view of Islam. His theological formulations could arouse a certain suspicion among Christians, as they might be taken to imply that Islam was an alternative path of salvation. He was a Catholic, however, and in later life became a priest of the Greek Catholic Church, and his basic position lies within the spectrum of possible Christian attitudes. He believed that Islam was a genuine expression of monotheistic faith, claiming descent from Abraham by way of Ishmael, and that it had a positive spiritual mission: to act as a reproach to the idolaters who did not confess that there was one God.[76] Muslims could give Christians an example of faith; this was another familiar theme in the writings of some Catholics of the time, such as Charles de Foucauld and Ernest Psichari, the grandson of Renan. Because of this, Christians, he thought, had a duty which they owed to Muslims: the Stranger who visited Massignon at the moment of crisis was an image of God, but also of the human exile, the wanderer knocking at the door to be let in. In Massignon's mind, hospitality was a cardinal virtue, because it implied loyalty and courage. In later life this was to lead him into active opposition to French policy in the period of colonial revolt: in Madagascar, Morocco and, above all, Algeria. In his earlier years he had had connections, like most of his generation, with the imperial mission of France, but later he came to see imperial rule as an 'abuse of hospitality', an expression of 'our secular rage to understand, to conquer, to possess'.[77] Beyond the sphere of political action, he believed it was the calling of Christians to bring Muslims to the fullness of truth through prayer and intercession, and by offering their lives and sufferings in substitution for them. The Christian could perform this role in a community of prayer with Muslims. This explains Massignon's concern for those places where Christians and Muslims could join in prayer: Jerusalem, the tomb of Abraham at Hebron, and a shrine in Brittany sacred to the 'seven sleepers of Ephesus', known in Christian tradition and also mentioned in the Qur'an.

---

[76] L. Massignon, 'Trois prières d'Abraham' in *Opera Minora*, ed. Y. Moubarac (Beirut, 1963), vol. III, pp. 804–16.
[77] L. Massignon, 'Tout une vie avec un frère parti en désert' in *Parole donnée*, p. 71.

Holding such beliefs, it was natural that Massignon should have a special concern for one stream of Muslim spirituality, that of the Sufis who tried not only to obey the will of God as revealed in the Book, but to draw nearer to Him by turning away from the things of the world, and by spiritual discipline. Much of his work as a scholar was given to the study of mysticism. In a sense, his was orthodox work, within the philological tradition of the nineteenth century: the discovery and editing of texts, the analysis of them with care for the precise meaning of words; he wrote on the development of the technical vocabulary of Sufism, and also of Islamic philosophy.[78] He was concerned to show how Sufism had grown, not by importation from eastern Christianity or Hinduism, but by an internal development, as some Muslims took the teaching of the Qur'an seriously, meditated on it and tried to draw out its implications for the spiritual life. He had a sense of the supreme importance of the Qur'an in the inner life of Muslims, as possessing a 'verbal repertory' containing a history of the universe, a collection of maxims for action, and a manual of moral self-examination and concentration of the soul on God.

Massignon's most famous work is his study of al-Hallaj (d.922), a mystic, poet and theologian who was accused of casting doubt upon the need for strict observance of Muslim duties: he is said to have asserted that one could make the Pilgrimage in one's own room instead of going to Mecca, and that the Ka'ba, the sacred edifice which lay at the heart of the Pilgrimage, should be destroyed so that it could be rebuilt in wisdom. Beyond that, there was a suspicion that he was teaching that, at the moment of mystical union, the human personality of the mystic could be absorbed into that of God. There was a famous saying attributed to him, although it is not certain that he ever said it: *ana al-haqq*, 'I am the Truth' or 'I am God'. This could be taken to imply a pure monism which would be incompatible with the idea of the transcendence of God. There may also have been political reasons for his arrest; he was tried, condemned and executed in Baghdad.

The study of al-Hallaj was Massignon's doctoral dissertation, virtually finished by 1914 and published in 1921; he continued to work on the subject for the rest of his life, and a revised version was published after his death.[79] It is a work of great erudition and

---

[78] L. Massignon, *Essai sur les origines du lexique technique de la mystique musulmane*, new edn (Paris, 1954); *Muhadarat fi tarikh al-istilahat al-falsafiyya al-'arabiyya* (Cairo, 1983).
[79] *La passion d'al-Hosayn-ibn-Mansour al-Hallaj, martyr mystique de l'islam*, 2 vols. (Paris, 1921); revised edn, *La passion de Husayn ibn Mansur martyr mystique de l'islam*, 4 vols.

original thought, using the fragmentary sources to construct a narrative of al-Hallaj's life and show the stages in the development of the vocation of a mystic, through penitence, renunciation and purification to some kind of experience of union with God. It shows also the relationship of his sayings and writings with the earlier development of Islamic theology, law and mysticism. This is placed within a description of the milieu of 'Abbasid Baghdad, where al-Hallaj lived; by a careful accumulation of detail, a medieval city of which almost no trace remains is brought to life – its streets and buildings, its people, the food they ate, the ways in which they earned their living, studied, worshipped and were buried.

In conformity with his idea of the chain of witnesses or substitutes, exercising an influence after their deaths and handing their mission on to others, Massignon sees the life of al-Hallaj as prolonged beyond his execution. In a remarkable survey of the spiritual life of Muslim communities, he shows how the fame of al-Hallaj survived, in discussion among the learned, and in popular devotion expressed in the process, and from being an 'outlaw' he was reincorporated into the community.

Some doubts have been expressed about Massignon's work. Running through it is a theme common to the French Catholic writing of his youth: the belief in secret societies, in vast conspiracies aiming to seize power or overturn the social order. Some of his interpretations of the sources have not been accepted by other scholars: the existence of trade-guilds and their links with esoteric religious movements, and the connection between certain Islamic sects and movements of social protest. More fundamental to his work is his treatment of the figure of al-Hallaj. Massignon has shown that al-Hallaj is a remarkable figure in the history of Muslim spirituality, and that by following the Sufi path he reached an unusual degree of understanding of the operations of divine grace. There is a warning, however, in his own words: 'I have added to the historical facts the further meditations which they have suggested.'[80] There seems to be an attempt to fit al-Hallaj into a Christian pattern; he is made to appear as if he regarded his own death as an act of vicarious suffering, even seeking martyrdom because 'there is no more pressing business

---

(Paris, 1975); English trans., H. Mason, *The Passion of al-Hallaj, Mystic and Martyr of Islam*, 4 vols. (Princeton, N. J., 1982).

[80] Ibid., new edn, vol. I, p. 32; English trans., vol. I, p. lxviii.

for the Muslims than my execution', wishing 'to die accursed for
the salvation of all'.[81]

9

By the originality of his ideas and the force of his personality,
Massignon had a deep influence on Islamic studies in France, and
indeed on French views of Islam; he was perhaps the only Islamic
scholar who was a central figure in the intellectual life of his time.
His work was a sign of a change in the Christian approach to
Islam, and even perhaps one of the causes of it. In the last two
generations there have been attempts by Christian thinkers and
scholars to define what has always been the puzzling phenomenon
of Islam, so close in some ways, so distant in others: a God who
seems to be the God of Abraham, who speaks to mankind and
makes His will known, and holds out the prospect of a final Day of
Judgement, but who speaks through a Book which Muslims do,
and Christians do not, accept as literally the word of God. These
attempts have been made largely by scholars in France, or at least
writing in French, for some of them are Christians from the Arab
countries but of French intellectual formation.

   Thus G. C. Anawati and Louis Gardet have written works on
Islamic theology and mysticism. As Christian theologians they
have tried to define the status of Islamic mysticism. Is it 'natural'
or 'supernatural'? For them it lies in a middle state between the
two: it tends towards the supernatural, that is to say, the
experience of divine love in the soul, given by supernatural Grace,
but is limited by the essential Islamic idea of the inaccessibility of
God, the veil which lies between God and man, whose true
worship is obedience to His word. Sufism therefore is marked by
'spiritual states which are capable of more than one interpretation'.[82] J. Abdel-Jalil, a Moroccan Muslim by birth but a convert
to Christianity and a Franciscan friar, studied those lines of
Islamic thought and spirituality which, if prolonged, might lead a
Muslim to Christianity; in *Marie et l'Islam*, he showed the special
status given to the Virgin Mary in the Qur'an.[83] This sense of
Islam as a religion formed by acceptance of the one God, but
tending towards completion in something other than itself, was

[81] Ibid., vol. I, p. 336; English trans., vol. I, pp. 95–6.
[82] *Mystique musulmane* (Paris, 1961), pp. 95–6.
[83] *Aspects intérieurs de l'islam* (Paris, 1949); *Marie et l'islam* (Paris, 1950).

shown also in the formulations of the Vatican Council of 1962–5, the first considered attempt by the Catholic Church to define its attitude towards Islam:

The Church looks with esteem upon the Muslims, who worship the one living God, merciful and all-powerful, creator of heaven and earth, who has spoken to men.[84]

In this formula there is an echo of the terminology of the Qur'an itself.

Similar voices have been raised in the Protestant churches, for example by Kenneth Cragg, a bishop of the Anglican Church,[85] and the World Council of Churches has made a sustained attempt to organize dialogue between Christians and Muslims. This line of thought is crossed, however, by another one, which also has deep roots in Christian theology. There has always been a strand of thought which has emphasized the uniqueness of the revelation of Christ: God cannot be known by human efforts, only by His own self-revelation, which has been perfected in the person of Jesus Christ and is recorded in the Bible; all other religious teachers, and the books in which their teaching is enshrined, can express no more than human strivings for something which cannot be attained by human effort. All that man can create for himself are idols; thus Karl Barth stated bluntly: 'The God of Muhammad is an idol like all other idols'.[86] In the same way, Hendrik Kraemer, a Dutch missionary and theologian, said that Islam is a man-made religion, not the true faith derived from God's unique revelation of Himself:

Man wants God, but somehow he wants Him in his own way . . . Nowhere do we find a repudiation of every possible man-made spiritual world.[87]

There is a significant difference of tone, however, between Kraemer's voice and that of similar voices in the past. Kraemer was an Islamic scholar with a deep knowledge of Muslim societies in south-east Asia, and a person of moral and intellectual sensibility; in his work there is no derogation of Muhammad and his followers, and he gives full weight to the human achievements of Islamic civilization.

[84] *Concile oecumenique Vatican II: Documents conciliaires* (Paris, 1965), p. 215.
[85] *The Call of the Minaret* (Oxford, 1956): *Sandals at the Mosque* (Oxford, 1959); *The Event of the Qur'an* (London, 1971).
[86] Quoted in G. Parrinder, *Comparative Religion* (London, 1962), p. 48.
[87] *Religion and the Christian Faith* (London, 1956), p. 334.

10

The central tradition of Islamic studies has continued to exist throughout the last half-century: the exploration of the ways in which what was given to Muslims by or through Muhammad was articulated into systems of theology, law and practice, an exploration carried on by the method elaborated by philologists, that of the careful study of written texts. Side by side with it, however, there has been an increasing interest in Islam as a living system of practices within specific societies. This interest can already be seen in the work of Goldziher, Hurgronje and Massignon, but it has been expanded by the entry into this field of scholars trained in other disciplines of mind – in history and the social sciences.

One cause of this change has been the growth of interest in the world of Islam in the great American universities. The tradition of European Islamic scholarship was carried to the United States by a number of European teachers, among them two Scotsmen. One of them, D. B. Macdonald (1863–1943), had studied in Germany with Nöldeke and Fleischer, and taught at Hartford Theological Seminary from 1893 onwards. The other was H. A. R. Gibb, who left Oxford in 1955 to become professor of Arabic at Harvard.

Both Macdonald and Gibb were keenly interested in the life of the Muslim world. Macdonald wrote a book about it, and Gibb, in a survey of modern trends in Islam, warned of the danger of studying only the consensus of the learned, and ignoring that of the people.[88] Such ideas aroused echoes in the minds of American students trained as historians or social scientists, and from the 1950s onwards some universities began to develop centres of 'area studies', where those whose minds had been formed by different disciplines, but who had acquired a special knowledge of the languages, culture and society of a particular region, could interact with each other.

Among much else, there has appeared both in European and in American scholarship a growing interest in what is often called 'popular Islam', and in particular the Sufi brotherhoods, which from at least the time of Goldziher have come to be recognized as the channels through which the mainstream of Muslim spirituality

[88] For Macdonald, see Waardenburg, L'islam, pp. 132ff; for Gibb, see A. Hourani, 'H. A. R. Gibb: the vocation of an orientalist' in A. Hourani, Europe and the Middle East (London, 1980), pp. 104–34; D. B. Macdonald, The Religious Attitude and Life in Islam (Chicago, Ill., 1909); H. A. R. Gibb, Modern Trends in Islam (Chicago, Ill., 1947).

has flowed. There are various ways of studying it. Islamic scholars have done so through the texts in which the mystic's path towards direct experience of God, and the ideas of God and man implied by it, have been expounded; social anthropologists have begun to study the penumbra of popular beliefs and practices which have grown up around the brotherhoods, the cult of saints, the practice of pilgrimage to their shrines, the belief in the validity of their intercession, and in invocations and visions. They have also studied the social role of shrines and their guardians as points around which communities and, in some circumstances, political movements can crystallize, and of brotherhoods as providing the link between different regions or social groups, or between men and women.

Work done on these lines during the past generation has posed a question: once we go beyond the normative definitions of theologians and lawyers, what do we mean by 'Islamic society'? In view of the great variety of customs and institutions, of artistic forms and collective mentalities of the 'world of Islam' which stretches from the Atlantic to the Pacific, from Morocco to the Philippines, is there a sense in which they can all be called 'Islamic'? This is a question to which a number of social anthropologists have addressed themselves. Clifford Geertz, in his *Islam Observed*, made use of material from Java and Morocco to answer the question, in what senses can two societies, standing at opposite ends of the world in which Islam is the main inherited religion, be called Muslim societies? What is the 'family resemblance' which makes them both 'Islamic'?[89] Michael Gilsenan, in *Recognizing Islam*, suggests that 'Islam', when seen in its social context, is not a single unitary object which by itself determines the behaviour and customs of a society; it is a word which can be used to refer to certain concepts, symbols and rituals which have helped to mould the collective consciousness of various societies, but have also been moulded by them. Islam is

a word that identifies varying relations of practice, representation, symbol, concept and world-view within the same society and between different societies. There are patterns in these relations, and they have changed in very important ways over time.[90]

---

[89] *Islam Observed: Religious Development in Morocco and Indonesia* (Chicago, Ill., 1968).
[90] *Recognizing Islam* (London, 1982), p. 19.

However carefully the word 'Islam' is defined, it may still be asked whether it can be used in any sense as a category of explanation for the history of the societies most of whose inhabitants are Muslims. Few writers would now assert this as categorically as some might have done a generation or two ago, because writers of a different kind are now thinking about the history of those societies. There was an age, not long since ended, and even now not wholly ended, when virtually the only scholars who wrote about the history and society of the 'Muslim world' were those whose primary task was to study and teach the Arabic, Persian and Turkish languages and the texts written in them. They brought to their writing about broader subjects the categories which were familiar to them. In the last generation, however, the field of study has been entered by scholars trained in different disciplines. Some scholars whose minds have been formed by historiography or the social sciences have begun to turn their attention to the 'world of Islam', and there is also a new concern with 'world history' and 'comparative history', with processes and movements which extend beyond the 'world of Islam' to the whole world, or at least to large parts of it. The change is a slow one, however; in most universities, in the English-speaking world at least, history is still taught with the main emphasis upon that western civilization which is regarded as having moved from ancient Greece westwards to the countries along the Atlantic coast, and then to have covered the whole world in its modern form. In a good universal history used widely in teaching, out of 900 pages or so on history since AD 600 only fifty or so are devoted to the world of Islam (but they are sensitive and well informed).[91]

In some countries, however, and notably in France and the United States, historians and social scientists are bringing their own categories of interpretation, drawn from the historical or sociological culture of the age: in particular, Marxist or post-Marxist categories, or those refined by historians associated with the French periodical *Annales*, or – in recent years – concepts derived from modern literary theory. To take a few obvious examples: Fernand Braudel, in *La Méditerranée et le monde méditerranéen à l'époque de Philippe II*, tried to explain the nature and development of the whole world lying around the Mediterranean Sea, and thus introduced a concept at once broader and narrower

[91] J. M. Roberts, *The Hutchinson History of the World* (London, 1976).

than that of the 'Muslim world'.[92] In the same way, in a book edited by Julian Pitt-Rivers, *Mediterranean Countrymen*, a number of anthropologists showed themselves to be concerned more with similarities than with differences between countries where Christianity, in its Catholic or Orthodox form, or Islam was the inherited religion; their interest lay in the values of honour and shame by which peasant societies live.[93]

The category of 'Islam' scarcely enters into one of the seminal works of Middle Eastern history written in the present generation: André Raymond's *Artisans et commerçants au Caire au 18ème siècle*. The principal factors of explanation are the administrative and fiscal system of the Ottoman empire and its local deputies in Egypt, and the system of industrial production in its relation to international trade; 'Islam' only enters into the analysis as a subsidiary factor, in so far as Islamic law affects inheritance and the distribution of property.[94] Maxime Rodinson, in *Islam et capitalisme*, examines the common view that there is something in the doctrines and laws and customary behaviour of Muslim societies which has prevented the development of a modern capitalist economy. The book is a product of the debate begun by Max Weber in *The Protestant Ethic*, and Rodinson attempts to show that, if capitalism developed first in countries where Christianity and not Islam was the dominant religion, the explanation cannot be found in the nature of either religion.[95] An international colloquium on 'the Islamic city', held in 1965, considered the idea that Muslim cities had characteristics, both of physical formation and of social structure, which are derived from the teaching and laws of Islam; it came to the conclusion that the concept of the 'Islamic city' was less useful as a category of explanation than, for example, those of the medieval or pre-industrial or Near Eastern or North African city.[96]

Such a change in emphasis can go too far, however. Those in particular who are concerned with the earliest period of what is normally called 'Islamic history' can scarcely ignore the rise of a new religion, its spread in countries of ancient civilization, its

[92] *La Méditerranée et le monde méditerranéen à l'époque de Philippe II*, 2nd edn (Paris, 1966); English trans., S. Reynolds, *The Mediterranean and the Mediterranean World in the Age of Philip II*, 2 vols. (London, 1972–3).

[93] *Mediterranean Countrymen* (Paris, 1963).

[94] *Artisans et commerçants au Caire au 18ème siècle*, 2 vols. (Damascus, 1973–4).

[95] *Islam et capitalisme* (Paris, 1960); English trans., B. Pearce, *Islam and Capitalism* (London, 1973).

[96] A. Hourani and S. M. Stern, eds., *The Islamic City* (Oxford, 1970).

articulation in theology and law through the medium of the Arabic language, and the foundation of an empire claiming authority in its name; even in later periods, there was a sense in which Muslim countries tended to live in comparative isolation from others. The most ambitious attempt to combine explanations in terms of Islam with other kinds of historical explanation, and to place the world of Islam also in the context of universal history, is that made by Marshall Hodgson in *The Venture of Islam*.[97] The subtitle of the book is *Conscience and History in a World-Society*, and this is significant of Hodgson's concern for the relations between the individual and the collectivity, and also his awareness of the place of the Islamic world within a broader unity: the Oikoumene, the whole world of cities and settled agriculture stretching from the Atlantic to the Pacific. He sees the history of Islam also within a broader temporal framework, as a continuation of an older cultural tradition, that of the Fertile Crescent, Iran and Egypt, stretching back to Babylonia and ancient Egypt, but now expressing itself in a new language, Arabic, and in intellectual and artistic response to a new holy Book.

Within this broad context of space and time, Hodgson puts forward a certain view of the historical process, in terms of the interaction of three forces: the gradual development of cultural resources and traditions within the limits of a certain physical environment, the growth and persistence of a collective solidarity, and the subtle working of individual thought and conscience which, in some circumstances, can give a new direction to cultural traditions and collective solidarity. The implications of this view of history are far reaching. Hodgson broke with the generally accepted idea of Islamic history as consisting of three centuries or so of achievement, with the Arabic language as its medium and the Fertile Crescent as its centre, followed by a long period of stagnation or decline. He saw the climax of Islamic civilization as coming much later in date and further east in space: in the early modern period, and in the region of Persian high culture, stretching from central Asia through Iran into northern India. This view has implications for world history also: Hodgson broke away from the familiar idea (expressed, for example, in the thought of Hegel) of history as being a westward march. Until the eighteenth century, he maintain, it is Muslim civilization which dominates

97 3 vols. (Chicago, 1974).

the world of cities and settled agriculture, with its languages of high culture, its law providing a framework of shared expectations within which commercial and other kinds of intercourse could take place, its literature and art giving symbolic expression to a vision of this world and the next. It was only in the nineteenth century, he suggests, that the power and cultural independence of the Muslim world began to be seriously challenged, as a result of a mutation of human society which first appeared on the far western fringes of the civilized world.

I I

In these discussions other voices are now beginning to be heard. In Europe and America, research and thought about Islamic culture and history are now carried on in the presence of those about whom western scholars and thinkers are writing. This is true in more senses than one: we are all conscious of a Muslim world which is living and changing, and is not just something which existed in the past and is now – to use Hegel's terms – sunk in 'oriental ease and repose'. Research and thought, moreover, are now being carried on in collaboration and dialogue. The international community of Islamic studies is more of an open community. We may compare a conference held sixty years ago with those held today. At the seventeenth international congress of orientalists, held in Oxford in 1928, scarcely more than a dozen out of some 750 subscribing members were Muslims, and they played a small part in the proceedings;[98] in present-day conferences of the Middle East Studies Association of North America, a large proportion of the members are from Muslim countries, and they include some of the most active and prominent of them.

Most kinds of study are neutral, in the sense that they can be pursued by the same methods and understood in terms of the same categories by those who have different cultural formations: the editing of texts, the exploration of government archives, the history of economic change or of art. In some fields, indeed, the balance is shifting between scholars in Europe and America and those in the Muslim world itself: all specialists in Ottoman history, for example, have felt the impact of the work of Halil Inalcık and other Turkish historians. There are likely to be

---

[98] *Proceedings of the Seventeenth International Congress of Orientalists, Oxford 1928* (London, 1929).

differences of approach, however, in regard to more sensitive matters: the interpretation of a religious tradition and the culture intimately bound up with it. In recent years, two kinds of criticism of Islamic, or more generally of 'oriental' studies have been expressed vigorously.

One of them comes from devout adherents of the faith of Islam, for whom the Qur'an is, in the literal sense, the word of God revealed throught the Angel Gabriel to the Prophet Muhammad, and who find it impossible to accept the kind of scholarly analysis which would reduce the Qur'an to a product of the mind of Muhammad, or would depict the person of Muhammad in a way which would cast doubt on the claim that he had been chosen by God to be a messenger of His word. Such reservations should be treated with respect by those who do not share them; they express a faith by which men and women have lived and died, and a way of thought and life which has shaped their personalities, both individual and collective. Some measure of the depth of these reservations has been given in an analogy suggested by Wilfred Cantwell Smith. For Muslims, he points out, the Qur'an is not simply a record of God's revelation, it is that revelation itself:

If one is drawing parallels in terms of the structure of the two religions, what corresponds in the Christian scheme to the Qur'an is not the Bible but the person of Christ – it is Christ who is for Christians the revelation of (from) God. And what corresponds in the Islamic scheme to the Bible (the record of revelation) is the Tradition (*hadith*) . . . the counterpart to Biblical criticism is *hadith* criticism, which has begun. To look for historical criticism of the Qur'an is rather like looking for a psychoanalysis of Jesus.[99]

If such doubts and hesitations are to be resolved, it cannot be done from outside, but only by way of the debate between 'modernists' and 'traditionalists' which has continued in every Muslim society for the last century or so. The terms of the debate have been well stated recently by the late Fazlur Rahman, a distinguished Pakistani scholar at the University of Chicago, in *Islam and Modernity*. The main work of the history of Islam, he points out, has been done by western scholars, but the task should now be that of Muslims themselves. It is essential, he believes, to preserve the Qur'an as the basis of faith, understanding and moral behaviour, but it should be seen as a book of guidance for mankind (*huda li'l-nas*). Legal writers have gone wrong in taking

[99] *Islam in Modern History* (Princeton, N. J., 1957), p. 18, n. 13.

particular statements of the Qur'an in isolation, and drawing from them, by strict analogy, laws and rules for all time; it is necessary to look at the Qur'an as a unity in the light of modern scholarship, discerning its 'leading intentions', and drawing from them specific injunctions appropriate to the circumstances of particular times and places. Similarly, it is necessary to look at the *Hadith* in a critical way; this 'should not only remove a big mental block but should promote fresh thinking about Islam'.[100] There is, therefore, a need for a new kind of Muslim education, in order to form scholars who can look at Qur'an, *Hadith* and law in the light of reason.

There is another range of criticism which comes from among scholars themselves, and not only from those whose inherited culture is that of Islam. The critique of 'orientalism' which has become current in recent days is partly an expression of the conflict of different generations, partly of different intellectual formations. There appear to be three main lines of attack. It is said, first of all, that western scholarship has tended to be 'essentialist': that is to say, to explain all the phenomena of Muslim societies and culture in terms of the concept of a single, unchanging nature of Islam and what it is to be a Muslim. There was some truth in this during an earlier period of Islamic scholarship, and echoes of it are still to be heard in popular writing and the mass media, but it has not been the dominant attitude of those in the central tradition of scholarship, at least since the time of Snouck Hurgronje. Most of them would accept a formulation such as his: that Islam, as articulated in laws, rituals and institutions, has provided a norm which affects societies where it has been the dominant religion, but the nature of any particular society can only be explained in terms of the interaction between this norm and the specific traditions and situation of that society, and even the norm itself changes in different times and places.

It is suggested, secondly, that western scholarship has been politically motivated: in the period of European power – and now in that of another kind of western ascendancy – it has been used to justify domination over Muslim societies, by creating an image of Muslim societies (or oriental societies in general) as stagnant and unchanging, backward, incapable of ruling themselves or hostile; fear of the 'revolt of Islam' haunted the mind of Europe during the

[100] Fazlur Rahman, *Islam and Modernity* (Chicago, Ill., 1982), p. 147.

imperial age, and has now come back to haunt it once more. Again, there is some truth in this accusation, in regard to a certain period, but the attitude to which it points was not necessarily an ignoble one, nor universal. It was natural that British, French and Dutch scholars should feel some responsibility for the way in which their governments exercised power; no doubt some of them did accept those broad divisions of mankind, between east and west, Christianity and Islam, advanced and backward, which could be taken to justify western domination, and this has been prolonged into the present age by the elaboration of such broad distinctions as that between 'developed' and 'underdeveloped' countries. Not all 'orientalists' did accept such distinctions or their implications, however. Some were strong opponents of the imperial policies of their countries: E. G. Browne in England was a supporter of the constitutional revolution in Iran, Louis Massignon of the Algerian movement for independence; others, such as Hurgronje, used what influence they had in favour of a more sensitive and understanding attitude towards those whom their nations ruled. What became the central tradition of Islamic studies in the nineteenth century, that expressed in German, was not so deeply marked by such attitudes, since neither Germany nor Austria had direct rule over Muslim countries in Asia or Africa; here too, however, certain distinctions of this kind were implied in such ideas about world history as those of Hegel.

The third line of criticism is that western thought and scholarship have created a self-perpetuating body of received truths which have authority in intellectual and academic life, but bear little relation to the reality of the object which is studied. There is undoubtedly some truth in this. Perhaps it is inevitable that scholars and thinkers should work in this way. In trying to understand a subject, we have to bring to it certain categories of explanation, which serve at least as principles of selection and emphasis; it is inevitable that these should be drawn from our own intellectual tradition, and they tend to perpetuate themselves. There is no other way of working effectively, but what may perhaps be said is that the categories which many of those who have worked on in the study of Islam have used are not those of the most vital modern thought, and are not likely to produce results which will be of great interest to those outside the ranks of specialists. The basic categories are still, to a great extent, those formulated by Goldziher, drawn from the speculative thought and philological scholarship of the nineteenth century. Compared with Chinese or South Asian history, that of most of the Muslim countries is still an underdeveloped field of study. This is so partly because serious studies of Muslim history and societies, formed by the specific discourse of these subjects, are comparatively new, and there are few specialists in the field; partly also because thinkers and scholars working within those societies have not – with some exceptions – been able to impose the authority of their own categories of explanation.

This may be changing now, as more scholars of a new generation enter the field, and make use of categories drawn from new bodies of thought. It is clear, however, that we should not expect to see emerging the same kind of consensus as existed in the past. There will be differences of approach between various lines of scholars, and there may well be also a difference of emphasis between those who look at the world of Islam from inside and those who look at it in terms of an inherited western culture. For example, the concern with Islam as an intermediate stage between classical civilization and that of Europe since the Renaissance is likely to be deeper among western scholars than among those in Muslim countries. When the German scholar C. H. Becker said, 'Without Alexander the Great, no Islamic civilization',[101] he was striking a note which might have a deeper resonance in western minds than in those who have inherited the tradition of Islamic culture, and for whom it represents not a bridge from one thing to another, but something original, and a culmination.

Western scholars may be more concerned with origins than with development. In the study of *Hadith*, for example, the best European work, from Goldziher onwards, has been devoted to the way in which the body of Traditions grew up, its origins, and development and the formation of a recognized corpus of Traditions over the centuries. There is another way of looking at the subject which may have more significance for Muslim scholars: the role of *Hadith* in Muslim thought and society. What are the different meanings which have been attached to it at different times? Which particular traditions have been used, and for what purposes? When the Mamluk rulers of Egypt heard the French had landed in Egypt in 1798, they sent to the Azhar to instruct the

---

[101] *Islamstudien* (Leipzig, 1924), vol. I, p. 16.

shaikhs to read the *Sahih* of al-Bukhari, the leading Sunni collection of *Hadith*.[102] Why did they do this? Which *hadiths* were read? What effect did the reading have on the mobilization of the people of Cairo in face of the invasion? Such questions may have a deeper resonance for someone who shares the collective consciousness out of which those acts and ideas arose than for someone who does not.

Such divergences of emphasis and opinion are inevitable in a developed field of study shared by those of different intellectual formations. They need not lead to conflict, if we remember, in the words of Pope Gregory VII, 'the charity which we owe one another'.

[102] al-Jabarti, *Aja'ib*, vol. III, p. 6.

2

WEDNESDAY AFTERNOONS
REMEMBERED

I

IN his book, *The Intellectual Origins of Egyptian Nationalism*, Jamal Mohammad Ahmed makes a kind reference to me:

Had it not been for the Wednesday afternoon sessions with Mr A. H. Hourani during the 1952–3 scholastic year in Oxford, this book would not have been conceived.[1]

Those sessions remain in my memory too, for more than one reason: they were the beginning of a long friendship, and for both of us – I the apprentice teacher, he the mature graduate student – they were part of an initiation into a scholarly tradition. Behind us there stood the great figure of H. A. R. Gibb, the Laudian Professor of Arabic. I remember him taking part in one at least of our sessions, and even when physically absent he was spiritually with us, the *murshid* guiding our steps in different ways.

In a famous article, 'Islamic biographical literature', Gibb explained the importance of the *tabaqat*, the biographical dictionaries, in Islamic culture:

It is clear that the conception that underlies the oldest biographical dictionaries is that the history of the Islamic Community is essentially the contribution of individual men and women to the building up and transmission of its specific culture.[2]

For him, the real history of Islam was not that of the rise and fall of ephemeral rulers of the world, but the growth and preservation of a cultural tradition at the hands of an unbroken chain of teachers and students. If this is true of the Islamic religious sciences, it is no

---

[1] *The Intellectual Origins of Egyptian Nationalism* (London, 1960), p. vi.
[2] 'Islamic biographical literature' in B. Lewis and P. M. Holt, eds., *Historians of the Middle East* (London, 1962), p. 54.

less true of other intellectual traditions. There are concepts, methods of work, intellectual styles and sensitivities which do not find their way into the textbooks, but can best be learned by living contact with a master. This is particularly true of rather marginal subjects of study, where a strong and self-perpetuating tradition has not been created. Such was the tradition of 'oriental studies' in England at the time of our meetings. I was then a young lecturer in the Faculty of Oriental Studies, and Jamal was a graduate student in it; perhaps what follows may help to explain what was the tradition into which our meetings on Wednesday afternoons, a generation ago, helped to draw us.

2

'Oriental studies' and 'orientalism' have become suspect words in the last few years. The time has gone when orientalists could speak of themselves, without fear of contradiction, as contributing from the purest of motives to the spread of knowledge and mutual understanding. At the seventeenth International Congress of Orientalists, held in Oxford in 1928, the American historian of the ancient Near East, J. H. Breasted, could give this definition of the work of the orientalist:

It is our task too to lay our hands in reverence and devotion upon the marred and weathered vision of the Past, with infinite pains to recognize what those venerable features once were, and then to restore them to proclaim their message to the modern world in all their pristine beauty.[3]

The President of the Congress, in closing it, was able to exclaim with pride, 'the comity of nations is safe in the ministering hands of Orientalists',[4] and such sentiments found an echo in the words of one of the few Asian scholars to attend the Congress, the Indian Yusuf Ali:

As an Eastern man, he wished to pay a tribute of admiration to those great and noble men and women who took up the study of the East at a time when the East was hardly interested ... 'I believe', concluded the speaker, 'that the East cannot understand itself until it sits humbly at the feet of the West, just as I believe that the West will find its own interpretation of life incomplete until it also sits at the feet of the wise men of the East'.[5]

---

[3] *Proceedings of the Seventeenth International Congress of Orientalists, Oxford 1928* (London, 1929), p. 102.
[4] Ibid., p. 103.   [5] Ibid., p. 99.

In the last twenty years the assumptions of such an attitude have been called into question by a succession of writers. The criticism has been mainly on two lines connected with each other: that orientalists have misunderstood the Orient, and in particular the Muslim Orient, out of prejudice or because they have tried to interpret it in terms of the wrong categories; and that their work has been too closely linked with the political interests of their countries. The attack has been mounted most strongly in Edward Said's now famous book *Orientalism*. The term 'orientalism', he maintains, can be used in three different senses. It can refer first to an academic discipline, the study of the 'Orient'; secondly, to a style of thought based upon a distinction between something called the 'Orient' and something called the 'Occident'; and thirdly, to 'a corporate institution for dealing with the Orient, for describing and controlling it'. These meanings are closely connected with each other: at the basis of what Europe and America think about the 'Orient' lies the reality of power, and it is this power which perpetuates the distinction between 'them' and 'us', and by so doing distorts even what may seem to be the most academic and detached work. As a discipline of mind, orientalism has become a closed system, having an internal consistency, 'self-perpetuating, with little essential relationship with the reality it purports to be describing, having less to do with the Orient than with "our" world'.[6]

3

There are a strength and force in Mr Said's methods of expression which at times bring him near to caricature, but what he says is not to be ignored. It can help those who profess 'oriental studies' to understand better what they are doing.

Mr Said is right to say that 'orientalism' is a typically 'occidental' mode of thought, but perhaps he makes the matter too simple when he implies that this style of thought is inextricably bound up with the fact of domination, and indeed is derived from it. It may be true that the ability to look at the world in a new way sprang from the confidence which western Europe derived from the expansion of its military power and its commerce. The enlargement of the horizons of Europe in the eighteenth century, through travel and trade on the oceans of the world, must have

[6] Edward W. Said, *Orientalism* (London, 1978), pp. 2f.

helped to arouse a new kind of curiosity, a desire to study the infinite variety of the human and natural world, and to study it without fear, and with freedom from the kind of judgement which limits curiosity. As in the natural sciences, this intellectual curiosity found expression to a great extent outside the universities; Sir William Jones in the British East India Company's new colony of Bengal was the leading and characteristic figure of this first phase.

The information and manuscripts brought back by travellers and traders were used by scholars and thinkers in the service of the great scholarly endeavours of the nineteenth century, and it is here that the intellectual origins of 'orientalism' must be sought. One of the dominant ideas which moulded it was the idea of world history: the idea that human society had developed from one period to another, and that each period had a 'spirit' and civilization of its own, which came to it from its predecessors and which it handed on to its successors. Seen in this perspective, the Islamic period was that in which the civilization of the Greek world was preserved, to some limited extent developed, and then handed on to western Europe. Linked with this was the idea of families of languages. Language, the greatest and most fundamental of human creations, and indeed that which makes us human, could be analysed, and structural similarities between different languages would make it possible to classify them in a number of families derived from the same roots; these families of languages were also families of what was expressed in them, religions, myths, civilizations and 'national character'. Thus the study of the structure of languages, or comparative philology, could reveal the natural history of mankind.

Another stream of thought was no less important. Textual criticism of the Bible gave rise to new methods of interpreting the history of religions. The study of the Old Testament led to a new version of the development of a religious community, and that of the Gospels to theories about the way in which religious traditions develop, by progressive accumulation of narratives and doctrines around a historical figure. These methods of investigation could be used in the study of other religions than Christianity; so to use them might throw light upon the origins and development of Christianity itself, but it might also lead to the construction of a 'science of religion', a comparative study in which all religious systems could be seen as products of the human mind and imagination, as expressions of the spirit of an age or the consciousness of a people.

4

It was from such roots as these that there grew a special manner of looking at the civilizations of Asia which traders, travellers, soldiers and officials were revealing – to use Edward Said's phrase, a 'new style of thought'. Its starting-point was the mastery of a language or a group of them, and the use of it to discover and publish texts, in particular those which cast light upon the origins, development and nature of one of the great religious traditions. In this study, languages, literature and cultural history were seen from a perspective so different from that of indigenous scholars immersed in the tradition which was being studied, that close and equal co-operation was scarcely possible. Another kind of collaboration could, however, take place: that of the scholar and his 'native informant', who provided information for purposes which he did not share.

This system of 'oriental studies' was a fragile growth. It was carried on by a handful of scholars, mostly in the great universities of Europe, corresponding with each other, meeting from 1873 onwards in periodical congresses, and training students to carry on the *silsila*, the chain of transmission. Most of those working in Arabic and Islamic studies belonged in fact to a single *silsila*, that which went back to Silvestre de Sacy, professor at the Collège de France in the early years of the nineteenth century, to whom students came from all over Europe. It was through membership of a *silsila*, and immersion in the tradition which it transmitted, that students were trained, although in the lives of some of them there was a period of apprenticeship, usually brief, in the world of Islam itself: Goldziher studied at the Azhar, Snouck Hurgronje lived in Mecca, and then in Indonesia.

Of the major states of Europe, nowhere was the tradition weaker than in the United Kingdom. This was made clear in a document published in 1909, the report of a commission appointed by the British government in response to a delegation from the Senate of London University, which had drawn attention to the need for a school of oriental languages in London. The report was known by the name of its chairman as the Reay Report.[7]

Attached to the report were the minutes of evidence given to the commission, and the responses to a questionnaire sent out to institutions of oriental studies in the main cities of Europe. These responses showed how far Britain was behind other countries in the provision it made both for the organized, academic study of oriental subjects, and for the training of those going out to Asia or Africa as government officials, businessmen, missionaries or doctors. In several European cities oriental languages were taught both in universities and in special training schools, like the Seminar for Oriental Languages in Berlin and the Ecole des Langues Orientales in Paris, and history, law and geography were taught as well as languages. In a few places, the number of students and teachers was sufficient to form a 'critical mass', a scholarly community which could create and perpetuate a tradition by interaction; in Paris, ninety-four students were reported to be studying colloquial Arabic at the Ecole des Langues Orientales, sixteen were studying classical Arabic, sixteen Persian and fifteen Turkish; and there were other students attending classes at the Collège de France, the Ecole Pratique des Hautes Etudes, and the Ecole Libre des Sciences Politiques.

The situation in the United Kingdom was in sharp contrast to this. The study of biblical Hebrew and cognate subjects was widely diffused, but that of Islamic languages and subjects was virtually confined to Oxford and Cambridge, and was carried on there on a limited scale. At Oxford only one student took the Honours BA in Arabic and Persian in the five years 1910–14, and there was a limited number of others following a special one-year course in preparation for entering the Indian and Egyptian and Sudanese civil services. There was a professor of Arabic, another teacher of Arabic provided by the Egyptian government for the probationer civil servants, and a teacher of Persian, mainly for the Indian civil servants. Apart from instruction in languages, virtually no instruction in any Middle Eastern subject was given in any other faculty of the university. The situation was much the same in Cambridge, and in London there was almost no teaching of any kind.

---

[7] *Report of the Committee appointed by the Lords Commissioners of HM Treasury to consider the Organization of Oriental Studies in London*, Cmd. 4560 (1909).

5

The commission had no doubt that the situation needed a remedy. Some general remarks in its report show the point of view from which it looked at the problem and throw some light on the spirit of the times. They reflect the certainties and doubts of the imperial age. The basic need for which the commission felt itself obliged to provide an answer was for 'the preliminary training of persons who are going out to the East or to Africa, either for public service or private business'.[8] Such training was particularly important because 'the foreigner has brought with him and introduced to the East the surroundings of the West'; there was a need to penetrate beyond the screen of those who spoke English, into the heart of society, and this was more difficult now than before; there were 'less knowledge and contact than there used to be', as foreign communities grew in size and self-sufficiency. The need was also more urgent, because of the awakening of the peoples of the East; they had begun to look at their rulers with new eyes. Those who went to the East should have 'some familiarity with the social manners, and with the peculiar notions and prejudices of Oriental peoples', so as not to make 'an unintentional breach of etiquette or an offence against some religious prejudice'.[9] The French, the Russians and, in particular, the Germans who went to the East were better trained in languages and a knowledge of the social manners and culture of those among whom they went, and seemed to be more successful in business.

In such statements, there is little sense to be discovered of any possible interchange of culture, any idea that, by studying Arabic or Chinese, or the culture of which it was the medium, a person could enrich himself. On the contrary, there was even a certain contempt implied in such references as those to 'the peculiar notions and prejudices of Oriental peoples'.

For whatever reason, languages, customs and cultures needed to be studied, and the commission recommended, on the basis of all the evidence it had received, that those who were going out to the East should receive their preliminary training in England, in a special school created for this purpose and attached to London University. The report made clear the principles on which the school should be based. They were principles of balance. First of

[8] Ibid., p. 3.   [9] Ibid., p. 18.

all, there should be a balance between pure scholarship and practical training. Most of those who gave evidence, officials and businessmen as well as scholars, laid emphasis on the need to create a scholarly tradition; as the report put it, in the language of the time, 'the existence of a nucleus of disinterested Oriental scholars of the first rank, training other scholars as well as our future Indian and colonial officials, is a matter of vital importance to the Empire'.[10] There should also be a balance between the teaching of classical and of living spoken languages, and between teaching languages and teaching the history, religion and laws of the societies which used them. All these different kinds of study should, it suggested, be carried on in the same school.

6

From this report there came, in due course, the foundation of the School of Oriental and African Studies in London. This was a major achievement, but when, a generation later, another committee was appointed to consider the same subject, it did not find that the situation had changed very much. In 1944, the Foreign Office took the initiative in setting up an interdepartmental committee to consider the present state of oriental, Slavonic, east European and African studies. Known generally as the 'Scarbrough Committee', from the name of its chairman, it presented its report in 1947.[11]

The language of the report shows that it was written in a new world of which the outlines were just beginning to emerge. The age of empire was ending; the British withdrawal from India, a major displacement of world-power, took place in the year in which the report appeared. In the new age, decisions affecting half the world would no longer be made in London and Paris, and what had been questions of colonial rule would become questions of international diplomacy. It could be hoped, however, that if the diplomacy were carried on with knowledge, skill and sensitivity, Britain could still have a position of paramount influence; this was the age of Attlee and Bevin, the great attempt to create a kind of moral empire to replace that which was ending. The spirit of the age was reflected in the way in which the committee saw its task:

[10] Ibid., p. 16.
[11] Foreign Office, *Report of the Interdepartmental Commission of Enquiry on Oriental, Slavonic, East European and African Studies* (London, 1947).

'cooperation between the nations [is] the basis of world peace and future prosperity'; 'a nation which does not possess a sound foundation of scholarship is ill-equipped to deal with world-affairs'.[12]

Once more, the committee found that Britain was not providing what was needed, out of insularity and neglect: 'we cannot go on ignoring the manners and customs of the greater part of the world's population.'[13] The study of Asia and Africa did not form part of general education. In most universities, there was no systematic organization of these studies; in so far as they existed, they were confined to linguistic studies. Teachers had limited facilities for research and travel, and libraries were inadequate. Whatever facilities existed were used by very few students.

The School of Oriental Studies provided a partial exception to this. It had about a dozen teachers of the living languages of the Middle East, but it had few students: between 1930 and 1944 only three British students took the Honours BA in Arabic and Persian. In a few other universities, such teaching as existed was carried on by one or two teachers. In Oxford, in 1939, there was a professor of Arabic (this was the year in which Gibb took up the post), and a lecturer in Persian appointed to teach probationers for the Indian civil service, and who also had to teach Urdu and Hindi. The influence of Gibb could already be seen in a certain broadening of the instruction offered. He lectured on Islamic history, but his lectures were not advertised on the list for students of modern history, and the lists of faculties other than of oriental studies contained no offerings in Middle Eastern or Islamic subjects. The number of full-time students for degrees had scarcely risen since 1914; in the five years 1935–9, only two students took an honours degree in Arabic and one in Persian. In 1939 there seems to have been only one graduate student.

7

By the time the Scarbrough Committee reported, however, there was some sign of a change. The war had aroused the imagination and intellectual curiosity of soldiers who had served in the Middle East, and some of those who returned to British universities brought with them new demands. In the years between 1947 and 1949, in Oxford alone, more than a dozen students, most of whom

[12] Ibid., p. 24.   [13] Ibid., p. 25.

had served in the forces, took the Honours BA in Arabic or Persian.

It was in response to new needs and demands, of which the increase in the number of students was a small symptom, that the Scarbrough Report made its recommendations. It returned to the idea of a balance, put forward in the Reay Report, between pure scholarship and practical training, linguistic and other studies classical and modern studies. Once more, it had no doubt that the first need was an academic one: 'the building up of an academic tradition comparable in quality and in continuity with those of the major humanities and sciences.'[14]

To this reiteration of the principles of the earlier report, the Scarbrough Committee added two new elements. First, it laid emphasis upon the need for closer contacts with the countries which were being studied; this would involve not only visits by teachers and students, but the creation of institutes similar to the British schools of archaeology in Rome and Athens, to provide a setting within which young scholars could spend years of residence and study, and act as organizing centres for research. The implications of this suggestion were in harmony with the spirit of the age: oriental studies could no longer be carried on only by transmission from one generation of orientalists to another, they demanded immersion in the 'orient' itself, so that it should no longer be strange and 'other', and equal partnership of western and indigenous scholars.

The second new suggestion was that efforts should be concentrated in a limited number of universities. If there was to be a stable tradition, 'comparable with those of the major humanities', this could not be maintained by isolated scholars scattered throughout the country; what was needed was to create in a few places a 'critical mass' of scholars teaching different subjects and students learning from them, large and varied enough to make possible a fruitful exchange of ideas out of which could emerge a self-perpetuating body of knowledge and thought.

8

Oxford was chosen as one of these points of concentration, and it was the sudden expansion in the next few years which perhaps

14 Ibid., p. 28.

brought Jamal Ahmed to Oxford, and certainly created the intellectual climate in which our meetings and talks took place. By the time he arrived, the solitary Professor of Arabic had acquired colleagues: full-time teachers of Arabic, Persian and Turkish, teachers also of Islamic jurisprudence, theology, and philosophy, Near Eastern archaeology and modern Middle Eastern history. Some of them had been appointed in the hope that they might be able to work in collaboration with other teachers of their disciplines, and so arouse interest in the history and society of the Middle East. A seeker after knowledge of the region would have been able to attend lectures or seminars on the Qur'an and Hadith, Arabic and Persian poetry, Ibn Rushd and Maimonides, Ibn Khaldun and Naima, and eighteenth- and nineteenth-century history.

The number of undergraduates had not increased much, once the returning soldiers had finished their studies and departed. What was more important was the sudden and rapid growth of graduate studies. By the time Jamal Ahmed arrived, there were almost twenty students, some of them from Arab countries, pursuing advanced study of the Middle East in the faculties of modern history, oriental studies, social studies, and anthropology and geography.

By this time, then, the nucleus of a community of Middle Eastern specialists was being created. What held them together was not only a common interest in the region, but the all-pervading influence of H. A. R. Gibb, then at the height of his powers as a teacher and scholar, in the middle period of a long career which took him from the School of Oriental Studies to Harvard by way of Oxford. The last of the universal Arabists, not only necessity but also inclination led him to move between pre-Islamic Arabia and the modern politics of the Middle East, theology and literature, history and sociology. This was indeed an expression of his view of what an orientalist should be. In one of his last lectures, 'Area studies reconsidered', he gave his version of the orientalist's creed. He should not only have technical competence in his branch of oriental studies, he should also have first-hand knowledge of the area and should 'pursue his own studies into their modern and contemporary developments with ... flexibility of mind and concern for actuality'. He should be able to take the facts and ideas produced by those trained in the social sciences, and set them 'in the broad context and long perspective of cultural habit and tradition'.[15] Gibb's animating influence was everywhere, and it is worthwhile to try to suggest what were the preoccupations of his mind at that time, which somehow cast their spell over our discussions.

He was approaching the end of two tasks, which might have appeared to be separate but were closely linked in his mind. First was the study of the historical development of Islam, that is to say, the gradual and unending articulation of the message communicated by the Prophet Muhammad; his thoughts about this theme were expressed in his apparently simple but subtle introductory book on Islam and some shorter writings.[16] The other was *Islamic Society and the West*, a study of the changes brought about by the expansion of European trade, empire and ideas in the world of Islam. Conceived on too large a scale for the knowledge and resources of the time, it was never finished, and all we have are the two volumes on Ottoman Islamic society in the late eighteenth century;[17] in a sense these are an attempt to take up themes expressed in his writings on Islam, and to trace the historical development of Islam (or at least of Turkish and Arab Sunni Islam) during the last phase when it was still a comparatively autonomous development, producing its own principles of change from inside itself.

Of the more recent stages of development, his short but important book, *Modern Trends in Islam*,[18] gave a general view. Two themes are intertwined in it. One of them is that of the ways in which certain groups of Muslim thinkers responded to the challenge of modern European ideas by trying to reinterpret the doctrines and social morality of Islam. Gibb regarded this as a legitimate endeavour. In the only personal statement in his published work, he said that 'it is certainly not for Protestant Christians to refuse to Muslims, either as a community or individuals, the right to reinterpret the documents[19] and symbols of their faith in accordance with their own convictions'. He believed also, however, that the endeavour had its dangers, and

---

[15] *Area Studies Reconsidered* (London, 1963), pp. 14–15.
[16] *Mohammedanism: An Historical Survey* (Oxford, 1949); 'The structure of religious thought in Islam' in H. A. R. Gibb, *Studies on the Civilization of Islam* (London, 1962), pp. 176–218.
[17] H. A. R. Gibb and H. Bowen, *Islamic Society and the West: Islamic Society in the Eighteenth Century*, part 1 (London, 1950), and part 2 (London, 1957).
[18] (Chicago, Ill., 1947).   [19] Ibid., p. xi.

many of those who had taken part in it had not avoided them; in their eagerness to reconcile Islam with what they regarded as the most valid modern thought, they had tended to abandon the intellectual traditions built up by generations of scholars and thinkers, and in this way what had begun as an attempt to protect Islam by reinterpreting it tended to end as a discussion of the possibility of creating a secular society with nationalism as its animating principle, and with Islam as its inherited culture rather than a guide to social action.

He suggested also that such a movement might arouse reaction. The historian of ideas should be aware of two kinds of movement, that of the systematic thinkers, and that – slower, less articulate, less easy to discern but also less easy to control – of a whole community. What would happen in the end would be a product of the interaction of these two processes. In a striking phrase, writing of the place of Sufism in modern society, he contrasted the *ijma'* of the learned with that of the people:

No one who has ever seen that mile-long procession of brotherhood lodges with their banners, trudging in the dust after the Holy Carpet on its annual progress through Cairo, can fail to be impressed by the vitality of the forces which they represent. Not for the first time, the *ijma'* of the people is opposed to the *ijma'* of the learned.[20]

The relationship of the 'learned' and the 'people', of cultural tradition and innovation, of the Middle East and the West, of ideals and social action: these are some of the ideas which I remember discussing with Jamal Ahmed on Wednesday afternoons, and which run like threads through his book.[21]

---

[20] Ibid., p. 38.
[21] Some sentences in this essay have also been published in 'Middle Eastern Studies today', *Bulletin*, British Society for Middle Eastern Studies, 11 (1984), pp. 111–20.

3

MARSHALL HODGSON AND THE
VENTURE OF ISLAM

WHEN Marshall Hodgson died in 1968, he was known to be working on a major book on Islam and drafts of various parts had been shown to friends and colleagues. It had already acquired a kind of fame before it was published, but few could have suspected how unusual and original a book it would turn out to be.[1] To say this is not to imply that every idea in it sprang fully-grown from his own head. On every page there is evidence of wide reading, in original sources as well as secondary works, and the footnotes form a commentary on the work of other historians. There is evidence, too, of a fruitful exchange of ideas with colleagues, and in a sense this book could have been written nowhere except at the University of Chicago in the 1950s and 1960s. There are echoes in it of Nef on industrial civilization, McNeill's *The Rise of the West*, Eliade's studies of religion, Adams's *Land Behind Baghdad*, and the discussions of sociologists and anthropologists. In the Islamic field, the influence of von Grunebaum and younger colleagues can be seen, blended with those of Massignon, Cahen and above all Gibb; some parts of the book indeed elaborate certain ideas suggested by Gibb.

It is the mark of original minds to take ideas and continue them in some new direction or to arrange known facts in a new order. This is what Hodgson has done, through a combination of great powers of explanation with exceptional gifts of human insight. When dealing with human minds and their creations, his method is one learned from Massignon:

what Massignon calls the psychosociological 'science of compassion'. The scholarly observer must render the mental and practical behaviour of a group into terms available in his own mental resources ... must broaden his

[1] *The Venture of Islam: Conscience and History in a World Civilization*, 3 vols. (Chicago, Ill., 1974).

own perspective so that it can make a place for the other ... however risky the method is, it is less risky than any more external method (vol. I, p. 379, n. 6).

Some of the descriptions of human achievements cannot be forgotten, for example the accounts of al-Ghazali and Jalaluddin Rumi, the studies of the development of Sufi thought, and the explanations of what poets and writers were trying to do. Hodgson tells us how to read 'Islamicate' poetry (I shall explain this term later): designed as it was for public recitation, no unexpected context should interfere with the appreciation of its virtuosity and no private reference detract from the public decorum (vol. II, p. 297); even in love-poetry, the realm of private sentiment, etiquette and courtesy reigned, and the poet's aim was to handle public images with grace and splendour (vol. II, p. 303); exaggeration in both poetry and prose was used deliberately, since the best way of illustrating a point was by citing an extreme case (vol. III, p. 310). Writing of Islamicate art, he reminds us that it is the most purely visual and the least symbolic art that can be imagined:

the mosque, like any other object of art, was not allowed to serve as representational symbol ... There was every reason, therefore, for mosque architecture – and with it other building ... – to move, like figural art, in the direction of pure visuality and the autonomy of the visual surface (vol. II, p. 523).

Design was all, and in some buildings it could only be perceived in movement: 'Islamicate architecture in general often stressed less the static unity of the plan of a monument than what may be called its unity of passage, its unity as one passes through it' (vol. II, p. 529).

Some of Hodgson's ideas may prove incapable of bearing the weight he lays on them, and we mention them here not to express agreement or disagreement but to illustrate a certain quality of his mind. Although there are passages of very abstract thought, the book as a whole is not at all abstract or dry. It conveys a special kind of excitement, that of a mind which responded vividly to all it perceived, one which could express warmly and freely the whole range of its responses.

Hodgson, himself, has described what kind of book this is, when writing of the Islamicate literature of the middle period. It is a 'mythic-visional' book, one of such works of evocation as, unlike science, are primarily moral interpretation of experience already given: yet unlike more fragmentary rhetorical or lyric writing, attempt a comprehensive vision of the totality of life (vol. II, p. 313).

In the end, such visions deal with the experiences of individual human beings. Behind the majestic vision of the venture of Islam, we can see the figure of Hodgson himself: one who could only face the terror and splendour of life by calling on all his resources of courage and lucidity to impose order on it, but who knew that there remained some initiative from elsewhere which could not be ordered:

Often, in mystical lore, God appears in the guise of enemy, or at least of opponent in a context ... sinfulness can become almost a function of human greatness, a real and very dangerous by-product of the fact that humans are nearer to God than are other animals or even, perhaps, than the angels ... None but the King (that is, God) is great enough to hunt him. In becoming the prey of such a huntsman lies true human triumph (vol. II, p. 254).

This product of Hodgson's vision has been edited by his close colleague, Reuben Smith, and published by the press of his own university in the most sensitive and scrupulous way. In his preface, the editor delineates the author's personality with a few skilful strokes and points out the difficulties of editing a book left almost, but not quite, finished. Hodgson was a careful writer; his style could be awkward and had features which any publisher's editor might wish to change, but it expressed every nuance of his thought. He would have disapproved strongly of any attempt to reduce it to ordinary correctness, and his wishes have been respected. Editor and publisher have confined themselves to 'external' changes, and special praise should be given to the maps and charts, compiled from the author's notes. In one respect they might have gone further: the bibliographies are admirable, but there might have been added to them some references to the books and articles which have appeared since the author died.

Hodgson's vision is not of an imaginary world, but of what has happened to man in space and time, and it is shaped by a certain view of what historians should do and what has occurred in history. The book can only be understood within a broader framework. He intended to write a history of the world, but left only parts of it which cannot be published; this book, however, gives some indication of his general view of history, and the reader should begin by studying carefully Hodgson's own statement of what he was trying to do, contained in an appendix which the editor has wisely placed at the beginning of the first volume and which will serve as Hodgson's *Muqaddima* (there are so many echoes of Ibn Khaldun in the book that it is difficult to keep them out of a review).

Although he had read Spengler and Toynbee and learned much from them, Hodgson's approach was different from theirs. They thought of themselves as dealing with processes which had recurred in much the same way, while his starting-point was 'dated and placed events' (vol. I, p. 23), all of them part of a unique and irreversible process which is human history. In regard to those events, social scientists ask certain kinds of questions, but historians ask others. This is what makes history a separate discipline: it has 'a body of interdependent questions that can be discussed in relative autonomy from other bodies of questions' (vol. I, p. 23). Some of its questions begin with 'how'; they deal with the relations between different events and processes. Others begin with 'why'; why did this happen and not that? ' "Might-have-beens" are built into the inquiry of any historian, whether explicit or not' (vol. I, p. 26, n. 16). There is yet another range of questions the historian should ask, about the significance of the process of history: what has each age, each society and each 'civilization' done to ' alter the moral context of human life', to 'set irreplaceable standards and norms', to create human beings of a different kind, who by their very difference must somehow have affected all other human beings?

The humanistic historian must concern himself with the great commitments and loyalties that human beings have borne, within which every sort of norm and ideal has been made explicit; and he must concern himself with the interactions and dialogues in which these commitments have been expressed (vol. I, p. 26).

Such a view of the historian's task implies a certain view of the historical process. Man's history, Hodgson suggests, has been moulded by the interaction of three factors: ecology, group interest and creative individuals. By ecology he means the whole environment, cultural as well as physical, which has been produced by the cumulative investment of human resources. 'Group interests' are the more or less stable aims pursued in common by groups of human beings within the limits of their environment and social power. The creative individuals are those who, at the interstices of history when 'habitual, routine thinking will no longer work', can produce new alternatives, which in turn can lead to the formation of a new cultural environment and the pursuit of new interests by the same or different groups (vol. I, p. 26).

The process of interaction is endless, and the lines of influence run in all directions. There is never a time when one of the factors can completely stultify the others. Hodgson here implies a criticism of a system of ideas derived from Max Weber, which rests on a broad distinction between 'tradition' and 'modernity': 'traditional' societies tend to preserve an existing system of customary actions and relations, even at the cost of rationality; only 'modern' western society is committed to rationality even at the expense of custom. Hodgson believes that 'every generation makes its own decisions ...; a generation is not bound by the attitudes of its ancestors, as such, though it must reckon with their consequences' (vol. I, p. 37). Every age has its rationality, within the limits imposed by its environment; in every age, a society must make its own decisions about the pace and direction of change.

Of these three factors, Hodgson tends to give his main attention to the third, the creative individuals and the cultural environment they make and change. He can justify this emphasis in terms of his own definition of the historian's task. It is the creative individuals who produce those works which are, in his sense, the most significant:

When we speak of a great civilization, we mean above all a consciously cultivated human heritage ...; in studying a given civilization our first interest is in those aspects of culture that have been most distinctive of it ... During much of history, at least, this has meant the artistic, philosophic, scientific life, the religious and political institutions, in general all the more imaginative activities among the more cultivated of the population (vol. I, p. 92).

Not only are the products of these activities significant in themselves, they are closely connected with the group-interests which on the whole assert themselves in political and social life:

It is what may be called a 'political idea' which gives individuals and groups a historical basis for expecting that the state will endure as a power to be reckoned with despite any given current crisis. This implies not merely the subjective prestige of legitimacy (important though that is) but also concrete geographical, economic, military and sociocultural components which gather together standing group interests effectively enough to give most groups concerned a practical reason for hoping the state will survive, or at least for accepting that others will so hope. On this basis they will, willingly or by way of precaution, forgo short-term interests if they conflict with the long-term interests of the state power (vol. I, p. 12).

In a statement like this we can see two of the influences on Hodgson's thought. The idea of a creative minority is Toynbee's, although he never explained clearly how the minority was able to communicate its ideas to society as a whole. The idea of a system of ideas as providing a link between the ruling power and the interests of society recalls what Ibn Khaldun says about the role of the *shariʿa* in preserving the rule of a dynasty.

Within what field, in space and time, can the interaction of these three factors be studied? Here Hodgson diverges from Spengler and Toynbee. His intelligible field of study is not a 'civilization'; it is the 'Oikoumene', that is to say, the whole Afro-Eurasian historical complex, from the beginnings of recorded history until the present day (vol. I, p. 50). The implications of this are far-reaching. It is necessary to avoid seeing Islamic and other history from the point of view of the West: in other words, believing that the only significant history is that which the modern West has chosen to identify with itself, including the history of the eastern Mediterranean at certain times in the past but not at others, or else believing that the modern civilization, which began roughly in 1800, is something essentially western and cannot be fully absorbed by those brought up in other cultural environments. (To ask why the modern age began in western Europe and not elsewhere, however, is one of those 'why, why not?' questions which are the specific concern of historians.) Even if this danger is avoided there remains another, that of interpreting what has happened in other parts of the world in terms shaped by western European or American experience. Great care needs to be taken in the use of words, since they make us think in certain ways. Hodgson's sense of the precise meaning of words leads him to invent some new ones: not all are likely to be generally accepted, but each has an exact meaning which older and more familiar words do not express so well.

It would be no less dangerous, however, for a writer on those parts of the Oikoumene where Islam has been the basis of the dominant cultural tradition to take too exclusively Islamic a view and assume (as Muslim authors themselves did) that the rise of Islam began something completely new rather than giving a new form and direction to a civilization which already existed, or to look for internal explanations for everything which happened in this region. Its relations with the rest of the Oikoumene should always be kept in mind. Historians are not likely to forget this when writing of the modern period and what is usually called the 'impact of the west', but they may forget something else which Hodgson always has in mind: the relations between the Islamic world and China. During a great part of Islamic history, China was the most powerful and creative region of the Oikoumene: in the period of the 'Abbasid Caliphate there 'began a long period of limited but unmistakable Chinese cultural ascendancy in the Oikoumene as a whole' (vol. I, p. 233), and two centuries later the Chinese economy 'was moving ... into the early stage of a major industrial revolution' (vol. 2, p. 4).

There is yet another danger about which Hodgson has important things to say: that of looking at Islamic history from an Arabist's point of view and assuming that the Arab lands lying around the eastern rim of the Mediterranean have always been the centres of Islamic civilization. It is one of Hodgson's main theses that the core of the Islamic world is composed not of these lands alone, nor of the Arabic-speaking lands as a whole, but of an 'Irano-Semitic' region of which they form part; and in later Islamic times the centre of gravity of the Islamic civilization lay in the eastern part of this core-area, the Iranian highlands where high culture expressed itself in Persian rather than Arabic. Distortion, he suggests, has been caused by the fact that western scholars have tended to look at the Islamic world from the standpoint of Cairo and, to some extent, through the eyes of modern Arab writers who interpret the past in terms of a certain kind of Islamic modernism moving in the direction of Arab nationalism.

Hodgson divides the history of the Oikoumene, before the beginning of the modern age, into two main phases. The first began with the emergence, at various points in the Afro-Eurasian area, of 'citied agrarianate societies': societies in which cities dominated the countryside and were able to order their relations with it in such a way as to gain control of the agrarian surplus and use it in their own interests. Whether the surplus came in the form of taxes or rent was a secondary matter; the concept of 'land-ownership' is of limited importance in dealing with societies of this kind. (The ocurrence of such statements, strongly worded, in the work of one who seems to have an idealist view of history may cause surprise; but Hodgson had thought much about economic history even if he wrote less about it than about the history of culture.)

In the cities which dominated such societies, a special kind of urban life grew up. The city supplemented the wealth derived from agrarian manual production by manufacturing goods and exchanging them over a wide area. The wealth derived from trade and dependent agriculture made possible the emergence of governments of a kind impossible in the countryside: governments which maintained an overriding military power and organized bureaucracy, with systems of law and legal or religious hierarchies to interpret and administer them. Rulers, religious specialists and merchants acted in different ways as patrons of a 'high culture', a lettered tradition and art, and this in its turn produced those political ideas which could bring together the power of the ruler and the interests of socially dominant groups. But such combinations of state power, group interests and political ideas were fragile; sooner or later they dissolved and new ones had to be created. (Hodgson tends to explain the process of dissolution mainly in terms of the failure of political ideas, and perhaps he lays too much emphasis on those features in history which can be fully explained and too little on the irrational factor of sheer power.)

In the period stretching roughly from 800 to 200 BC, all the agrarianate societies of the Oikoumene, interrelated by trade and mutual influence, passed into a second phase of history. Following Jaspers, Hodgson calls this period of change the 'Axial Age'. The Oikoumene now articulates itself into four main regions, each distinguished by a high culture, a cumulative tradition of dialogue and self-conscious reflection on the cultural monuments of the past, expressing itself in various forms of literature and art. Because cultures, political ideas and forms of socio-political power are so closely connected, each area of high culture also tended to embody its cultural unity in distinctive political forms.

In each region there was a 'core-area' where the high culture developed and from which it radiated. These were the northern Mediterranean littoral, from Anatolia to Italy, where Greek and Latin were the main languages of high culture; the area stretching from the Nile to the Oxus, where culture was expressed in various Semitic and Iranian languages; India and the lands lying to the south-east of it, with Sanskrit and Pali as their languages of culture; and China and its neighbouring countries.

Hodgson's main concern is with the area lying 'between Nile and Oxus'. The cultural area which includes the Nile Valley, Fertile Crescent, Iranian highlands and the Oxus valley is an indivisible whole, although it includes some countries which we should now regard as Arab and others as Persian. At the time when Islamic history began, it already had a distinctive society and culture, some features of which help to explain Islamic history. The comparative aridity of most of the area meant that the agrarian basis of society was fragile: some parts of the area could not be cultivated, others only if rainfall was good or irrigation works maintained. On the other hand, the urban mercantile element was comparatively strong, because the area lay between other regions of 'high citied civilization' and was able to profit from trade between them.

The high culture of the Axial Age had also taken a special form here. There was a religious tradition based on belief in one God who demanded righteousness of his creatures, in one life by which men will be judged, and in one righteous society tending to embody itself in a 'confessional' state. (The author's perception of the similarities between the Judaic and Christian traditions, expressed in Hebrew and Syriac, and the Mazdean tradition, expressed in Pahlavi, is helpful; but he may go too far when he traces links between these religious traditions and the interests of urban mercantile groups.)

The region has another important feature. Much of it is peculiarly exposed to invasion and conquest from outside. Only in the eastern part, the Iranian highlands and the adjoining plain of Iraq, did the political ideas implicit in the religious culture embody themselves in an indigenous 'confessional state', that of the Sasanians. In the western part, political power fell to invading groups from the occidental area, and the culture patronized by the government was Greek and not Semitic in expression. Beyond the range of the state and the cities where its strength was rooted, however, society continued to be 'Semitic', and when the empire became Christian it turned into the kind of 'confessional state' implied by the culture of the area.

Hodgson's views of the nature and development of Islam are linked with this concept of an Irano-Semitic society and of its core-area between Nile and Oxus. At a certain point, the development of this society and its culture was given a new direction by something which began not in the core-area but on its margin.

There is a question here, and in his view it cannot be answered only in terms of the cultural or political weaknesses of the area in which Islam expanded. This is indeed an essential part of the answer: Irano-Semitic civilization had reached a point of development which demanded a creative movement of the conscience and imagination. But that the movement came from where it did, and took the form it did, must be explained in terms of what was happening in western and central Arabia: a special kind of society with a pastoral rather than an agrarian basis was emerging; linked with three areas of high civilization (Byzantine Syria, Sasanian Iraq and the Yemeni-Ethiopian area), it was beginning to create its own high culture. Behind this explanation, however, there lies another: the message mediated through Muhammad, and evoking from him and his associates a series of decisions, by way of which a religion was shaped and an empire conquered.

Here a second question arises: what did the conquest mean to the conquered countries? In Hodgson's view, the Arab conquerors gave their empire two things, a religion and a ruling elite. In so doing, they changed the nature of society but did not create something new. The coming of Islam and the Arab rulers did not destroy the Irano-Semitic society but released or redirected its energies, and the most important question to ask about this process is not how the new Arab elite absorbed the Greek and Irano-Semitic culture of the lands they ruled, but how and why the existing culture absorbed Islam and the new ruling elite. This question gives rise to two others. How can we explain the break in continuity, the total abandonment of the former languages of high culture and acceptance of a new linguistic medium for it? What were the steps by which the traditions of that culture were reformulated in response to the challenge posed by the Qur'an?

The continuous development of the Irano-Semitic cultural tradition in an Islamic form, and within a certain ecological framework, is the central theme of Islamic history, and Hodgson distinguishes six main phases in it. It may seem strange that, in a book largely concerned with cultural history, the division adopted is basically political, but Hodgson might have replied that, in his view of history, basic political changes are connected in more ways than one with other kinds of change: in urban control over the rural hinterland and its wealth, the direction and volume of trade, patronage of the arts, and the formation of those political ideas which support or challenge the structure of political power.

The first period runs from the beginning of Muhammad's mission to the end of the first generation of the Umayyad caliphate (662–92). It is significant of Hodgson's view of history that he begins, not as most books do with an account of western Arabian society seen in isolation, but with a survey of the three high civilizations to which that of western Arabia was marginal; and he calls this period that of the 'Islamic infusion', the creation of a new kind of political order in a society which already existed.

The second phase is that of 'the high caliphate' (692–945); it saw the creation of an absolute bureaucratic empire with an agrarian basis, modelled on that of the Sasanians, and with a 'classical civilization' expressed in Arabic. This civilization was given its shape by the Qur'an and Islamic faith, but not all its manifestations can be explained wholly in terms of Islam. We therefore need, Hodgson suggests, new and less ambiguous terms than 'Islam' and 'Islamic' for the society and culture associated with the religion of Islam. The society in which Muslims and their faith were prevalent and socially dominant he calls 'Islamdom', by analogy with Christendom; the 'culture, centered on a lettered tradition, which has been historically distinctive of Islamdon' he calls 'Islamicate'. The terms are strange, but he uses them to express his ideas clearly.

Much of this second part is given to an analysis of the forms taken by classical Islamicate culture, in particular the different kinds of response to the challenge of the Qur'an. One such response was *shariʿa*-mindedness, legal correctness, and this was to be a continuing theme in Islamicate culture. Another was that of personal piety, and this took two main forms: one which identified itself with the community, in the belief that truth is normally dominant among mankind, and one which identified itself with the Imams, in the belief that truth can be defeated and driven into hiding but never destroyed. Here lie the origins of Jamaʿi (a word Hodgson prefers to Sunni) and Shiʿi attitudes, although they were not yet sharply distinguished from each other. At this time also certain ways of explaining the universe, those of the mystics and the philosophers, begin to appear, and beside the religious culture there develops a culture of the state secretaries, *adab*, embodying secular as well as religious norms and aiming at elegance in the use of Arabic.

In these chapters about the development of Islamicate culture, certain problems of method reveal themselves. Does Hodgson's desire for complete explanation carry him too far when, for example, he identifies certain forms of piety with the merchant class and *adab* with the 'gentry'? When he explains the different kinds of piety in terms of 'responses' to the 'challenge' of the Qur'an, is he using a concept of dramatic confrontation, and categories like 'decision' and 'commitment', which have been developed in the course of some modern protestant interpretations of Christianity? Such questions will have to be asked before the lasting value of Hodgson's work can be assessed. Whatever the verdict, these chapters on piety and religious culture will remain the most memorable of the book; based on a careful study of individual writers, they have a psychological insight, philosophical clarity and felicity of expression which are unusual.

The political form characteristic of this second period, that of the universal caliphate, which tended towards absolutism, failed in the end, Hodgson maintains, partly because of the fragility of its agrarian base and the decline of the system of irrigation in Iraq, and partly because the *adab* of the secretaries did not produce the political idea which could rally the dominant social groups to its support and so create a universal ruling class. A third period now begins, the early middle period (945–1258), marked by political fragmentation but also by the emergence of a universal social and cultural order.

The political fragmentation took more than one form. A number of virtually separate states emerged, often short-lived, and in most of them there was a division between two elites, which might work together but between whose ideas and interests there could only be a gulf, the *umara* and *a'yan*. On one side were the politico-military groups, mainly of Turkic origin, coming from the reservoir of military energy on the northeastern frontier by way of nomadic migration or recruitment into armies, drawn into the political struggles of Islamdom by the need of the cities for an external power to maintain urban order and control the countryside, but standing in a sense outside urban society. On the other, were the dominant groups of that society, religious specialists (*'ulama*), great merchants and masters of the crafts. These groups gave the military rulers support and legitimization but stood aloof from them as parts of an international social order independent of any political regime; this society had a political idea which could legitimize all governments and was not tied to any of them, a law regarded as standing above the will of rulers, and a universal system of commercial exchange.

This division of *umara* and *a'yan* showed itself at every level. There was a social division between those who derived wealth from control of the land and those who derived it from trade, the 'gentry' and the merchants (once more we may have doubts about so neat an explanation) and a distinction also between two kinds of culture. The Arabic culture of the *'ulama* grew by way of further articulation of law, piety and cosmic explanation; and the most significant development was that of Sufism. The polite culture of rulers and courts expressed itself mainly in Persian, now revived in an Islamicate form. Quite rightly, Hodgson stresses the importance of this distinction. From this point on Islamicate culture is at least double: religious thought is expressed mainly in Arabic, polite literature in Persian or one of the 'Persianate' languages which developed under its influence, Ottoman Turkish, Chaghatay or Urdu. The creative advances begin to take place in these languages, and those in the Arabic-speaking countries who do not know them scarcely take part in the advance. At this point, Hodgson pays less attention than other writers to the regions which lie outside the creative core of later Islamicate culture: not only Spain and the Maghrib, but Egypt and Syria.

When he comes to the fourth period, that of the predominance of a new Turco-Mongol ruling elite (1258–1503), the scale of Hodgson's treatment becomes smaller. This is partly because the period has not been studied much: 'Generalizations ... cannot expect to be better than educated guesses' (vol. II, p. 373). There is another reason: by this time the Islamicate universal order was strong and stable enough to absorb new rulers without being fundamentally changed by them. The coming of the Mongols into the Irano-Semitic world had a result very different from that of the Arab invasion: the energy of the new elite was placed at the disposal of society; it gave a new direction to the visual arts and other forms of culture, but it brought no radical change in the social order. This does not mean that there is no change, still less that there is what can be called cultural decadence; but a society with a firmly established structure changes in a different way from one which is responding to new challenges.

In this section, therefore, Hodgson can take the inherited structure for granted and lay emphasis on what appears to be new. First of all, why did there appear a new political elite, Mongol, or rather Turco-Mongol? Detailed research has not yet been done, but Hodgson suggests that the answer lies partly in a decline in agriculture, particularly in Iraq, the only country with a massive system of irrigation; and partly in the expansion of a pastoral economy in central Asia, dominated by Turkic horse-nomads. There is, however, a problem here: how could nomads living at a comparatively low level of technology and in small social units come together into a stable, organized, and rationally directed force which could overrun cities and found states? We have here something different from the gradual seepage of nomads into settled areas along the steppe gradient or their enlistment in slave armies. Hodgson seems to think it was a spontaneous process:

> In these vast shifting populations, it became possible for powerful aggre-gations of tribes under united leadership, such as sometimes arose in inter-tribal struggles, to snowball, gathering the potentially military forces of the nomads of extensive areas for plundering expeditions that could over-whelm whole settled nations (vol. II, p. 401).

This however is to state the question rather than answer it.

Once established, this ruling elite created a type of state here called the 'military patronage state', one 'ruled by men who took independent achievement – "action" in the sense of leaving a magnificent personal impress, for good or ill – as their express goal' (vol. II, p. 403). The new rulers protected the civilization of cities, to some extent closed the gap between *umara* and *a'yan*, and patronized the visual arts. The main discussion of Islamicate art, therefore, comes in this section.

In this period, Islamdom expanded beyond the core into Anatolia, the Balkans, India, south-east Asia and sub-Saharan Africa; and in the next period (1503–1800), the greater part was integrated into three large states, Safavid, Ottoman and Timurid (a term which Hodgson prefers to 'Mogul'), and some smaller ones. This process he explains in terms of the adoption of innovations in the art of war; he calls the new states the 'gun-powder empires', by a risky generalization from Ayalon's study of the use of firearms by Mamluks and Ottomans. All three large states had Turkic ruling elites, all in different degrees were bureaucratic, and all gave special attention to investment in the land. All too had a kind of legitimacy in the eyes of dominant social groups: there was a certain 'integration of the political power of Islam and its public conscience' such as had not existed since early times (vol. III, p. 111).

Most writers on this period would probably give their main attention to the Ottoman empire. For Hodgson, however, it is the Safavid empire which is central, not only in the obvious geographical sense, but because the areas it included were still the centres of creative advance in architecture, poetry and the metaphysical constructions of the later Sufi thinkers. For all their splendour, the Ottoman and Timurid empires were marginal: their court culture was Persianate, and the lands in which their power was rooted, the Balkans and India, came late into Islamdom and had large non-Muslim populations.

Most writers, again, would see this period as one when those forces were gathering which would lead to western domination of the world, Hodgson reminds us, however, that it was the period when Islamdom played its largest part in the history of the Oikoumene:

> though probably less than a fifth of the world's population were Muslims, yet the Muslims were so widely and strategically placed that the society associated with them did embrace in some degree the greater part of citied mankind; 'microcosm' is no longer just the word for Islamdom. World history and Islamicate history had become very hard to disentwine (vol. III, p. 11).

There was almost a Muslim hegemony in a large part of the world. In spite of the deepened gulf between Jama'is and Shi'is, the Muslim states formed 'a single far-flung diplomatic world' (vol. III, p. 81). The expansion of European sea-power in the sixteenth century did little to shake it, and the European Renaissance, although it raised the culture of the Occident to a high level, scarcely touched the rest of the Oikoumene.

In the eighteenth century, Hodgson detects a certain deterioration, both in the quality of cultural creation and in the strength of the bureaucratic agrarianate empires. This came at the same time as a completely new process, the 'Great Western Transmutation'. The extension of the area of occidental culture to North and West, the Renaissance, the expansion of sea-borne trade and other factors involved a human investment of a kind and degree such as to bring about a fundamental change. The agrarian age comes to an end, and from about 1800 the world passes into a new age. Its characteristics first appear in the occident, and for a century or more there is European domination of the world. In the long run, however, the transmutation affected the whole world. In a sense it caused Islamdom to disappear, just as it abolished other divisions within the Oikoumene:

In this sixth period the Islamicate society is ceasing to exist . . . The common basis of the lettered culture . . . is now for the most part . . . one which [Muslims] share with non-Muslim peoples . . . To the extent that the Muslim lands can still be studied as an active cultural grouping, it is not as an Islamicate *society* but as sharing the Islamicate *heritage* (vol. III, pp. 166–7).

The most significant element in this heritage is 'religion and the religious conscience' (vol. III, p. 412), which faces a new challenge presented by confrontation with other religious traditions. This may lead to a reassessment of the *shari'a*, the nature of the community and the meaning and significance of the Qur'an.

These are some of the themes of this extraordinary book, so far as they are clear to one reviewer after one reading. It will need time for any reader to come to terms with it, but it should be taken seriously by all those concerned with Islamic history, and discussion of it may play an important part in that dialogue (to use a favourite word of the author's) which should lie at the heart of our studies.

Such discussion can take place at two levels. Hodgson's interpretation of particular themes will arouse controversy and may have to be changed as research casts doubt on his 'educated guesses'; to take examples at random, what he wrote about cities shows the influence of Massignon's untenable theories, recent work places the migrations of Beni Hilal in a new light, and not all would agree with what he says about Islamicate art. Beyond these points of detail, there is bound to be discussion about his general categories of explanation. The analysis of historical processes in terms of ecology, group interests and creative individuals; the concepts of the Oikoumene, agrarianate society, the Axial Age and the Irano-Semitic civilization; the dissection of Islamicate society in terms of military elites, bureaucrats, and notables; the distinction between different kinds of piety and culture, and the emphasis on the role of Persianate culture: do such ideas and methods help us to understand Islamicate history better? It is too early to say, but one reader closes the book with the first impression that Marshall Hodgson has given us a framework of understanding which may be no less valuable than that of his great ancestor Ibn Khaldun

4

ISLAMIC HISTORY, MIDDLE EASTERN HISTORY, MODERN HISTORY

FIRST of all, may I express my gratitude for the honour of this award,* which has pleased and touched me deeply, and which I do not think I deserve. Nothing will persuade me that I can be compared with the great scholars who have received the medal before me, or that anything I have written will last as long as what they have written. At moments like this, I think of the words of Adlai Stevenson, 'Praise isn't harmful if you don't inhale'; let me then try to define the sense in which I can safely accept the award. I take it as a sign that the modern studies with which I am concerned have become respectable, and I may have played some part in this: I can say of my works something like what the poet Yeats said of his metaphysical theories, that he did not quite believe in them but they were the scaffolding within which other things could be built.

The medal is also precious to me because it is linked with the names of two distinguished men. The spirit of Gustave von Grunebaum is still present in this place, and there is little I can say about him which has not already been said by friends, colleagues and students. I remember in particular his generosity towards younger colleagues, his quickness to detect promise and his warmth in trying to bring it out, and also the imaginative quality in what he said and wrote. His interest in poetry expressed his lifelong concern with the images and dreams which make men what they are; let me mention here his essay on 'Self-image and approach to history',[1] and his introduction to the book he helped to edit on *The Dream and Human Societies*, where he analyses with

---

* The Giorgio Levi Della Vida Medal was presented to the author at a conference at the University of California, Los Angeles, on 27 April 1979.

[1] In B. Lewis and P. M. Holt, eds., *Historians of the Middle East* (London, 1962), pp. 457–83.

delicacy the Muslim view of dreams as a means of communication between man and the supernatural powers.[2]

Giorgio Levi Della Vida I met once only, but I have learned something of him from a book he wrote towards the end of his life, *Fantasmi Ritrovati*.[3] In it he speaks of friends of his youth, the growth of his own mind, and the way in which his scholarly vocation declared itself. From an early age he was aware of the majesty of his own Jewish tradition, which his family had put aside but not formally renounced, but stood close enough to Catholic Christianity to feel its attraction. Before he could choose between them, he wished to study them both, and other faiths as well, in their original texts. In this way he came under the influence of the German biblical exegesis of the nineteenth century, which raised the most important of questions, that of the authenticity and authority of holy scripture, and this in turn led him to the study of philology; Renan, he tells us, became 'the idol of my adolescence and tutelary divinity of my first steps on the path of scholarship'.[4]

This vocation was pursued within the framework of a rich and complex culture. Running through the book are great themes which were central to the Italian culture of the first half of the twentieth century. One is that of Catholic modernism in its Italian form. By the time he wrote the book, he was critical of the modernist emphasis on the immanence of God in the world, which might turn Christianity into a kind of religion of humanity; he found this too in the thought of his first master, the orientalist Caetani, for whom democracy was the religion of the future, the manifestation of the divine in the life of man. By now Levi Della Vida himself had moved towards a recognition of transcendence as giving the answer to the great mysteries of human life, those of knowledge and of suffering; nevertheless he saw the historical importance of modernism in the life of the Church.[5]

He writes also of the growth of Fascism, the child of the 'Great Fear' of the bourgeoisie in the 1920s. He himself had been an early victim of it, because he had refused to take the oath of allegiance demanded of university professors, and there is a note of firm although charitable authority in his judgements. Writing

[2] 'Introduction: the cultural function of the dream as illustrated in classical Islam' in G. E. von Grunebaum and Roger Caillois, eds., *The Dream and Human Societies* (Berkeley, Calif., 1966), pp. 3–21.
[3] (Venice, 1966).   [4] Ibid., p. 133.   [5] Ibid., p. 160.

of Gentile, the philosopher of Fascism, he criticizes his desire to be near the centre of things, and a certain capacity for self-deception which led him to attribute to the rhetoric of Fascism a depth and meaning it did not possess; but he acknowledges the dignity and sincerity of his character. When the professors who would not take the oath were dismissed, he says, the tears that Gentile shed were crocodile's tears, but at least they were those of a good crocodile, who was really sorry that the dialectical process of history had compelled him to eat his victims.[6]

The book tells us something important about the nature of what were called 'oriental studies' in his time: they were rooted in the great intellectual concerns of the age, and made a contribution of their own to them. The same lesson emerges from another book, which can be taken as expressing the collective consciousness of those engaged in 'oriental studies': the *Proceedings of the Seventeenth International Congress of Orientalists*, held at Oxford in 1928.[7] A reading of the book may leave certain clear impressions. The first is that of the domination of a certain method of work, which proceeds by a careful analysis of the precise meaning of literary texts; thus, to take examples, Farmer gave a paper on Greek musical texts in Arabic, Mittwoch on Arabic medical texts and Levi-Provençal on Ibn Bassam. This method, of course, was far from being as simple and limited as might appear to those who did not know it. It made use of all kinds of ancillary sciences to throw light on the texts, and it did so in order to explain far more than the history of a literary and scholarly tradition. Here we come once more on the roots of 'oriental studies' in the great science of philology, one of the seminal sciences of the nineteenth century. It was not just a science of languages seen in their relations with each other, it aimed at giving a kind of natural history of mankind: to study the relationships between languages was also to study races, cultures, religious systems, and the myths which express the consciousness of a people. The relationships to be studied were not only those of similarity and difference, but also those of descent and kinship; the existence of families of languages indicated that of families of races and cultures. We are conscious now of the dangers in this way of thinking, the ideas of superiority and inferiority to which it may give rise, but at the time it was a

[6] Ibid., p. 244.
[7] *Proceedings of the Seventeenth International Congress of Orientalists, Oxford 1928* (London 1929).

liberating force: religious systems were seen as human products, or as human efforts to express some experience of the divine, and they could be examined and judged with the same freedom as other expressions of the human spirit.

Closely connected with this idea was another one which gave a direction to scholarly work: the idea of the history of cultures, that what is of intrinsic value in human history is what men have produced in the way of beliefs, systems of thought, artistic forms and institutions, and that each phase of history is marked by a certain spirit, such that all the products of its culture bear a resemblance to each other and are manifestations of the same reality. This idea could be developed in different directions. The civilization of the modern West, from the Renaissance onwards, could be seen as the culmination of history, and all earlier cultures would then be judged by what they had contributed to the process by which the modern West had emerged; or else the cultures produced by the human spirit could be regarded as separate from each other, standing on the same level, and each having a value of its own.

This indeed seems to have been the prevailing view at the Congress of 1928. There was general agreement that the work of its members was contributing to human understanding and therefore to peace and happiness. There may have been a special reason for the note of self-congratulation in the formal speeches: this was the first Congress to be held since World War I had disrupted the community of scholars. Something of more general importance, however, was involved. Those present thought of themselves as working to recall 'the East' to knowledge of its true self, and also to bring the light of 'the East' to bear on the common problems of humanity. At the banquet, Professor Breasted said: 'It is our task . . . to lay our hands in reverence and devotion upon the marred and weathered visage of the Past, with infinite pains to recognize what those venerable features once were, and then to restore them to proclaim their message to the modern world.'[8] In his reply, the President of the Congress, Lord Chalmers, exclaimed: 'The comity of nations is safe in the ministering hands of Orientalists.'[9]

There seems to have been a warm sense of community among those present. They were all priests of a mystery. With all its limitations, this was the only kind of gathering at which, at that

[8] Ibid., p. 102.   [9] Ibid., p. 103.

time, any aspect of the culture, history or society of 'the East' could have been discussed with serious knowledge and concern. There were virtually no specialized conferences (the first serious meetings held to discuss the problems of modern Arab society and culture were three *Entretiens* held in Paris in 1936, 1937 and 1938).[10] Moreover, most of those present were conscious of intellectual affinities. Like Sufis, they knew their own *silsila*, the chain of teachers through whom they had been initiated. The members of the Far Eastern section went together to lay a wreath on the grave of James Legge, translator of the Chinese classics,[11] and the Islamic section passed 'enthusiastically' a motion to send a telegram to Theodore Nöldeke, calling him 'the great teacher whom we all revere'.[12]

What brings out most clearly the special nature of this community of scholars is the relative absence of those who did not belong to the *silsila*, and in particular of those whose cultures and histories were being studied. Some of them were there it is true: from Turkey, K. Z. M. Fouad Bey, better known later as Fuat Köprülü; from Egypt, Taha Husain and ʿAli ʿAbd al-Raziq; a few from India. But there were not many, and the framework of discourse into which they had to fit was not perhaps that which they themselves would have chosen. Fouad Bey gave a paper on a Turkish dictionary; Taha Husain offered two papers, one on the use of the pronoun in the Qur'an, and the other on some curious similarities between Leibnitz and the Muʿtazilites; Muhammad Kurd ʿAli injected no note of controversy when he spoke on Muslim studies in Europe.[13] At the banquet, the Indian scholar Yusuf Ali spoke in deferential terms, but with perhaps an overtone of surprise:

As an eastern man he wished to pay a tribute of admiration to those great and noble men and women who took up the study of the East at a time when the East was hardly interested ... In the West, classical studies were pursued in the spirit of an inquiry into the working of the human mind rather than merely into the archaeology of ancient civilizations, and he could conceive it possible that a similar spirit might come over Oriental studies. ... 'I believe,' concluded the speaker, 'that the East cannot understand itself until it sits humbly at the feet of the West, just as I believe that the West will find its own

---

[10] *Entretiens sur l'évolution des pays de civilisation arabe*, 3 vols. (Paris, 1937–9).
[11] *Proceedings*, p. 68.
[12] Ibid., p. 85.
[13] 'Fi mu'tamir al-mustashriqin al-duwali', *Majallat al-majmaʿ al-ʿilmi al-ʿarabi*, 8, 11–12 (1928), pp. 680–5.

interpretation of life incomplete until it also sits at the feet of the wise men of the East.'[14]

To read such a quotation will remind us how much the climate of thought and scholarship has changed in the last fifty years. The criticism now being directed at the tradition of oriental studies, and in particular of Islamic studies, is by now too familiar to need to be described at length, but since in a way it forms the starting point of our discussions, it may be worthwhile to summarize it briefly.[15] It is suggested, to begin with, that the method of the orientalist – the analysis of a certain kind of written text, the product of a high religious culture – is not adequate if a scholar wishes to say something significant about human character, or history or society, or literature. At the very least, this kind of work needs to be extended by the use of other disciplines relevant to the subject-matter. More than that, the older method may even be dangerous if it leads us to believe that there is some unchanging essence in Islamic or 'oriental' societies, expressed in the writings of the high religious culture and only to be understood through a study of them, and that this essence is unchanging, so that those societies can never in any real sense develop.

It is also suggested by the critics that, even when students of the Muslim East recognize the need for some specific discipline of mind beyond that of the analysis of texts, and for inserting their work into a living tradition of thought, they have not been able to make full use of the creative ideas of our modern culture. They are still in thrall to certain traditions of comparative philology, or old-fashioned views of literature or history, and what they produce is therefore marginal to the scholarly life of our age. For the critics, this weakness is linked with the fact that western scholars look on the world they study as passive or lifeless, incapable of creating a self-image which will compel them to change the image which they have inherited. This in turn is linked with a certain relationship of power, which appeared in the nineteenth century and still exists, although in a different form: a relationship which, as always, is less obvious to those who have the power than to those over whom it is exercised.

[14] *Proceedings*, p. 99.
[15] E.g. Anouar Abdel-Malek, 'L'orientalisme en crise', *Diogene*, 44 (1963), pp. 103–40; Abdallah Laroui, 'Les arabes et l'anthropologie culturelle: remarques sur la methode de Gustave von Grunebaum' in *La crise des intellectuels arabes; traditionalisme ou historicisme?* (Paris, 1974), pp. 59–102; Edward W. Said, *Orientalism* (London, 1978).

I do not intend to go into this whole system of ideas. I agree with some of them, disagree with others, and there are others again which I do not quite understand; but at least I am sure they should be taken seriously. The voices of those from the Middle East and North Africa telling us that they do not recognize themselves in the image we have formed of them are too numerous and insistent to be explained in terms of academic rivalry or rational pride. It may be that, if the Arabs or Persians have not been able to impart their images of themselves to those who study them from outside, the explanation is to be found in their own culture and societies as well as in those of Europe and America, and it may be true too that, if our studies are marginal to the general culture of the age, a complex explanation is needed. At least it is worthwhile to ask such questions, and in particular to ask them in regard to what we may think of as our guiding concept, that of Islam itself, of an Islamic civilization and society. This is the starting-point of our discussions, which have brought together a number of scholars in order to think about what they are doing or ought to be doing, and what others in the past, standing in the *silsila* of our great teachers, tried to do.

In a sense, of course, those who pursue what we call Islamic studies do not need to justify their work in any terms except their own. When we study a religion which starts from the belief that God has revealed His will to man in a Book, it is valid and important for us to try to understand the way in which the Book has been interpreted and its teaching articulated into formal systems of thought. This is the central tradition of Islamic studies. It produced the great works of Goldziher and others of his generation, and is now being renewed and carried further in work of much importance and originality: investigations of the origins of Muslim thought, and in particular the Muʿtazilite strand in it, a new awareness of the importance of the Hanbali tradition, a more subtle view of the process by which Sunnism and Shiʿism separated from each other, a more adequate view of Islamic philosophy, as a way of thought which was used by Muslims for Islamic purposes, down to the great metaphysical systems of early modern times. These researches have begun to have an influence on the way in which Muslims think of their own past: a certain kind of modern Arabic thought appeals to the example of the Muʿtazilites, whether or not it interprets them correctly, and philosophy has reappeared as a living mode of belief.

It is possible, moreover, to hold a view of history which sees the handing on of knowledge of God from one individual to another as the only significant process, and therefore the process most deserving of study. This was the belief of Louis Massignon, the one man of overwhelming personal genius drawn into this field of study. His conception of history is clearly expressed in a series of writings which reveal him with peculiar force, his letters to the poet Paul Claudel.[16] The meaning of history, he believed, is to be found not in the impersonality of social evolution but in the divine work in the individual seed,[17] and this work is done through human mediators. It is in the encounter with the 'other' that there may appear the transcendent figure of God. Such encounters can take place within the ordered framework of an established tradition, but they can also be sudden confrontations: the unexpected 'other' breaks in on ordinary life, shattering and transforming it. In a moment of illumination a man can transcend his worldly images and see beyond them another beauty. History is a chain of witnesses entering each other's lives as carriers of a truth beyond themselves, and a chain which can run across the habitual frontiers of different religions.

Massignon believed that he himself had been drawn into this chain, in an event of which it is difficult to accept all the details as he has described them, but which certainly decided the direction of his life. It was through the human witness of Muslims that the mystery of transcendence had come down on him like a sword: 'It is in Arabic ... that I recognized God for the first time, in Arabic that I made my first prayer to Him.'[18] This event was his initiation as a witness, a participant in the mystery of substitution, by which a man can provide for others what they cannot obtain for themselves. Having acquired through Muslims the knowledge of transcendence, how could he himself serve as the channel through which they could come to knowledge of Incarnation? His correspondence with Claudel concerns his search for a stable vocation, the need to choose between renunciation of the world, ending perhaps in martyrdom, and a lifetime of scholarship within a recognized discipline of science. In the letters, it is Massignon who insists. Claudel is hesitant. In a sense he pushes the other towards a heroic destiny, haunted as he is by the thought that he himself had turned his back on it. It is, he suggests, the only valid

[16] Michael Malicet, ed., *Paul Claudel – Louis Massignon (1908–1914)* (Paris, 1973).
[17] Ibid., p. 104.   [18] Ibid., p. 111.

response to the grace of overwhelming conversion: a conversion is a kind of catastrophe, almost like a change of sex. But Massignon's exaltation of spirit makes him uneasy, as a man of good sense and prudence, and it is with a certain relief that he receives the other's decision to remain a scholar: 'You are no longer romantic and interesting, Massignon, but it is a very good thing to be neither the one nor the other.'[19]

This is a possible view of history, but not for everyone. Most of us work on 'the impersonality of social evolution', or at best try to trace the connections between it and 'the divine work in the individual seed'. For us the question is bound to arise: to what extent and in what ways can the history and nature of the societies where Islam is the inherited faith of the majority be understood in terms of Islam?

I want to say something about this question in so far as it arises for someone who works on modern history. I have recently been preparing for publication a collection of essays written at various times, and have been thinking about the ideas and methods I used in them.[20] They now seem to me to have been written within three different, but overlapping, systems of ideas, which can be called those of 'Middle Eastern history', 'modern history' and 'Islamic history'.

By 'Middle Eastern history' I mean the history of a region defined in terms of something other than itself, and specifically, in the modern period, by its relations with the growth and decline of European power. Its main subject, then, is the expansion of Europe, and the special relationships between the European powers generated by the dissolution of the great Muslim empires of early modern times. In such a history, the peoples of the region appear either as passive objects reacting to what is done to them by occasional spasms of anger, or else in a relationship of dependence, trying to prevent the expansion of Europe by creating a reformed autocracy, or to obtain a favoured position with the imperial system, or to win political autonomy within a system of continuing economic dependence.

The basic idea of what I call 'modern history' is that of a process called 'modernization', which takes place in various

---

[19] Ibid., p. 217.
[20] *Europe and the Middle East* (London, 1980); and *The Emergence of the Modern Middle East* (London, 1981).

stages arising by natural progression from each other: modernization is defined in terms drawn from the social sciences, to mean,
for example, the extension of bureaucratic authority over society,
the expansion of urban control in the countryside, the commerciali-
zation of agriculture, the beginnings of large-scale industry, the
emergence within the cities of classes recognizably the same as in
western industrial societies, or the formation of an elite educated
in a certain way.

'Islamic history', within the modern context, can be defined in
terms of the continuity of a tradition of high literate culture,
created around a core of religious doctrine and laws, and its
gradual interaction with ideas coming from outside, and in
particular with the complex of ideas to which we can give the
name of 'nationalism'.

All three approaches seem to me valid, and the problem they
pose is that of the limits within which each of them can be used
with profit. The danger inherent in using the first or the second is
that of extending it to the point where the specific nature of the
region and its peoples is obscured, and they are seen simply as
examples of a single, inexorable, world-wide process. We can only
avoid this danger if we make some careful distinctions. The
history of British and French power in the Middle East and North
Africa, for example, can be seen as being different from that of
British power in India, because it takes place to a great extent
within the limits imposed by the survival of the Ottoman, Persian
and Moroccan states. The powers have to pursue their interests
within that framework creating informal protectorates, acting at
times as a single body, the 'Concert of Europe', at others in
rivalry; and they pursue their rivalries through local client states
and communities, so that the history of the Middle East, when
seen in this perspective, becomes the history of a complex
relationship between great powers and small local forces, a
relationship uneasy and tragic, ending from time to time in the
destruction of ancient communities.

In the same way, if we want to see the history of the Middle East
in terms of 'modernization', we have to take into account its
specific nature: first, the fragile and shifting balance between
settled agriculture and transhumant or nomadic pastoralism in
the semi-arid zones of the world, which means, as Marshall
Hodgson has reminded us, that the agrarian basis of civilized

society is weak and its cultural achievements liable to be lost;[21] and, secondly, the modes of social action peculiar to societies which do not possess formal and persistent institutions that define the ways in which power is acquired, used and transmitted. In such societies, social action must be analysed in terms of alliances, systems of patronage and changing relations between political manipulation and bureaucratic control, and of the intermediate roles played by those ambiguous groups we are now accustomed to call 'notables', at the same time leaders and mobilizers of opinion and agents of authority.

The danger of the third approach, that which I have called 'Islamic history', is rather different. It is that of seeing history in terms of an endless repetition of certain patterns of behaviour, derived from an unchanging system of beliefs. Thus, to take examples from ideas which are current nowadays, modern nationalism is seen as being no more than a new version of an 'Islamic' idea of political domination, and certain weaknesses of modern Middle Eastern societies are explained in terms of the absence of the idea of the State, or the weakness of the rational tradition in Islamic thought.

It is the problems posed by this third approach that I wish to consider now. Is it possible to interpret modern history in specifically Islamic terms, without falling into the trap of believing in an unchanging essence of Islam defined in terms of its written formulations?

We can find the beginning of an answer to this question in the ideas, by now becoming quite familiar, of social thinkers such as Clifford Geertz.[22] Seen from the point of view of a sociologist or historian, a religion is not only a system of propositions about the nature of God and man, but a system (if that is not too formal a word) of symbols: that is to say, images, objects, words or ceremonies which serve to express a certain conception of the universe, an idea of some ultimate harmony between the nature of reality and our habitual ways of acting, thinking and imagining. It is these symbols which give meaning to social action, and which therefore give a direction to it, for they are never simple reflections of whatever exists, they also contain within themselves some kind

---

[21] *The Venture of Islam: Conscience and History in a World Civilization*, 3 vols. (Chicago Ill., 1974), vol. I, pp. 107–9.

[22] *Islam Observed: Religious Development in Morocco and Indonesia* (Chicago, Ill., 1968), pp. 90f,; *The Interpretation of Cultures: Selected Essays* (London, 1975).

of principle by which acts can be regarded as worthy of praise or blame, and so define the limits of what should or can be done. Such symbols should not therefore be interpreted in isolation, but in their connection with the social actions which they express and direct. So, when they change, we need to ask whether this reveals some important social change, and there are moments of social dislocation or disintegration when symbols themselves dissolve and are replaced by bare ideas or ideologies not yet fully enough accepted to be embodied in stable and generally recognized symbols. Even when they do not appear to have changed, we must still ask whether they express the same social reality as in the past. Here we can perhaps find an analogy with those tribal names which persist over centuries and whose persistence can, if we do not look beyond them, conceal from us the reality of change. When we read of Palestinian villages in the nineteenth century expressing their quarrels in terms of the ancient tribal conflict of Qais and Yemen, or of two groups competing for land and water in the Sudan in the eighteenth century and claiming descent from Umayyads and 'Abbasids, we should beware of ascribing a continuity which does not really exist.

It follows from this that it would be dangerous to draw a sharp distinction between the 'true' Islam and something else, or to give a privileged position to the formal statements of textbooks of law or theology. Seen in this perspective, whatever people have believed to be Islam *is* Islam, and what we used to call 'popular' Islam may have a special significance, however much the lawyers or theologians may condemn it. From this insight there has come an important extension of our studies of Islam. Popular religion is no longer seen simply as reprehensible innovation or a bundle of quaint superstitions. The role of rural shrines and saintly lineages has been studied in such a way as to reveal the dynamics of rural society, and we are beginning to understand the importance of looking again at those popular movements which have used the language of *jihad*, and seeing them as something more than movements of purposeless 'fanaticism', but also as movements of more than one kind, for the language of *jihad* can express many different realities.[23]

My intention here, however, is not to study these popular

---

[23] Ernest Gellner, *Saints of the Atlas* (London, 1969); Edmund Burke, III, *Prelude to Protectorate in Morocco: Precolonial Protest and Resistance 1860–1912* (Chicago, Ill., 1976), p. 124.

movements, but to confine myself to the high, urban, literate tradition of Islam. Even if the historian should not regard it as being the only 'real' Islam, it is still important for him. Once more, when we study a religion which springs from the belief that God has revealed himself to man through His word, and a society which was dominated by cities, as centres of government and social control, we should not ignore or underrate the importance of the moral ideals enshrined in its literature, and particularly in those kinds of literature which are regarded as having some connection with the revealed word of God. In such writings we can find, if we look, not only legal and moral precepts, but – what may be more significant – certain ideal types of human personality, certain ways of thinking and acting which are regarded as being somehow sanctified, as being ways of serving God's purposes for the human world.

A good method of approaching the study of these ideal types in a historical context is by way of the biographical dictionaries. In a famous article, H.A.R. Gibb suggests that the essential purpose of the dictionaries was to record the true inner history of Islam, that of the development and transmission of a body of truth and culture, by an unbroken chain of men and women, witnesses to the truth.[24] This is true, but something should be added: in what the dictionaries record and what they omit, and in their characteristic modes of expression, there is contained a certain human image, an ideal type of what the concerned, literate, law-respecting Muslim should be, and this image not only describes a historical reality, it has helped to mould it, has acted as one of those forces which give form to men's view of themselves and therefore to their lives.

Such works, of course, have to be interpreted with care. The image they enshrine was one which evolved slowly over a long period and in many countries, and we should not neglect differences of place and time. In what I say I shall be concerned only with the latest phase in the development, the last two centuries or so, and only with those countries, from Tunisia to Iraq, which underwent the deep and lasting experience of Ottoman rule; Morocco, Iran and northern India might perhaps need to be thought of in rather different terms.

Every writer, moreover, has his own principles of selection and

---

[24] 'Islamic biographical literature' in B. Lewis and P. M. Holt, eds., *Historians of the Middle East* (London, 1962), pp. 54–8.

emphasis; he writes with a purpose of which we should be aware. To take two examples from the nineteenth century, the Tunisian Ibn Abi'l-Diyaf writes at the level of the inner group of statesmen and high officials, and his emphasis is on state service and worldly success;[25] 'Abd al-Razzaq al-Baitar, recording the lives of learned and pious men in and around Damascus, does so from the point of view of the provincial notability with religious culture and some record of local service, and his emphasis is more on learning and social leadership.[26]

Again, there is something equivocal in what such writers say. They are not only describing what men were like and what they did, they are also – whether they know it or not – fitting them into a pattern of what they should be and do. The same terms of praise recur again and again. To take an example from Baitar: among the lives of saints and scholars he includes one of Ahmad Pasha, who was governor of Damascus at the time of the massacre of Christians in 1860, and was executed by the Ottoman government for his supposed complicity in it. Baitar belonged to that group of notables of the Maidcn quarter who condemned the massacre, and he clearly thought Ahmad Pasha to have been guilty of some neglect of his duties, but his criticisms are expressed by implication, almost in the conventional language of eulogy. He begins the biography by telling us of Ahmad's religious lineage: he was learned in *fiqh* (jurisprudence) and an initiate into the Khalwati order. His piety is made a kind of excuse for his ineffectiveness: he was so intent on fasting, prayer and submitting himself to God that he neglected the things of this world, and left the way open for bad men to do bad things. When he dies, his death too is fitted into a familiar pattern: he is called a martyr, *al-shahid*.[27]

With these reservations, it is possible to extract from the biographies an image of human personality which had an influence not only on the way in which the writers viewed those whose lives they wrote, but on the way in which the subjects may have thought of themselves and tried to shape their lives. It is a complex, varying image which needs to be defined in more than one way. First, it is the image of the 'doctor' rather than the

[25] *Ithaf ahl al-zaman bi akhbar muluk Tunis wa 'ahd al-aman*, vol. VIII (Tunis, 1971).
[26] *Hilyat al-bashar fi ta'rikh al-qarn al-thalith 'ashar*, 3 vols. (Damascus 1961–3).
[27] Ibid., vol. III, pp. 26of.

'saint'. This distinction has now become a familiar one:[28] It refers to two ways of acquiring and transmitting knowledge of God, and corresponding to them two different kinds of social role. The 'doctor' is he whose essential function is to develop and transmit the body of religious sciences derived from the Qur'an and the Hadith (Traditions of the Prophet), and who therefore performs certain functions in society, as teacher, judge (*qadi*), interpreter of the law (*mufti*), or preacher in a congregational mosque, but who also, more generally, can act as leader and spokesman of urban opinion. The 'saint' is the mystic or Sufi, he whose essential purpose is to pursue a path of spiritual and moral training, passing through recognized stages and culminating in experiential knowledge of God, and who also performs certain specific social functions, as teacher of this path and spiritual director of those who wish to learn it, as a channel through which divine graces can come to human beings; in rural societies, a saint, or a family which maintains his tomb after his death, can also perform a more general function, as the neutral point where different social groups meet, disputes can be arbitrated, and, in times of need, a leadership which transcends the differences of groups can arise. To these two types there correspond two families of words embodying different conceptions of the ways in which God can make himself known to man: those derived from the root '-*l*-*m* ('*ilm*, '*ulum*, '*alim*, '*ulama*), and those coming from the root '-*r*-*f* (*ma'rifa*).

In the later period with which we are concerned, the distinction between the two had become less clear than it may once have been. Most 'doctors' ('*alim*, pl. '*ulama*) were members of Sufi orders (*tariqa*, pl. *turuq*), and some held high positions in them; for the most part, they belonged to those *turuq* which insisted on strict observance of the law (*shari'a*), but we hear of one high Tunisian '*alim* who belonged to one of the wilder orders, the 'Isawiyya.[29] Since the biographical dictionaries are mainly an urban form of literature, the emphasis in them lies towards the doctor rather than the saint, towards the attainment of learning rather than rare spiritual states or the working of wonders, and this expresses a reality of urban life: members of Sufi orders, guardians of the tombs of saints, tended to be drawn into the system of '*ilm* to the

---

[28] Ernest Gellner, 'Doctor and saint' in Nikki R. Keddie, ed., *Scholars, Saints and Sufis: Muslim Religious Institutions since 1500* (Berkeley, Calif., 1972), pp. 307–26.
[29] Arnold H. Green, *The Tunisian Ulama 1873–1915* (Leiden, 1978), p. 58.

extent to which they became fully a part of urban society.[30] Thus Ibn Abi'l-Diyaf records the history of a family associated with a shrine in a popular quarter of Tunis, Bab Suwaiqa: the grandson of the rural saint who founded it goes to the Zaituna mosque, studies *fiqh* to a high level, and then returns to be shaikh of the *zawiya* (shrine).[31] A Sufi teacher who would not accept the restraints of urban learning would arouse some resistance: a historian has recorded the shock felt in the society of Damascus by the coming of a Kurdish saint whose teaching rejected the compromises of urban life, and whose influence on the governor of the province, also a Kurd, was believed to be bad.[32]

The ideal type of the doctor can be defined in terms of another spectrum which ran between service to the ruler and distance from power and the affairs of the world. In societies where all social roles tended to be ambiguous, the specialists of Hadith and *fiqh* balanced precariously. They accepted for the most part the later tradition of Sunni social thought, that of obedience to authority and co-operation with it, as necessary to preserve an ordered and civilized society, but they also maintained a certain moral distance from the rulers. An *'alim* often displayed at least a formal reluctance to accept the office of *qadi*, although not so much perhaps that of *mufti*, and this reflected a social reality; as holders of leadership and prestige in urban society, the *'ulama* wished to maintain a position in which they would not be obliged to do all that the rulers demanded of them, or to become directly involved in disputes between rulers and ruled, or between one faction or family and another. At times they would express disapproval of the ruler's acts, although in a prudent and circumspect way, so as not to lose the access to authority without which they could not act effectively as social leaders.[33]

This attitude to authority was only one aspect of an ambivalent relationship with society and its concerns. The ideal life of the

---

[30] Keddie, *Scholars, Saints and Sufis* (in particular, Leon Carl Brown, 'The religious establishment in Hussainid Tunisia', pp. 47–92; Edmund Burke, III, 'The Moroccan ulama, 1860–1912; an introduction', pp. 93–126; Kenneth Brown, 'Profile of a nineteenth-century Moroccan scholar', pp. 127–48); Green, *The Tunisian Ulama*; Haim Shaked, 'The biographies of 'ulama in Mubarak's *Khitat* as a source for the history of the ulama in nineteenth-century Egypt', in Gabriel Baer, ed., *The 'Ulama in Modern History* (Jerusalem, 1971), pp. 41–76.

[31] *Ithaf ahl al-zaman*, vol. VIII, p. 73.

[32] Ibrahim al'Awra, *Ta'rikh wilayat Sulaiman Basha al-'adil* (Saida, 1936), pp. 94–5.

[33] Ahmed Abdesselem, *Les historiens tunisiens des XVIIe, XVIIIe et XIXe siècles: essai d'histoire culturelle* (Paris, 1973), p. 103.

'alim was one devoted to learning, with a certain disdain or distrust of the things of the world. This ideal expressed itself in certain modes of speech and action: the *'alim* avoided places of popular resort, did not indulge in loud speech or laughter, his manners were dignified and his language elevated. Inescapably, however, he was involved in the life of the city. Holders of religious offices controlled much of the wealth of the city. They had salaries or received fees and administered religious endowments; those who came from families with a tradition of religious learning and office in a certain city might have connections of marriage with families of merchants or masters of crafts; they might be in partnership with local officials or merchants for the exploitation of the resources of the city and countryside. Their attitude towards the city might, therefore, move between detached observation guided by moral principle and concern for the interests of a family or a social order; and the attitude of the urban population towards them might vary in the same way. (In the countryside, too, the family descended from a saint or the guardians of his tomb might in some sense comport themselves as if set apart from the cares and ties of society, but in time they would acquire wealth and social position, could be closely associated with the lords of the district or themselves become lords, and people would look at them with a mixture of respect and cynicism.)

This complex and ambiguous human image provided a pattern not only for the lives of professional *'ulama*. The concept of the *'alim*, indeed, is not by itself a sociological category. Among those who participated to some extent in the high religious culture there were at least three different social groups. In the capital city of a dynasty which was strong and deeply rooted enough to be able to control urban society, there was a small group of high professional *'ulama*, *qadi*s, *mufti*s, and teachers, who were an integral part of the machinery of government: such were those who held the highest legal offices in Istanbul and the small group of court *'ulama* in Tunis. They tended to form privileged and closed bodies, being drawn from special schools and also from certain kinship groups, and perhaps connected by marriage with high officials or the ruling dynasty; in Tunis, they were separated from most of the population by the fact of belonging to the Hanafi school of law. Secondly, there were holders of legal and religious posts below the highest, and in particular the deputy *qadi*s, *mufti*s, teachers and preachers in provincial cities. Thirdly, there were all those who were not full-time *'ulama* but had the same education, at least up to a certain level, and conformed therefore to the same human type; they might include merchants, masters of crafts, secretaries of the local government, guardians of tombs or *zawiya*s. The concept of the *'alim* therefore defines a social order or estate, but not a class.

By the eighteenth century, there seems to have been achieved a certain stability in the ideal human type here described: that of the man learned in tradition and law, initiated into a Sufi order within the bounds of the *shari'a*, respectful of authority, willing to serve it but keeping his distance from it, giving leadership to the urban population, linked by interest with the preservation of a fabric of ordered and prosperous city life, and having a certain fear and disdain of the forces of the countryside. This type remained more or less unshaken until the middle of the nineteenth century. In some ways our usual periodization of history may be wrong, and the beginning of the nineteenth century may not be so important a turning-point, in all respects, as it seems at first sight. By that time, it is true, there had taken place what Marshall Hodgson has taught us to call the great western mutation,[34] that acquisition of technical skill which enabled western Europe to free itself from the shackles of its agrarian base, and this change had led to a vast expansion of European trade, and to an event which was in the long run to be decisive in the history both of Europe and of Asia: the establishment of British rule in Bengal in the 1760s. Half a century later, at the end of the Napoleonic wars, the expansion of trade in a new form led to an irreversible process, the division of labour on a world-wide scale between European industrial producers and providers of raw materials. In its early stages, however, this process still took place for the most part within an administrative and legal framework maintained by indigenous rulers. For another half century or so, the political life of the Middle East, as of other parts of Asia, could still be interpreted in terms of that tension between central governments and provincial authorities which had appeared much earlier, and, outside small groups of high officials serving the autocrats, the changes which were taking place in Europe had scarcely begun to affect men's minds. Even an event which now appears to us to have been decisive, the French occupation of Algiers in 1830, may at first have seemed to be one more episode in the long struggle for

[34] *Venture*, vol. III, pp. 176f.

control of the North African ports: it was only forty years earlier that the previous episode had taken place, when the Dey of Algiers seized Oran from the Spaniards.

During the first half of the nineteenth century, then, it was possible for the interplay of social forces to take place in much the same way as before, and for the self-image which both mirrored and moulded it to continue to exist. We can find an example of this – not quite typical but still significant – in the biographies of the Algerian hero ʿAbd al-Qadir. We have at least two of them written by scholars in Damascus, where he spent his later years of exile: one by Baitar, and one by the historian of the Naqshbandi order, ʿAbd al-Majid al-Khani.[35] They are able to see his career in traditional perspectives. His spiritual lineage is first established: descent from the Prophet, studies in *fiqh*, initiation into Sufi orders – the Qadiriyya in Baghdad, at the hands of the descendant of the saint and guardian of his shrine, and the Naqshbandiyya in Damascus by Mawlana Khalid, whom he had met on pilgrimage. His struggle against the French is seen in terms of *jihad*: the formal recognition of his rule (*bayʿa*), his assumption of a title implying divinely sanctioned authority, that of *amir al-muʾminin*. So too for his years in Damascus: the biographers tell us of his pilgrimages, his initiation into another order – the Shadhiliyya, taken from Shaikh Muhammad al-Fasi – his study of Ibn ʿArabi with a group of students, and his burial near Ibn ʿArabi's tomb. No doubt there is a conventional element in this, but it seems that ʿAbd al-Qadir himself shaped his own later life on a traditional pattern. Although there may have been elements of innovation in his policy during the years of struggle with the French, his encounter with European power does not seem to have shaken him deeply. In Damascus he lived as urban notables had lived, although with this difference, that to the forces between which he balanced, that of the ruler and that of urban society, there was now added a third, that of the European consuls. His public acts can be explained more easily in terms of the role of the notable than in those of the political ambitions which were sometimes ascribed to him, and these public acts were not his whole life. The long series of Sufi meditations which he wrote in exile, the *Mawaqif* or 'Spiritual Stations', perhaps more fully expressed the reality of his

[35] Baitar, *Hilyat al-bashar*, vol. II, pp. 883f; ʿAbd al-Majid al-Khani, *al-Hadaʾiq al-wardiyya fi haqaʾiq ajilla al-naqshbandiyya* (Cairo, 1890–1), pp. 281f.

life, as he now saw it, than his action in what he called 'years when I did not know myself'.[36]

The moment when this image begins to be shaken, the point of social and moral disturbance, comes, at least in some parts of the Middle East, in the 1860s and 1870s, decades which are a watershed in the history of the region. There takes place a basic change in power: decisive changes in military techniques and an accumulation of capital, which makes control of markets and raw materials necessary, between them lead to an expansion of European control. Europe is no longer willing to conduct its business within an administrative and legal framework maintained by indigenous autocrats, and there is a series of decisive interventions: the Spanish attack on Morocco in 1860, the establishment of financial control in the Ottoman empire, the occupation of Tunisia in 1881 and Egypt in 1882. At the same time, there grows up an educated class of a new kind. Modern schools are created: Galatasaray in Istanbul, Sadiqiyya in Tunis. Those educated in them have new means of communication at their disposal. The telegraph lines come to the Middle East in the 1860s, drawing it into a world market and opening it to the events of the whole world: the eastern crisis of the 1870s and other happenings of the decade are the first great events known all over the world as soon as they take place. The first newspapers of opinion appear, in Arabic and Turkish, and the cultural periodicals; there emerges something which we can call 'public opinion' and a new group which tries to articulate it, the intelligentsia.

To understand the disturbances caused by these rapid changes, we need to study the interaction of social changes and religious or national symbols in the great popular movements of the time: those in the Ottoman cities which culminated in the events of 1860 in Damascus, the Tunisian revolt of 1864, and the Algerian revolt of 1871, which led to the full imposition of the colonial system. At another level, we can notice in this period a deep disturbance in the lives of educated men, not only those trained in the new schools but those formed in the traditional ways of thought; not only do their careers take different paths, but the ways in which they see their own lives begin to change.

---

[36] 'Abd al-Qadir al-Jaza'iri, *Kitāb al-Mawaqif fi'l-tasawwuf wa'l-wa'z wa'l-irshad*, 3 vols. (Damascus, 1966–7). I owe this reference to Jacques Berque, *L'intérieur du Maghreb* (Paris, 1978), pp. 506f.

Once more, let us consider two examples of lives which are by no means typical, but which can teach us something. The first is that of Muhammad Bairam, whose life we know both from what he himself wrote and from a biography by his son.[37] The fifth of that name, he was born in 1840 into a Tunisian family of Ottoman origin, which had held the offices of Hanafi chief *mufti* and *naqib al-ashraf* (doyen of the descendants of the Prophet) for the greater part of a century: a family closely identified with the court and linked by marriage with the ruling dynasty. His early career was conventional: studies of *fiqh* with both Hanafi and Maliki teachers, as had become customary in Tunisia, a teaching post at the Zaituna at an early age, rapid promotion by favour of the Bey. Then we begin to notice a change in the pattern: he goes against his family and most of the 'ulama in supporting the reforms of Muhammad Bey and disapproving of the government's reprisals after the revolt of 1864; there is a hint of awareness of the oppression under which the peasants lived. In 1873 there begins a short period of power: Khair al-Din, the Prime Minister, asks him to take office. At first he refuses, saying that he does not want to be bound in a way which would prevent him doing what he thought right (conventional terms which perhaps were more than that to him); then he accepts, holds several posts, and is sent on missions to France. By 1879, however, his patron Khair al-Din has fallen from power, and he is under suspicion. He goes to Istanbul, urges the Ottoman government to intervene in Tunisia in order to prevent a French occupation, and then, when the occupation takes place, sells his property and cuts his links with Tunisia. In 1884 he leaves Istanbul for Cairo, where he plays a minor part as a client of Riaz Pasha, holds some official posts, but works mainly as a journalist.

Most lives are ambiguous, and Bairam's can be read in more than one way. It may seem to be the life of a politician who backed the wrong side and lost, but that was not how he himself saw it. In what he writes there is a sense of the decay of Islam; at one point he refused the family post of chief *mufti*, because 'the times are not propitious for restoring the glory of this office'.[38] He intended to finish his great work of history and travel, *Safwat al-i'tibar*, with an

---

[37] Muhammad Bairam, *Safwat al-i'tibar bi mustawda 'al-amsar wa'l-aqtar*, 5 vols. (Cairo, 1884–94); biography by his son at end of vol. V (page numbers designated by letters).

[38] Ibid., vol. V, p. 11.

epilogue modelled on the *Prolegomena* of Ibn Khaldun (knowledge of whose thought had come back into the collective
consciousness of Arabs and Turks mainly by way of the Ottoman
ruling groups in Istanbul, Cairo and Tunis); in it he would show
how to reform conditions and restore 'the age of youth of Islam'.[39]
His main function in exile was that of a journalist; the hereditary
'alim had become a member of the new intelligentsia, using a new
medium to instruct the people and move them in the direction of a
reform of Islamic law and society by way of the reopening of the
door of *ijtihad* (the use of individual reasoning). In what he writes,
and what others write of him, one is aware of a stranger living in a
world which had grown alien: 'He looked sadly out over a world
which appeared to him to have gone mad; he saw all that was
noble in the faith he revered stifled by parasitic growths; he noted
that Islam was tottering to its fall by reason of internal decay.'[40]

The second example is taken from the next generation and a
different milieu. Muhammad Rashid Rida was born in 1865 in a
Lebanese village. He has described his family and early life in a
fragment of autobiography.[41] His was a family of poor *sayyids*
(descendants of the Prophet), having no endowments to support
them, but with a tradition of learning: the village lay near Tripoli,
which had been a centre of Sunni learning since Mamluk times.
What he tells us of his family shows the conventional pattern of
the *'alim's* life. They preferred the company of the learned to that
of the rulers of Tripoli, and there are several stories (some of them
not quite convincing) about the way in which they resisted the
temptations of power; they practised and took pride in a certain
withdrawal from the world. His great-uncle, the head of the family,
only saw *'ulama* and friends, preferred solitude and prayer to
company, did not allow loud voices or laughter in his *majlis*
(reception room), and left a scrap of poetry glorying in the fact
that he visited nobody and was visited by none.[42]

As a boy, Rashid Rida tells us, he showed signs of intellectual
talent, a love of solitude, a carelessness of food and clothes which
went as far as self-neglect, and he was known in his family and
village to be the recipient of special graces: he saw visions of the
dead, and was able to heal the sick and predict the future, and it

[39] Ibid., p. 23.
[40] Earl of Cromer, *Modern Egypt*, 2 vols. (London, 1908), vol. II, p. 183.
[41] *al-Manar wa'l-Azhar* (Cairo, 1934–5); relevant parts reprinted in Shakib Arslan,
    Rashid Rida aw ikha arba'in sana (Cairo, 1937), pp. 20f.
[42] Arslan, *Rashid Rida*, pp. 23f.

was known that anyone who harmed him would be punished in this life. Looking back on his youth forty years later, he believed that most of these experiences had a natural explanation, but some might have been true visions and graces, of which a devout Muslim should not speak openly. At the time, however, his family and the people of the village thought him to be a saint in the making. Everything conspired to push him towards a certain vocation, and he himself was prepared to go in that direction: he was initiated into the Naqshbandi order and found satisfaction in its silent ritual (*dhikr*), which in that place took the form of 5,000 daily repetitions of the name of God, in silence, with the eyes closed and the heart linked with that of the shaikh, and through him with the masters of the order back to the Prophet.[43] Gradually, however, he broke away from this vocation. The study of al-Ghazali taught him that a man should act freely from sincere conviction and not be afraid of anyone's blame, and a Mawlawi *dhikr* which he attended was the occasion to apply the lesson. The dances and music brought home to him the dangers inherent in the use of images of worldly beauty; he condemned them openly, in spite of the advice of his teacher, who urged him to be prudent.[44] From this time there began a change in his life. He took to preaching the importance of strict obedience to the *shari'a*, and the evil of honouring the tombs of the dead. His sense of the moral decay of Islam was heightened by the contrast with what he learned of Europe from newspapers and periodicals. A copy of the '*Urwa al-wuthqa*, a periodical published in Paris by Jamal al-Din and Muhammad 'Abduh, calling for Islamic reform, showed him that there might be another path, and he finally decided to leave Tripoli for Cairo and the life of an '*alim* in the schools for that of a journalist.

Once more, it is possible to understand this life in more than one way. Some of what he tells us is consistent with a familiar process, that of the '*alim* turning his back on the *khurafat* (superstitions) of the countryside and seeking his career in the city. He himself saw it differently, however; it was a conscious rejection of a vocation, a deliberate choice of a new path, a sign of a disturbance in himself as well as in his world.

---

[43] Ibid., pp. 50f; cf. Albert Hourani, 'Rashid Rida and the Sufi orders', *Bulletin d'Etudes Orientales*, 29 (1977): *Mélanges offerts à Henri Laoust*, vol. I, pp. 231–41; reprinted in Hourani, *The Emergence of the Modern Middle East*, pp. 90–102.

[44] Arslan, *Rashid Rida*, p. 95.

Bairam and Rida are only two of a number of men whom we find, in the later years of the nineteenth century, breaking out of traditional patterns of thought and life. With them there takes place a kind of mutation in the ideal type of the 'alim, a mutation symbolically associated with the figure of Muhammad 'Abduh. If we want to understand what this mutation was and where its importance lay during the next two generations, we should ask what these men thought they were doing and what in fact they did; and we may find that what they did was not exactly what they hoped to do.

Their aim was to create a new school of 'ulama who should have much the same position in government and society as 'ulama had always had. Much of their time was given to careful development of the sciences of religion. They are often called 'modernists', but the word does not carry the same implications of doctrinal change as with the Catholic modernists. At every point they tried to link themselves with what they regarded as the central tradition of Islamic thought, and only a delicate analysis, such as that which J. Jomier had made of the Qur'anic commentary of 'Abduh and Rida, *Tafsir al-Manar*,[45] and Christian Troll more recently of Sayyid Ahmad Khan,[46] would show the points at which they diverge from their predecessors, by some new interpretation of a verse of the Qur'an or the use of one *hadith* rather than another.

However careful they might be, their work met with strong resistance from the general body of 'ulama. Rida was always on bad terms with the Azhar, 'Abduh was suspect there, and on his second visit to Tunis was received coldly by the teachers at the Zaituna;[47] the later group of Algerian reformists worked outside the framework of the established religious schools. Such influence among the 'ulama as their ideas had was partial and came late, at a time when the traditional education of the religious schools had become less central to the life of society, because it no longer taught men what they needed to know in order to understand the modern world, and no longer led to positions which gave wealth, prestige or power. So far as the 'ulama were concerned, the most lasting effect of reformism was perhaps to widen the gulf between

---

[45] *Le commentaire coranique du Manâr* (Paris, 1954).
[46] *Sayyid Ahmad Khan: A Reinterpretation of Muslim Theology* (New Delhi, 1978).
[47] Green, *Tunisian Ulama*, p. 184; Ali Merad, *Le réformisme musulman en Algérie de 1925 à 1940* (Paris, 1967), p. 214.

them and the Sufi orders; in later generations of 'ulama, active membership of a tariqa was to become rarer.

The main influence of the reformers lay rather in their ability to give a kind of Islamic legitimacy to people whose education and aims were very different from theirs, those who lived in a world of secular thought. Here there was a certain ambivalence in their position, typical of the 'ulama whose tradition they inherited. In the first stages – the last years of the nineteenth century, and the first of the twentieth – they were accused by their enemies of being too close to the rulers, even if they were foreign or absolute: 'Abduh was thought to be too subservient to the British, Bairam certainly believed that the Egyptians should try to profit from the British presence, the Tunisian reformists had a moment of co-operation with the French,[48] and Rida was accused of betraying the memory of 'Abduh by trying to win favour with the Khedive 'Abbas Hilmi.[49] Later, however, their links grew closer with the nationalists of the first generation, those born in the 1870s, 1880s and 1890s, educated in secular schools and following civil professions. The nationalism of this phase, whether Turkish, Arab, Egyptian or Tunisian, can be seen in fact as springing from a confluence of two streams of influence, that of certain ideas coming from Europe, and that of this group of reformist 'ulama, who provided an Islamic legitimacy which was necessary if the nationalists were to appeal beyond the small circle of the educated, or if they were to be at ease in their own minds. The alliance of the two groups was an uneasy one at times: 'ulama, however modern, might distrust some of the tendencies of nationalism, and they were not given and could not take a central political role, but they had, for a generation or so, a primacy of honour.

The meeting of these two streams of thought can be seen in the picture given by writers of this and the next generation about the growth of their minds. In the second volume of his autobiography, al-Ayyam, Taha Husain tells us what the example of 'the Imam', Muhammad 'Abduh, meant to one who had broken out of the disciplines of the Azhar and whose mind was opening to modern science and the literature of the world: 'Abduh gave him an assurance that he was not betraying the past.[50] The same picture appears in a book written by an Algerian, Malek Bennabi, a

[48] Green, Tunisian Ulama, pp. 163f.
[49] Taha Husain, Al-Ayyam, vol. III (Cairo, 1972), p. 13.
[50] Ibid., vol. II (Cairo, 1939).

generation later. *Mémoires d'un témoin du siècle*[51] describes the education of a young Algerian growing up in the early decades of the present century. Steeped in French romantic literature, seeing even his own society through the eyes of Pierre Loti, he rejects the Islam he knows, that of the Sufi chiefs of the countryside, who have brought religion into disrepute and served the purposes of the colonial power. His mind is open to the secular idea of nationalism, coming to him through the 'Young Algerian' group and the example of Mustafa Kemal, but he is reluctant to accept it entirely, and he is saved from his dilemma at the moment in the 1920s when 'Algerian taste became egyptianized',[52] the first gramophone records, those of Salama Hijazi, appear in the shops; news of Sa'd Zaghlul and the Wafd spreads; the group known as the Algerian *'ulama* begins to publish newspapers, through which the ideas of reformism come to Algeria with a time-lag of a generation. 'What I felt at this moment,' our author tells us, 'was a new sentiment which could never leave me all my life ... I was a nationalist ... I could define myself from this moment as politically revolutionary and psychologically conservative.'[53]

The final importance of the reformers is that they prepared the moral ground for a change which both modernizing governments, whether foreign or indigenous, and nationalist movements wanted to bring about: the extension of bureaucratic control over the whole of society, and with it the strengthening of the social control of the city over its hinterland. This process involved the destruction of rural authorities, in particular those which claimed a religious sanction. A type of Islam which was simple and universal, preached respect for the law but allowed for changes in it, and was opposed to the moral domination of the countryside by the tombs of saints and their guardians, could give a religious sanction to such changes.[54]

This was only a brief moment of modern history. In the 1940s and 1950s we come to another watershed, the beginning of a new phase which perhaps needs to be explained in different terms; but at least in the two or three generations before, there is something in the historical process which can still be called an 'Islamic' history.

[51] (Algiers, n.d.).   [52] Ibid., p. 123.   [53] Ibid., pp. 107, 166.
[54] Ernest Gellner, 'The unknown Apollo of Biskra: the social base of Algerian puritanism' in Ernest Gellner, *Muslim Society* (Cambridge, 1981), pp. 149–73.

5

T. E. LAWRENCE AND LOUIS MASSIGNON

A PHOTOGRAPH of the Allied entry into Jerusalem on 11 December 1917 shows, among the tall British officers with their air of confident authority, the small figure of T. E. Lawrence with downcast eyes, and, close to him, that of a French officer, erect and slim, his eyes staring ahead as if seeing, beyond the buildings which lead from the Jaffa Gate towards the Holy Sepulchre and the Dome of the Rock, a vision of another Jerusalem.

The figure is that of Louis Massignon, assistant political officer attached to the mission of Georges-Picot, French High Commissioner for the occupied territories in Palestine and Syria. He was then thirty-four years old, Lawrence was twenty-nine. Their meeting in Jerusalem marked the end of a brief moment in which the lines of two unusual lives crossed one another. Lawrence was in the middle of the adventure which was to leave an ambiguous mark on the history of his time; Massignon was already known to the learned world as an Arabic scholar of unusual gifts, and had joined the *Mission Picot* after service at the Dardanelles and in Macedonia. They had first met in August 1917 at the Arab Bureau in Cairo; there was a plan to attach Massignon to the 'Arab Legion', a force composed of Arabs who had rallied to the Sharif Husain's revolt, which was being trained near Ismailia by British and French instructors.[1]

There is no reference in Lawrence's published works to this meeting; his wide interests did not extend far into the history or culture of the Arabs, and the name of Massignon perhaps meant little to him then or later. To the French in the Near East, however, the name of Lawrence was beginning to be well known. At about the same time the French military attaché in Cairo,

[1] 'Mes rapports avec Lawrence en 1917' in L. Massignon, *Opera Minora*, 3 vols. (Beirut, 1963), vol. III, pp. 423–7.

de Saint-Quentin, a diplomat and a man of perception and judgement, called him 'probably the most striking figure of the British Army or administration in the East', a man whose very light eyes were lit up by the intensity of his thought, and who gave a profound impression of energy and intelligence.[2] In an article written towards the end of his life, Massignon described him in not very different terms:

I saw with surprise an Englishman who was still very young, so free from all conventions, almost an outlaw, but so discreet, at the same time sweet and bitter, with the timidity of a young girl, and then with harsh intonations, in a low voice, like those of a prisoner.[3]

In his article, Massignon claimed that it had been the intention of General Headquarters to attach him together with Lawrence to the northern Arab army under Faisal, which was to operate on the east flank of Allenby's army, but that Lawrence had threatened to resign if a Frenchman were appointed who could challenge his own ascendancy over Faisal; a professional soldier, Pisani, was therefore appointed in his stead. It may be that research in British or French archives will confirm this version of what happened, but until then it should be treated with caution, for one of the traits which the two men shared was a powerful imagination which could impose its own order on the remembered events of their lives. Massignon was certainly haunted – in a long life constantly meditated upon, with an awareness of doors opened but never entered – by the thought of a destiny which might have been his; but also by the thought that it would have been a false one. On the morning of the entry into Jerusalem, he tells us, Lawrence opened his heart and expressed his 'disgust at having been delegated to the Arabs in revolt, with whom we were allied, in order to use them and then abandon them'.[4] Again, this memory may or may not be accurate, but before the end Lawrence did have such a sense of having been placed in 'a situation with no honest way out'.[5] It was a feeling which aroused an echo in Massignon, who reproached himself and his fellow-countrymen for 'our secular rage to understand, to conquer, to possess', the abuse of sacred hospitality.[6] After the fashion of their

[2] Report of 20 August 1917: Service Historique de l'Armée, Chateau de Vincennes, carton 7, N489.
[3] *Opera Minora*, vol. III, p. 424.   [4] *Parole donnée* (Paris, 1962), p. 71.
[5] D. Garnett, ed., *The Letters of T. E. Lawrence* (London, 1938), p. 462.
[6] *Parole donnée*, p. 71.

generation, both men judged what their countries did against a high standard of national honour, an ideal of imperial mission.

In what Massignon wrote of Lawrence we can perhaps discern some sense of an affinity. The two lives which touched each other briefly were those of pilgrims in a world which was not for them. Both were self-conscious men of letters, capable of giving expression in words to the beauty of external forms. *Seven Pillars of Wisdom* is full of vivid and violent images recording the impact of a landscape, a town or a person, from the moment when 'the heat of Arabia came out like a drawn sword'.[7] Massignon, the son of an artist, could evoke the heart-breaking beauty of visible forms, which 'I have so much loved'.[8] For both, however, this world was somehow a forbidden one: they had a sense of exile, of loneliness in a desolate country, of seeking something which visible forms could not give. Lawrence wrote of 'my solitary unlikeness, which made me no companion, but an acquaintance, complete, angular, uncomfortable'.[9] Too much has been written about the origins in his life of this sense of difference: perhaps it has been too much explained in terms of sex, too little in those of class. In the England of his time, class was as much a cause of torment as sex; it may be that some sense of having, through the circumstances of his birth, lost the place in the world which should have been his added to the torments of the body. In another article on Lawrence, Massignon speaks of him as suffering from some 'incurable "cancer" of his flesh',[10] and it does not need great insight, only attention to his own words, to know that Massignon too had his own sufferings: in letters, as well as in published writings, he spoke of the 'horror of myself' by which he had been obsessed.[11]

To inquire what form the 'cancer of the flesh' took in each of them is less important than to understand the meaning they gave it. For both of them, life and travel in the world of Islam was the experience by which they became aware of themselves and through which they worked out their own destinies. For each, however, it was a different world. Lawrence's Arabia is the desert: 'the Arab East to me is always an empty place',[12] 'I wake up now, often, in Arabia: the place has stayed with me much more than the men and the deeds.'[13] His view of Arabia echoes that of

---

[7] T. E. Lawrence, *Seven Pillars of Wisdom* (London, 1935).
[8] M. Malicet, ed., *Paul Claudel – Louis Massignon (1908–1914)* (Paris, 1973).
[9] *Seven Pillars*, p. 562.   [10] *Opera Minora*, vol. III, p. 427.
[11] Malicet, *Claudel–Massignon*, pp. 143, 160; Massignon, *Parole donnée*, p. 67.
[12] Garnett, *Letters*, p. 372.   [13] Ibid., pp. 692–3.

C. M. Doughty, the geologist wandering in the desert in order to find the bare face of the world as it was when it began, like the hermits who 'fled wilfully ... to retrieve the first Adam in their own souls'.[14]

For Lawrence and Doughty, the desert was the outward form of the primeval world. For Massignon, it meant something not in itself but rather as a symbol of the barren waste of unredeemed human life, into which there can suddenly break an illumination from elsewhere: 'almost I have a nostalgia for the desert, this perfect, serene sea, balanced in its very immensity by the daily passage of the sun ... it is there that I was truly born, called by my name by the "Voice of one crying in the wilderness".'[15] His Arab East is not only the desert, however. 'You love the Arabs more than I do,' he quotes Lawrence as saying to him;[16] for him the East is filled with human beings, past and present. At its very heart lay Cairo, the greatest product of Arab Muslim civilization. Lawrence disliked Egyptians: 'the climate is good, the country is beautiful, the things admirable, the beings curious and disgusting', he wrote to Robert Graves who was going to teach there.[17] For Massignon, the city meant intense love and friendship, reinforced by many visits throughout his life and, in due course, by the generations of his students. It was also a visible expression of what was to be the object of his deepest concern, the transmission through the ages of a culture and moral consciousness derived from the teaching of the Prophet Muhammad. Cairo was not only a city of the living. Outside its medieval walls lay the 'City of the Dead', where teachers and saints as well as rulers were buried; in a famous article, he was later to commemorate their tombs, and the 'chain of witnesses' which was for him the real history of Islam.[18]

For both Massignon and Lawrence, too, the Arab East was also the place where they experienced something so deep and challenging as to have revealed their true selves and the orientation of their lives. For Lawrence, it was the total experience of the 'Arab revolt': the vividness of the adventure, shot through as it was with the sense of being in a false position, increased his loneliness. The symbolic moment was that day in November 1917 at Deraa

[14] Travels in Arabia Deserta, new edn (London, 1923), vol. I, p. 473; R. Bevis, 'Spiritual geology: C. M. Doughty and the land of the Arabs', Victorian Studies, 16 (1972–3), pp. 163–81.
[15] Malicet, Claudel–Massignon, p. 100.   [16] Opera Minora, vol. III, p. 425.
[17] R. Graves, Goodbye to All That (London, 1960), pp. 264–5.
[18] 'La cité des morts au Caire' in Massignon, Opera Minora, vol. III, pp. 233–85.

when, according to his own account, he was imprisoned, beaten and abused by Turks, and 'the citadel of my integrity had been irrevocably lost'.[19] In the life of Massignon the crisis had come earlier, in May 1908 when – according to his own account, many times repeated – he had been accused of being a spy while on an archaeological expedition in Iraq, held under constraint and threatened with execution. He had tried to commit suicide 'by sacred horror of myself', lost consciousness, then suddenly awoke to be aware of the presence of a Stranger 'who took me just as I was, on the day of his Anger, inert in his hands like the gecko of the sands.[20] ... sudden awakening, the eyes closed before the inner fire, which judges me and burns my heart, certainty of a Presence pure, ineffable, creative, suspending my condemnation through the prayers of invisible beings, visitors of my prison, of which the names strike my thought'.[21] Those 'invisible beings' included persons known to him, and some from the past, of whose intercession he was conscious at that moment.[22]

Once more, it is necessary to be cautious. Some writers have doubted whether the incident Lawrence describes at Deraa ever took place. R. Meinertzhagen, not a very reliable writer, said that the story was false;[23] Bernard Shaw and his wife, both more reliable and more charitable, said much the same, and Mrs Shaw called him an 'infernal liar'.[24] It may be to this episode that Lawrence refers when he says that, at one point in *Seven Pillars*, 'I funked the distinct truth, and wrote it obliquely'.[25] Similarly, there is something a little unconvincing about a French citizen being threatened with execution at that moment in Ottoman history. Reports by the French consul in Baghdad and the captain and doctor of the river-steamer on which Massignon was travelling are silent about any such threat or sentence, but show that he had a period of high fever, due to malaria or sunstroke, which may have affected his view of what was happening around him.[26] It

---

[19] *Seven Pillars*, p. 447.
[20] 'Visitation de l'étranger' in Massignon, *Parole donnée*, pp. 281–3; also published as 'L'idée de Dieu' in Massignon, *Opera Minora*, vol. III, pp. 831–3.
[21] 'Visitation' in Massignon, *Parole donnée*, pp. 66–7.   [22] Ibid., p. 67.
[23] *Middle East Diary* (London, 1959), p. 38.
[24] P. Knightley and C. Simpson, *The Secret Lives of Lawrence of Arabia* (London, 1969), p. 215.
[25] Garnett, *Letters*, p. 463.
[26] G. Harpigny, *Islam et christianisme selon Louis Massignon* (Louvain-la-Neuve, 1981), p. 57; D. Massignon, 'Le voyage en Mésopotamie et la conversion de Louis Massignon en 1908', *Islamo-Christiana*, 14 (1988), pp. 127, 199.

does not much matter; in however imaginative a form, both men were trying to describe some decisive confrontation with themselves. If not at Deraa then elsewhere, Lawrence knew that the citadel of his integrity had been lost; in prison or in the grip of fever, Massignon experienced the horror of himself and the incursion of grace.

To both men, from then onwards, this was the summons to find some kind of order in the chaos of life. For Lawrence there was no Stranger, no irruption of another life into his. The rigours of an Evangelical boyhood seem to have left in him no sense of an eternal order breaking into the temporal, only a distaste for the clergy: 'I wish these black-coated apes could see the light with which they shine.'[27] Yet he ardently wished for 'that vision of the wholeness of life'; which was 'not a visitor to me, but always there'.[28] Whatever order his life could hold would have to be imposed from within himself, but this was his problem. His own explanations of himself are always the best. He was aware of a dangerous combination between a will of exceptional power and the lack of a stable directing purpose: 'I saw myself a danger to ordinary men, with such capacity going rudderless at their disposal';[29] 'I haven't the impulse and the conviction to fit what I know to be my power of moulding men and things.'[30]

The revelation of this tragic disharmony between will and purpose is what his eastern adventure ultimately meant to him. He had believed in the Arab movement, 'not finally ... but in its time and place',[31] and therefore he had been able to 'write my will upon the sky in stars';[32] but before it ended he no longer believed in it, or in Britain's role in it, or in his own role, and in some deeper sense this was the citadel of his integrity which was lost.

Not all was lost, however. Deeper than anything else in him was the literary impulse, the desire to transmute all experience into words, and even to shape that experience in the light of literary models. When he first went to the Near East his mind was already formed by books read during his school and student years in Oxford: Homer, Icelandic sagas, medieval French romances, William Morris. He aimed at preparing himself for an Arabian journey from which another *Arabia Deserta* might come. Then the war offered him an epic subject; after it was over, he no longer

---

[27] Garnett, *Letters*, p. 582.   [28] Ibid., p. 758.   [29] *Seven Pillars*, p. 564.
[30] Garnett, *Letters*, p. 411.
[31] Ibid., p. 693.   [32] *Seven Pillars*, dedicatory poem.

believed in what he had done, but he could still make literature out of it. This was to be his guiding star for the next decade, until *Seven Pillars* was finished. Then the same question posed itself once more: in the end, did he believe in what he had done? His verdict on his own book is harsh, but probably just; it was 'built up of hints from other books, full of these echoes to enrich or side-track or repeat my motives';[33] 'the echoes of Oxford and academic respectability of my prose'.[34]

The subtitle of *Seven Pillars* is *A Triumph*, and whether this is taken to refer to the exploits or to the book itself, Lawrence uses it with conscious irony. Both, in his view, were failures, because both were attempts to solve a problem which was insoluble, in the terms in which he posed it: by an effort of will, how could he escape from the tyranny of will? In the famous chapter of self-analysis in *Seven Pillars*, it is perhaps significant that he always writes 'Will' with a capital 'W', as it it were a separate being.[35] (It may be to this chapter that he is referring when he speaks of writing about something not directly but obliquely: in what he says about 'Will', it is possible to catch overtones of a feared, insistent sexuality.)

In his last phase, he tried to subject himself to an order not of his own making but willingly accepted, and to acquire spiritual release through a 'disciplined and surrendered life', to quote a perceptive critic.[36] His model of human behaviour, in these last years, was Thomas Hardy, fulfilled, detached from the world, all passion spent: 'so pale, so quiet, so refined into an essence ... There is an unbelievable dignity and ripeness about Hardy: he is waiting so tranquilly for death, without a desire or ambition left in his spirit.'[37] (Whether this is the true Hardy is irrelevant.) In the last letters of Lawrence's life there is something of this peace, a turning away from all efforts to impress others or impose himself upon the world. It is not in defeat but perhaps with a kind of satisfaction that he writes, five days before his death, that 'there is something broken in the works ... my will, I think'.[38]

To Massignon the problem appeared in other, one might say precisely opposite terms. The Stranger, who had held him in his hands on the day of his anger, would henceforth be the pole of his

---

[33] Garnett, *Letters*, p. 371.   [34] Ibid., p. 517.   [35] *Seven Pillars*, chapter 103.
[36] R. P. Blackmur, 'The everlasting effort: a citation of T. E. Lawrence' in *The Lion and the Honeycomb* (London, 1956), pp. 97, 123.
[37] Garnett, *Letters*, p. 429.   [38] Ibid., p. 872.

life, to be sought and loved, not by an act of pure will, but by a total surrender: by purification from sin, and then renunciation of the joys of the world, it might be hoped to attain to that reality which had revealed itself, gratuitously, in a moment of vision. By what path to approach that goal is the main subject of the correspondence between him and the poet Paul Claudel, which began in August 1908, soon after the crisis in Iraq. The letters revolve around the choice which Massignon saw himself compelled to make: to turn his back on the world, become a priest, and accept Charles de Foucauld's invitation to join him in a life of prayer and solitude in the Sahara, or to pursue the vocation of a scholar in the world.[39]

The correspondence is between two men of very different temperaments. For Massignon, the world is a desert illuminated by rays from the Eternal; for Claudel, all is balanced and symmetrical, having its own order and beauty, ravaged by sin like a building struck by lightning, but restored by divine grace. Each man must find his proper place in the structure and accept the limitations of that place, and in the end there are only two kinds of order between which to choose, that of marriage and that of priesthood; a man who has received neither of them is imperfect, his powers will be dissipated.[40] Claudel was clearly fascinated by the personality of Massignon, and something which the other told him called back a memory of that love-affair which is reflected in his *Partage de Midi*. 'These terrible confidences which you have given me and which find an echo in my heart' remind him of 'the horrible affair where I just missed losing my soul and my life'.[41]

It was not only a memory, but some sense of a missed vocation which led him to urge upon Massignon the vocation of priesthood: 'I consider my own life as a life wasted';[42] 'the taste for art has prevented me from having that terrible simplicity of intention without which there is no intimate friendship with God';[43] 'when we have written some articles, composed like me some plays full of artificial sentiments, *quid hoc ad aeternitatem?*'[44] Massignon's conversion was a sign that something special was

[39] Malicet, *Claudel–Massignon*.
[40] Ibid., p. 54; cf. J. de Menasce, quoted by S. Fumet in J. F. Six, ed., *Louis Massignon* (Paris, n.d.), p. 407.
[41] Malicet, *Claudel–Massignon*, pp. 55, 66.   [42] Ibid., p. 125.
[43] Ibid., p. 131.
[44] Ibid., p. 88.

demanded of him: 'God has rescued you by a miracle from the death of the body and the soul ... You belong to Him and not to yourself.'[45]

There was that in Massignon's nature which inclined him in the same direction. He was aware of those forces in himself which could lead to 'the death of the body and the soul'; the conversion in Iraq had come, he tells us, at the end of a period of 'violent escapades, disguised as a *fellah*, among outlaws'.[46] For him, earthly beauty was a temptation:

There are two beauties in this world, and it is necessary to destroy the first in oneself in order to have the purity of regard which alone permits one to become the second.[47]

He declared himself to be 'paralysed by the horror of myself and the incapacity to love others purely'.[48]

In the end, however, the decision went the other way, and when Massignon tells Claudel that he is to marry and to remain in the world as a scholar, there is a note of regret, however delicately expressed, in Claudel's response:

I feel only a sentiment of selfish disappointment. I hoped that you would transcend me, and it is hard for me to see you at the same level as myself... I salute your marriage tenderly and call upon you the help of God. You are no longer romantic and interesting, Massignon, but it is a very good thing to be neither the one nor the other.[49]

Perhaps Massignon's choice expressed a conviction that, for him at least, the path of the world was more arduous than that of renunciation, but it sprang also from a sense of some debt which he owed to Arabs and Muslims. His conversion had taken place in the Arab East, the first prayer he was able to say was in Arabic, an Arab family of Baghdad had shown him kindness and hospitality in his hour of need. Whatever the motives, the path once chosen must be followed to the end; in the years when Massignon was writing to Claudel he was also finding a way in which the life of the world – in his case that of a scholar studying Arabic manuscripts – could be consecrated to the service of God.

The work in which he faced this problem was his doctoral thesis – virtually finished by 1914 but not published until 1922 – on

[45] Ibid., p. 80.   [46] *Parole donnée*, p. 66.
[47] Malicet, *Claudel–Massignon*, p. 140.
[48] Ibid., p. 205.   [49] Ibid., pp. 215, 217.

Mansur al-Hallaj, a Sufi teacher executed in Baghdad in 922.[50] He was accused of teaching that the ritual observances of Islam were unnecessary: the Kaʿba at Mecca should be destroyed and a Muslim could make the pilgrimage in his own room without going to Mecca. Behind this, however, lay the suspicion that he was teaching that, at the end of the mystical way, the separation between man and God could be overcome in a union of essences. Massignon believed these accusations to be false: Hallaj was teaching not the union of substances, but that of love between man and God present in his heart. He was conscious of a special affinity with Hallaj, some of whose words had brought back to him the sense of sin, and then the desire for purity; Hallaj was one of the intercessors of whose presence he was aware at the moment of crisis.[51]

The thesis, *La Passion de Husayn ibn Mansur Hallaj*, is a very different kind of book from *Seven Pillars*, and yet they have a certain similarity of intention. In each, a literary artist of high imaginative power achieves a kind of self-knowledge through the depiction of something other than himself; they are spiritual autobiographies by implication. This is a perilous task: the artist is working with material which is not wholly malleable, hard facts may resist the efforts of the imagination to impose a unity of form upon them. Many doubts have been cast on Lawrence's interpretation of the 'Arab revolt', but it remains a more valuable source for the history of the period than its harsher critics will allow, and a flawed masterpiece of self-revelation. Of the depth and original-ity of Massignon's scholarship, the extraordinary range of his learning and the quality of his insights, there can be no doubt, but sooner or later it will be necessary for some other scholar not under his spell to look again at the sources for the life and teaching of Hallaj. Nevertheless, the achievement remains: one of the great works of European orientalism, and a permanent monument of French literature.

Had he wished, Massignon could have called it 'A triumph' without the overtones of irony that can be heard in Lawrence's subtitle. *Seven Pillars* ends in the total dissolution of the bond between the writer and his subject; the 'Arab revolt' goes its own

[50] L. Massignon, *La passion d'al-Hosayn-ibn-Mansour al-Hallaj martyre mystique de l'islam*, 2 vols. (Paris, 1922).

[51] *La passion de Husayn ibn Mansur Hallaj, martyr mystique de l'islam*, revised edn, 4 vols. (Paris, 1975).

way, and the fragility, or even the falsity, of its bases is already clear; the protagonist who is also the observer asks 'leave to go away', for him the event is sorrowful and the phrase meaningless.[52] There is no such separation in Massignon's work, rather the opposite; he has discovered and expounded a view of history which creates a link between him and his subject.

The true history of the human world, for him, is not that of the great collectivities, but of the divine work in the interior of each individual grain.[53] The bearers of this work are those human beings who are moving by prayer and sacrifice towards the final goal of life, union with God in love, and who take on themselves the sufferings and imperfections of others, the sinners, the ignorant, the poor and the oppressed. The possibility of substitution, of one person accepting a debt to God which others owe, was something he claimed to have learned from the writer Huysmans, whom he had met in adolescence, and who, on his death-bed, had offered his sufferings for Massignon's conversion.[54]

In this community sustained by prayer, there are some who, by the hard way of sin, contrition and purification, have reached a point where their prayers of substitution are of continuing validity. Their acts and words go on echoing after them; the line of their lives is prolonged by their survival in the lives of others. They form that chain of heroic souls, friends of God, which is the central thread of human history. One such was Hallaj, accepting the reproaches of his community, willing to die a martyr, but gradually, over the centuries, being absorbed into the moral consciousness of the Muslim world, and finally performing his work of substitution in the life of Massignon himself.[55]

No thinker is wholly original, and in this concept of a line of substitutes it is possible to see traces not only of what Huysmans wrote but of ideas current in the French Catholicism of the time, and of a certain 'occultism' which was also current, the belief in a hidden reality behind the appearance of things. The concept of a chain of witnesses to the truth, an invisible hierarchy of saints who keep the world on its axis, is an important theme of Sufi writing. Such ideas were used by Massignon in ways which were not without danger, but they formed a structure solid enough and well enough adapted to the needs of his temperament to provide a

[52] *Seven Pillars*, pp. 656, 660.   [53] Malicet, *Claudel–Massignon*, p. 104.
[54] Harpigny, *Islam*, pp. 42f.
[55] Ibid.

framework within which he could live, until his death in 1962 at the age of seventy-nine.

No one can say what the old age of Lawrence would have been like. It is possible that, with his temperament of a doer rather than a contemplative, he would have been drawn again into the public life of his country, had he lived beyond 1935 into the harsh years which followed; perhaps once more he would have found himself involved in the temptations of 'Will', perhaps they had been finally overcome. The image which remains is the last sad one, in the photograph taken as he left the Royal Air Force. Massignon's old age, however, is enshrined in the memories of innumerable colleagues, students and friends, and those who saw – with approval or distaste – his public interventions. Passionately desiring to belong to the chain of witnesses and substitutes, not without a longing for martyrdom in the desert, like that of Charles de Foucauld, the meaning of his life had come to be one of prayer and intercession by which he might give back to Muslims something of what he thought he had received from them. In the world of Islam he had known the oneness and greatness of God; the prayers of Christians might give them what Islam could not give, the Incarnation and the Cross; in spite of differences and conflicts, both belonged to the lineage of Abraham. To pray with and for Muslims was the special vocation of the Arabic-speaking eastern churches: this belief was expressed in the community of prayer which he founded, but above all in the most important event of his later life, his ordination as a priest of the Greek Catholic Church, long hoped for, finally achieved with papal consent, kept virtually secret as long as he lived.[56]

From this central core his activities sped in all directions: visiting prisoners, teaching Algerian immigrants, assisting innumerable students, to whom he was always obliging and helpful; practising non-violent protest against the excesses of French colonial rule, under the influence of Gandhi; going on pilgrimages, above all, in later life, to places associated with the Seven Sleepers of Ephesus, known both to Christian and Muslim tradition, and taken by him as symbols of the excluded and persecuted, and also of purity of faith.

Couve de Murville has described how, when he was ambassador in Cairo, the 'sombre, alert and tense figure of Professor Massignon' would appear in his office from time to time, and in

[56] Harpigny, *Islam*, pp. 124f.

what unexpected directions his talk would move. Most of those
who met him in his later life have similar memories, of a man
wholly unlike anyone else, at times disconcerting, and quite
unforgettable: always dressed in black, as if in mourning, emanci-
ated but with an austere beauty, his ravaged face lit up by
contrary passions, as if he were a battlefield of good and evil
spirits; exquisitely polite, very 'vieille France', combining force
and sweetness, anger and pity, with such intensity that some who
met him could not bear his presence, but most were overwhelmed
by a physical sense of the supernatural; always talking, in a flow
that took little account of time or place or his interlocutor, bearing
witness to his vision of human life, and returning, even on the
most unpropitious occasions, to the central moment of his own
life, the drama of sin and contrition and the divine light in the face
of the Stranger.[57]

[57] Six, *Louis Massignon*, pp. 109f, 237, 431, 433f.

6

IN SEARCH OF A NEW ANDALUSIA: JACQUES BERQUE AND THE ARABS

IN his valedictory lecture at the Collège de France,[1] Jacques Berque expressed once more, in personal and moving terms, the ideas which have guided him as a teacher and writer and the faith by which he has lived. At the heart of his concern has been the problem of alienation: how can men and women repossess a world which has grown alien to them, and do so without losing their authenticity? How can they avoid the two dangers of a stagnant reassertion of an identity inherited from the past, and a cosmopolitan and featureless modernity? For the Arabs, he believes, their identity as a separate people has two roots, Arabic poetry and the Qur'an, and the movement of his thought, in these last years, has led him to a deep meditation on their meaning and significance; from this have come his remarkable book *Cultural Expression in Arab Society Today (Langages arabes du présent)*[2] and his translation of the pre-Islamic odes.[3] He still has to give us his thoughts about the Qur'an and its meaning for the modern world; in spite of the example given by his former students Ali Shari'ati and Hasan Hanafi, he admits to a certain anxiety about the way in which a defensive attitude towards the Qur'an among modern exegetists can stifle creativity. He ends with an affirmation of faith, not only in the Arabs but in the larger entity of which they form a part, the Mediterranean world in its wholeness, Latin North and Arab South alike. He believes that the revival of its 'inherited landscapes', the creation of 'new Andalusias', is possible and necessary.

To look back from this to his inaugural lecture, twenty-five

---

[1] *Andalousies* (Paris, 1982).
[2] *Langages arabes du présent* (Paris, 1974); English trans. R. W. Stookey, *Cultural Expression in Arab Society Today* (Austin, Tex., 1978).
[3] *Les dix grandes odes arabes de l'Anté-islam* (Paris, 1979).

years ago, is to gain some sense of his steadfastness to a vocation.[4]
Given in December 1956, when the guns had scarcely fallen
silent on the Suez Canal and were still sounding in Algeria, it
takes up a sensitive theme: how can one know the 'other', how can
Europeans understand Islam? Speaking at the heart of the
western orientalist tradition, he suggests that oriental studies as
formerly concerned and practised are no longer sufficient. The
western scholar must henceforward work in partnership with
those who know their societies and cultures from within. He must
turn from the past to the present; and in the present he should look
beneath the surface of political and economic events to the
intimate movements of the individual heart, to that frustration
and anxiety which are the marks of those who no longer possess
the world they are compelled to live in, and to which a reaffirmation of Islam may seem to offer an antidote. Few western
observers at that time would have predicted the revival of Muslim
identity with which we are now familiar, and few in France or
England would have dared to confess their faith, at the end of
1956, that the ties between France and the Arab world would
remain. The Arab countries of the Maghreb 'are still for us the
place of our pride and of our tears';[5] the French language 'still
remains – I dare to proclaim it today – the hellenism of the Arab
peoples'.[6]

These two lectures, Janus-faced like all Berque's writings, look
backwards and forwards, seeing the shadows thrown by the past
on the present and future. They show clearly the theme, the
method and the tone of his writings. To take his own definition of
himself, he is a 'historical anthropologist', whose central subject is
the great theme of modern history, the scientific and technical
revolution and its effects upon the human world. Beginning in
northern Europe, in its first phase the revolution was owned in
monopoly by the great western nations; they took the profits of
trade and military power, and imposed their own signs on the
countries they ruled or dominated. Then came the age of nationalism, when the rest of the world reclaimed its rights over the
revolution and recovered at least the outward signs of its identity.
With independence, however, the real problem revealed itself,

---

[4] Collège de France, *Leçon inaugurale* (1 December 1956): reprinted as 'Perspectives de
l'orientalisme contemporain' in *Revue de l'Institut des Belles Lettres Arabes*, 79 (1957),
pp. 217, 38.
[5] Ibid., p. 32.   [6] Ibid., p. 31.

that of mastering the revolution in its depths and doing so while remaining true to oneself. In the first stage of independence, ruling elites kept for themselves the fruits of the national revival and tried to impose on their nation a modernity not rooted in the deepest soil of the inherited culture; opposition to it, the assertion of the need for the whole people to participate in its collective acts, could easily take the form of a reaffirmation of the heritage in a way which would inhibit progress. For Berque, there are two paths of escape from the dilemma: an Islam of modernity and a Socialism of authenticity. It is for the Arabs themselves to choose, no one can choose for them; one of the ghosts which haunt his work is that of T. E. Lawrence, manipulating other men's hopes for purposes which were not theirs.

To state the theme in this bare form is to give a distorted view of what will be found in Berque's books; they contain not a series of abstract ideas strung along a thin, straight line of exposition, but a continuous movement from the surface of society into the depths of the ideas which move and explain it, and back again. He states his method in the most personal of his books, *Arabies*, part autobiography, part meditation on the human world, in the form of a conversation with Mirèse Akar, who deserves praise for having induced him to reveal himself in this way, and having clothed his revelations in a faithful and elegant fashion:

When you talk to an individual, you look first of all at his face. If I talk to someone, I don't talk to his skeleton, still less to his actions, but first of all to his expression. It is the same with the study of societies. I know that beyond the expression of the face there lies that which moves and sustains it, something as real as what I am first aware of, the exchange of looks and breath between us ... I think of the two together as forming a single being, or rather two reciprocal beings, advancing, withdrawing and returning to the charge like Arab horsemen of the romantic era. Let us call the effect this has on us *frontalité*, the name historians of art give to the strange power of those archaic statues which follow you with their eyes and impose their obsessive presence on you. 'Presence': a word still more terrible than 'absence', and like it related to our reciprocity as living beings – a reciprocity of which the extreme case is love.[7]

It is this alternation of regard between the face of a society and its interior which gives life and excitement to Jacques Berque's books. His writing is at its best perhaps when it evokes most precisely the look and shape of a specific society: in his book on a

[7] *Arabies*, revised edn (Paris, 1980), pp. 80–1.

Moroccan scholar, *al-Yousi*,[8] and his study of a village in Egypt, *Histoire social e d'un village égyptien au XXe siècle*,[9] where direct observation and a reading of modern novels and stories are used together to paint a picture of a society and the forces which sustain and change it. In his larger book on Egypt, *Egypt, Imperialism and Revolution (L'Egypte, impérialisme et révolution)*,[10] the analysis of political and economic movements is interwoven with evocations of the sights and sounds of the city and countryside. Upper Egypt, the Delta, the popular quarters, the salons of Zamalek and Garden City, are mirrored precisely; only the English, awkward visitors from the Gothic North to the sunlit Mediterranean, perhaps elude him a little.

Berque's writings indeed are full of sights and sounds, smells and tastes. He has absorbed the Arab world through all his senses. The *'alim*, the traditional scholar, is not simply encountered in his books, but is someone seen walking in the narrow streets of Fez,

his eyes lowered, his prayer-rug under his arm . . . his step expresses disdain for the sights of the world about him . . . his slippery courtesy, his nerves of an old city-dweller, his ruse of an old courtier, his attachment to ornamental velvets and the sculptured plasters of magnificent houses, make him the intellectual champion of a culture which expresses itself equally well by the erudition of the scholastic, the fine hand of the craftsman, or the succulence of its cuisine.[11]

Just so the Algeria of his childhood is evoked in sights and smells – the opalescent light of the afternoon, the greasy smell of the *burnous*, the odour of spices – and Morocco by its royal dish, the pie of pigeons and almonds, the *bastila*. Such sense-impressions in his work become symbols of the specific nature of the Arabs, and of his own acceptance of it. He has none of that lack of ease which marked the contact of many scholars of an older generation with the human reality they studied. Quite simply, 'I go to the Arab countries because I am happy there'.

To move so easily between the surface and the depths is more than a method, it is an expression of a way of living. In his final

[8] *Al-Yousi, problèmes de la culture marocaine au XVIIe siècle* (Paris, 1958).
[9] (The Hague, 1957).
[10] *L'Egypte, impérialisme et révolution* (Paris, 1967); English trans., Jean Stewart, *Egypt, Imperialism and Revolution* (London, 1972).
[11] 'Ville et université: aperçu sur l'histoire de l'école de Fès', *Revue historique du Droit Français et Étranger*, 27 (1949), p. 107; English trans., K. Brown, 'Profile of a nineteenth century Moroccan scholar in N. Keddie, ed., *Scholars, Saints and Sufis: Muslim Religious Institutions since 1500* (Berkeley, Calif., 1972), p. 127.

lecture, Berque spoke of his need to integrate in his work insights gained from the social sciences, observation of the movements of a violent reality, and the memories and imperatives of his personal life. The greater part of his life has been spent in the Mediterranean world, and the vision of the antiquity of that sea-linked world is 'what is most deep in me'. The attempt to come to terms with his own life is shown clearly, for example, in his book of *French North Africa (Le Maghreb entre deux guerres)*.[12] Looking back on the world where his youth was spent, he describes how the two shores of the ancient sea grew apart from each other. For the *colons*, the men of the Maghreb became unreal, 'a menace, an uncertain quantity, something to be made use of or at best to be taken care of'. For the North African, the Frenchman in his country is real, but beyond him lies an image of another France, 'a constantly aggravated contrast between the France he desired and the France he knew by experience'. In such passages he is recording by implication his own steps towards acceptance that the colonial system was doomed. He does not pretend that this movement of his thought was swifter or simpler than it was; he did not fully accept the necessity of nationalism, as a preliminary step to human liberation, until he lived in an Egyptian village in the 1950s.

Childhood and youth are evoked more directly in *Arabies*, and a clear picture emerges of the way in which his vocation declared itself. At the beginning of the path there stands his father: 'my life has taken over my father's life'. Augustin Berque was a remarkable person in his own right, a high official of the Algerian government and a writer with something of the same power of evoking men and places as his son: his portrait of a rural notable in the Algeria of another age catches precisely the ambiguous relationship of colonizer and colonized:

Ardent and impetuous under his cold dignity, with a passionate ambition masked by indifference, and a generosity at the same time chivalrous and calculating, he excelled at the role of honest and naive devotion ... In this way he linked his interests with our cause, as formerly he had mixed them with those of our enemies.[13]

The standard by which Augustin Berque lived was that of imperial service at its highest, and this was the moral world in

12 *Le Maghreb entre deux guerres* (Paris, 1962), pp. 414–17; English trans., Jean Stewart, *French North Africa: The Maghreb between Two World Wars* (London, 1967), pp. 386–8.
13 A. Berque, *Ecrits sur l'Algérie* (Aix-en-Provence, 1986), p. 26.

which the son was raised. Some years of childhood were passed in Frenda, near the place where Ibn Khaldun retired to meditate on the natural history of dynasties; Ibn Khaldun's is another of the spirits which haunt his thought. In Frenda he would sit, a small boy in a corner by the chimney, watching his father administer justice; some sense of an easy and open relationship, before the contradictions of the colonial presence revealed themselves, was to remain with him.

Memories of the same kind are called back from early manhood. Unhappy as a student in Paris, detesting the Sorbonne of the time, he suddenly returned to Algiers, where his father arranged for him to spend some months with a tribe in the south, riding horses, learning Arabic, and receiving the imprint of an ancient patriarchal life. Then came his initiation into the service. As a very young man he found himself an official in the Moroccan countryside, called on to make decisions about men and societies he imperfectly understood. In another personal writing, 'Entrée dans le Bureau Arabe'[14] he depicts with affection and irony the fragile balance between ruler and ruled: the young inexperienced administrator, and the local *qa'id* giving judgements in the light of custom and his own interests, each possessing power of a kind but wary of having to use it, linked together by a common interest which time would soon erode. Looking back on this period of his life forty years later, he saw himself as 'the importunate guest come to seat himself at the hearth of Islam, but as master'. From the ambiguities of that position, and from the 'rage of desire of early youth', he was rescued by 'the passionate apprenticeship to a portion of earth and the beginning of a dialogue with its history'. The dialogue was carried further when he was transferred to Fez, and spent his evenings studying *fiqh* with a scholar of the city, in that kind of collaboration between men from the two shores of the Mediterranean, face to face and united by the desire to understand, which could serve as a paradigm of what he hopes will come about.

In a sense the dialogue has never ceased to take place in his own mind and heart. In *Arabies* he speaks of himself as Algerian on both sides; if his father belonged to the elite of service in the second generation, his mother's family belonged to the *petits blancs* of the countryside. On the other shore of the Mediterranean, his ancestral roots lie in a village of the Landes, on one of the great

[14] In *Nomades et vagabonds* (Paris, 1975), pp. 113–36.

pilgrim routes of Europe, but also, through his mother, in Spain. He can claim to be 'the last Frenchman of Algeria', but also 'the first Arabo-Latin of the Mediterranean'.

Whether or not the fusion implied in this name will ever come about, there is something of it which has been realized in his own life. It is a measure of the depth of the response of some French scholars to Islam, that they can claim to have helped the Arabs to understand themselves; one can say of him, as of Louis Massignon, that the idea which educated and thoughtful Arabs have of their own tradition, their definition of themselves, will be different because of what he has written and taught. He writes of Massignon with high regard, but a certain distance from his quest for high spiritual experiences and his tendency to give Islam a Christian visage. For him Islam is the 'other', to be apprehended and accepted in itself: a fitting task for a long and fruitful retirement, in St Julien-en-Born on the road to Santiago de Compostela.

7

⁘

CULTURE AND CHANGE: THE MIDDLE
EAST IN THE EIGHTEENTH CENTURY

LOOKING at the Muslim world in the eighteenth century from a later point in time, we can scarcely avoid searching for signs of what was to come, a new relationship of minds between Muslims and European Christians. There are such signs to be found, but we should not overestimate their importance. So far as Europe was concerned, the basic Christian attitude was still what it had been for a millennium: a rejection of the claim of Muslims that Muhammad was a prophet and the Qur'an the word of God, mingled with a memory of periods of fear and conflict, and also, a few thinkers and scholars apart, with legends, usually hostile and often contemptuous. Such attitudes had been modified but not replaced by others. The fear was less than it had been, and since the Reformation the claims of Islam had not seemed relevant to the great controversies of Christendom. If, therefore, the same language was used in regard to Islam, it was often used with a different purpose: in refuting Islam, writers might be using it as a symbol of enemies nearer home – Protestants arguing against Catholics, Anglicans against Deists, freethinkers against theological tyranny and prejudice.[1] There were, moreover, scholars who, working within a wider field of awareness, set themselves not to judge but to understand: in some of the great universities of western Europe and in the new British territory of Bengal, under the patronage of Warren Hastings.

For the most part, however, it was the imagination rather than the intellect which had changed: a new desire to seek and appropriate what was distant and strange moved travellers, collectors and those seeking to furnish the new and larger palaces

---

[1] A. Hourani, 'Islam and the philosophers of history' in A. Hourani, *Europe and the Middle East* (London, 1980), pp. 19–73; 'Western attitudes towards Islam' in Hourani, *Europe and the Middle East*, p. 1–18.

and mansions which the wealth and security of western Europe made it possible to build. For a brief period this movement of the imagination was not mixed with the contempt of the strong for the weak, or with a moral condemnation based on new ethical systems. Thus, in India, agents of the trading companies, indigo growers and military adventurers could venture far beyond the European settlements into the Mogul empire, marry into good Mogul families and found families of their own. Even in the factories there was some intercourse between Europeans and Indian Muslims of standing. It was only at the end of the century, as Spear has shown, that the British rulers of northern India began to draw apart from those they ruled and abandon all easy intercourse with them, because of an increase in the number of Europeans (and in particular of women), the influence of Evangelical and later of utilitarian ideas, the new policy, begun in the time of Cornwallis, of excluding Indians from higher posts, and, behind all these, the simple fact of power. The new relationship was symbolized by the ceremonial buildings erected by the British, above all in their capital of Calcutta: splendid but distant, owing nothing to Indian architecture, modelled on European buildings of neoclassical type, and built to a large extent by European bricklayers and carpenters.[2]

If this change had come in India by the end of the eighteenth century, in the Middle East and North Africa it was to come rather later. A European traveller in the Ottoman lands could feel reasonably sure, by the end of the century, that he came from a land stronger and better governed than those of the sultan; but he was not yet in a position to exercise power, and the signs of Ottoman power were all around him. He could still find much to admire, and some things where a comparison between East and West ran in favour of the first. Lady Mary Wortley Montagu was writing, it is true, at the beginning of the century when she said that the great mosque at Adrianople was 'in point of magnificence ... infinitely beyond any church in Germany or England'[3] and that the Turks are 'not so unpolished as we represent them ... 'Tis true their magnificence is of a different taste from ours, and perhaps of a better'.[4] Even at the end of the century, however, a

---

[2] P. Spear, *The Nabobs*, revised edn (London, 1963); S. Nilsson, *European Architecture in India 1750–1850* (London, 1968), pp. 101ff, 167ff.

[3] Letter to the Abbé Conti, 17 May 1717 in R. Halsband, ed., *The Complete Letters of Lady Mary Wortley Montagu*, vol. I (London, 1967), p. 359.

[4] Letter to the Abbé Conti, 19 May 1718 in ibid., pp. 414–5.

visitor to Istanbul might without absurdity have made a similar judgement.

On the other side, we can see much the same combination of an intellectual attitude which was almost unchanged with a new stirring of the imagination. There was no lessening of the basic religious hostility. When they wrote of Christianity and Christian Europe, Muslims placed them within the same framework of thought: Christianity had corrupted its Book, turning its prophet into a God and changing its one God into three; it denied the prophethood of Muhammad and the validity of the Qur'an. Once more, this attitude had been modified but not replaced by the end of the century. The calm assurance of strength had vanished, and religious hostility had been reinforced, in some places and among some classes, by a fear of European power. Indian Muslims observing the expansion of British power from the small factories on the coast into the heart of the Mogul empire, and Ottoman statesmen aware of the encroachments of Russia along the coasts of the Black Sea, which had once been an Ottoman lake, could already see the creeping shadows of things to come; even in the distant provincial town of Mosul, the Ottoman defeat in the war of 1768–74 was thought of as a sign that the Muscovites would soon eat up the world of Islam.[5]

It was partly, no doubt, this sense of something to be feared and faced which inspired what seems to have been a new curiosity about the ways in which Europeans lived and thought. Travellers from the West to Istanbul found some of the higher 'ulama willing to meet and talk to them, although in secret.[6] There were not only travellers, there were Europeans living in the cities of the Muslim world. In the growing and prosperous trading centres of the Ottoman Empire – Istanbul, Izmir, Salonica and Aleppo – as in India, Europeans could live alla franca, and there is some evidence of curious Muslims visiting them to see how they lived: for example, the travellers studied by S. Digby, Ghulam Husain Khan and 'Abd al-Latif Shushtari. A few travellers found their way to Europe itself. Ottoman officials went on business of state, like the famous ambassador Yirmisekiz Mehmed Said Efendi in 1719. There was also an occasional independent traveller:

[5] A. Hourani, 'The Fertile Crescent in the eighteenth century' in A. Hourani, A Vision of History (Beirut, 1961), p. 65.

[6] U. Heyd, 'The Ottoman 'ulema and westernization in the time of Selim III and Mahmud II' in U. Heyd, ed., Scripta Hierosolymitana: Studies in Islamic History and Civilization, vol. IX (Jerusalem, 1961), pp. 63–96.

S. Digby has told us of an Indian Muslim of Persian origin, Mirza Abu Talib Khan Isfahani, who visited England in 1799.[7]

To a great extent, Muslim writers who wrote of Europe, whether they had visited it or not, were concerned with power: what they observed and discussed were the details of government and policy, the sources of strength which the Ottomans or Moguls needed to acquire. Thus we have a series of travel reports (*sefaretname*) by Ottoman officials, and such works as those of the Christian convert Ibrahim Müteferrika, assessing the strength of the governments of Europe and their armed forces. In the same way, 'Abd al-Latif Shushtari tries to show how it was that the British had been able to obtain power in India: by their skill in piecemeal penetration aided by the negligence of Indian rulers.

What such writers noticed reflects what they were willing to learn from Europe: first of all, the arts of war and the sciences related to them. There was no lack of teachers: the Ottoman sultan could draw on European renegades like de Bonneval, or even at times on the help of European governments. India and the world of the Indian Ocean were full of military adventurers willing to take service with provincial rulers who were building up their power within the Ottoman or Mogul empires: the Mamluks of Baghdad, the Newab of Oudh, or the Sultan of Mysore. Through them, through travellers and through the naval and military schools in Istanbul, knowledge of some modern sciences came in. First of all came knowledge of geography: this was so important for statesmen, soldiers and sailors that the new European discoveries were assimilated without too great a timelag. The famous map made by Piri Reis in the early sixteenth century shows a knowledge of the discovery of the North American coast; a century later, the encyclopaedist Hajji Khalifa (Katib Çelebi) wrote a world geography which showed some knowledge of European works, and translated a Latin atlas; a century later again, the first Turkish printing press, that established by Ibrahim Müteferrika, published a number of geographical works. Beyond this, the officers of the new naval and military corps established in the 1730s onward needed some knowledge of mathematics and engineering for the management of ships and guns; here again, a few European works were translated and

---

[7] 'Changing horizons of thought in eighteenth century Muslim India', Colloquium on the Muslim world in the eighteenth century, unpublished paper (University of Pennsylvania, 1971).

published by the new printing press. Another science, that of medicine, was slower to change because it was so deeply rooted in the inherited Islamic culture, and because in many ways it had not been made obsolete by new discoveries; in the seventeenth century a European medical scientist could still learn from the works of Ibn Sina. It is not until the end of that century that we find signs of interest in European medical discoveries, but in those of the previous century rather than the more recent advances in anatomy and physiology. Some Greeks and Armenians of Istanbul, educated in Italy, did indeed know of these: Alexander Mavrocordato, the second Greek Dragoman of the Porte, wrote his thesis for the University of Bologna on Harvey's theory of the circulation of the blood. But their knowledge took time to spread, and it was only in the eighteenth century that some Turkish medical writers began to show a knowledge of what had been discovered in the previous one.[8]

Among some members of ruling elites there was something more than this: not just a need to borrow useful techniques, but a desire to learn and even imitate how others lived. Yirmisekiz Mehmed Said and his entourage mixed freely with the society of the French court, and Mirza Abu Talib Khan learned English and moved in good society in London. There seems to have been some stirring of the visual imagination, which we should not regard as more or less important than it was. It certainly signified some broadening of curiosity, but not yet a real change in values: to some extent it may have been no more than an expression of the desire of ruling and leisured classes for something new.

Articles by Kuran and Carswell show how far this movement had gone by the end of the century. As Kuran points out, there is little European influence to be found in the Ottoman architecture of the 'Period of Tulips'. There is a 'mannerism', an expression of a kind of boredom with the patterns of the classical Ottoman architecture – that of Sinan with its skilful use of domes, buttresses, slender minarets and fenestration – but it leads rather to an extension or distortion of these traditional patterns than to a rejection of them. It is not until the middle of the eighteenth century that we find, in the Nuruosmaniyeh mosque, something which 'comes close to the spirit of the European baroque': close, but no more, for what the architect of the mosque, and those of

[8] A. Adnan, *La Science chez les Turcs ottomans* (Paris, 1939).

later buildings modelled on it, has taken from Europe is not the new 'concept of space which seeks an expression of movement', but some surface features – broad stairs leading up to a portico, larger windows, greater variety. The need for a certain kind of uninterrupted space made it difficult indeed to build mosques in a new way; and it is for this reason, Kuran suggests, that the borrowing is most successful in small buildings like tombs, fountains and pavilions, where interior space plays little or no part.

Even this amount of change was more or less special to Istanbul, and elsewhere indigenous traditions of building continued or reasserted themselves. The rare examples of systematic town-planning – Isfahan in the seventeenth century, Nevşehir in the eighteenth – can be explained not as an imitation of Europe but as expressions of the traditional ambition of rulers to show their power by imposing their order upon space. In individual buildings the great architectural styles continued: the Ottoman in Istanbul and Asia Minor; the Syrian, reasserting itself as the Ottoman influence grew weaker and producing the great houses of Aleppo, Hama and Damascus, which have no parallel elsewhere in the empire at that time; the Persian, taken over and developed by the Safavis from the Timurids, then by Karim Khan in Shiraz; the Maghribi, in the mosques and palaces of Maknas.[9]

As both Kuran and Carswell show, the influence of Europe is stronger in some of the decorative arts. Kuran draws attention to kiosks and palaces in and around Istanbul which are Ottoman architecturally but purely French inside, with carved and gilded ceilings, rococo decorations and reliefs. Under Selim III, part of the Topkapı Palace was decorated in the European manner, with painted plaster-work, imported tiles, pilasters and crude landscape murals. The craftsmen here seem to have been largely European, often of mediocre talents. It is only to be expected that such craftsmen should have gone to seek their fortunes in a great capital. But Carswell has also studied a provincial tradition, that of Syria (and, inside Syria, of Damascus and Hama, cities which

---

[9] A. Kuran, 'Eighteenth century Ottoman architecture' in T. Naff and R. Owen, eds., *Studies in Eighteenth Century Islamic History* (Carbondale, Ill., 1977), pp. 303–27; G. Goodwin, *A History of Ottoman Architecture* (London, 1971), pp. 334ff; A. U. Pope, ed., *A Survey of Persian Art*, 3rd edn (Ashiya, Japan, 1972), vol. III, pp. 1165ff. G. Marçais, *L'architecture musulmane d'Occident* (Paris, 1954), pp. 381ff: J. Carswell, 'From the tulip to the rose' in Naff and Owen, *Studies*, pp. 328–55.

were not great centres of foreign trade), and found something similar: buildings constructed within an inherited tradition, with masses of different heights and sizes grouped around a central courtyard, and carrying a decoration in which European influences can be seen, particularly in the painted walls with their 'vases of Chinese porcelain filled with sprays of flowers painted in a manner betraying Western influence in every stroke', and their panoramas of cities, probably copied from engravings, and showing attention to topographical detail. The original furnishings, china and silverware are missing, as he says; but enough of them survive to support his suggestion of a new eclecticism and striving after novelty among the professional and merchant classes as well as at court. In another study, he has traced the development of Kütahya pottery to its apogee in the first half of the eighteenth century. Here, too, a close imitation of porcelain was produced, with Chinese and Japanese designs, as well as tiles of traditional design for mosques and churches; and production was for Armenian bourgeois clients, as well as the Ottoman ruling elite.[10]

The use of foreign forms, shown in the Kütahya pottery, appears in an even more surprising way in one particular visual art, that of painting in seventeenth- and eighteenth-century Iran. In the course of the seventeenth century, elements derived from European art – details of dress and decoration, the treatment of landscape and of figures – appeared in the two traditional types of painting: wall paintings, showing battle or hunting scenes, girls dancing or playing musical instruments, which decorated the palaces of rulers and nobles, and miniatures in manuscripts or albums. It is not easy to trace the process of reception: some European artists are known to have worked in Iran, both for the Shah and for Armenians in Julfa, but little is known about them; European paintings and engravings were brought in, notably by Armenian silk merchants trading with Europe; there were influences, too, coming from Mogul India, where European paintings and prints had been known since the 1580s, and western painters had worked soon afterwards. Before the end of the seventeenth century a new technique had been learned, that of painting in oil on canvas; Persian artists must have acquired this from Euro-

---

[10] J. Carswell, *Kütahya Tiles and Pottery from the Armenian Cathedral of St James, Jerusalem*, 2 vols. (Oxford, 1972), vol. II, pp. 1ff.

peans, and gradually a distinctive Persian tradition developed, which reached its height under the early Qajars.[11]

Literature lay much closer to the heart of the inherited culture, and here influences from outside were even more limited. They can be found, to a small extent, in an important genre, that of the writing of history: historians were not yet moved by new conceptions of the past or of how to write about it, but at least they used a limited number of European sources when dealing with a certain kind of subject. The Maronite historian Istifan al-Duwaihi (1629–1704) used European chronicles of the Crusades, works by European travellers to the Holy Land, and works of Church history in his history of the Maronites;[12] and the Ottoman writers, Huseyn Hezarfenn (d. 1691) and Muneccimbaşi (d. 1702), relied on European sources in those parts of their work which dealt with the world outside *dar al-Islam*.[13] In general, however, the tradition of Islamic historiography was too firmly rooted to be displaced. Ottoman official historians, compilers of biographical dictionaries, and historians of Arab cities went on writing in their own styles, and the end of the century saw at least one historian who can be compared with the great masters of earlier ages: al-Jabarti, with his clear understanding of the use of sources – 'I do not record any event before ascertaining its truth by means of independent and consecutive sources and by means of its becoming widely known' – and his vision of the rise and fall of rulers, set against a backcloth of ordered Islamic society.[14]

This continuity can be seen even more clearly in poetry, the expression and aesthetic justification of an existing moral order. If Arabic poetry (so far as it has been studied) seems to show no great originality in this century, there were two living traditions of

[11] A. Welch, *Shah Abbas and the Arts of Isfahan* (New York, 1973), pp. 103ff, 148; E. Grube, 'Wall paintings in the seventeenth century monuments of Isfahan', *Iranian Studies*, 7 (1974), pp. 511–42; E. Sims, 'Five seventeenth century Persian oil paintings' in P. and D. Colnaghi and Co., *Persian and Mughal Art* (London, 1976), pp. 223ff; J. Carswell, *New Julfa* (Oxford, 1968), pp. 21ff; S. J. Falk, *Qajar Paintings* (London, 1972).

[12] K. S. Salibi, 'The traditional historiography of the Maronites' in B. Lewis and P. M. Holt, eds., *Historians of the Middle East* (London, 1962), pp. 212–25; A. Hourani, 'Lebanon: historians and the formation of a national image' in A. Hourani, *The Emergence of the Modern Middle East* (London, 1981), pp. 149–69.

[13] B. Lewis, 'The use by Muslim historians of non-Muslim sources' in Lewis and Holt, *Historians*, pp. 180–91.

[14] D. Ayalon, 'The historian al-Jabarti' in Lewis and Holt, *Historians*, p. 396; P. M. Holt, 'Al-Jabarti's introduction to the history of Ottoman Egypt' in P. M. Holt, *Studies in the History of the Near East* (London, 1973), pp. 161–76.

Persian poetry: the Indian, which had grown up under court patronage, and combined a certain liberation from classical canons of style with a proliferation of elaborate images; and the Persian, with a poetry more closely linked to religious themes, and a style going back to classical models in reaction against artifice. Ottoman poetry reached its climax in this century; in style and language more Turkish, more liberated from Persian models; in spirit more secular, celebrating, as with Nedim, the magnificence of courts and the pleasures of the world, or, with other poets, more simple themes; in feeling less conventional, more expressive of personal experiences.[15]

Among Muslims and non-Muslims alike, the inherited culture had been moulded by the attempt to relate the whole of human life and knowledge to a religious revelation; or, to put it the other way round, to articulate the revelation in systems of thought, law and ritual. At this level, only the Christian communities (and not all of them) had been touched, at the end of the century, by movements of thought coming from western Europe; and the movements which touched them were religious, rather than the secular ones which were to be characteristic of a later age.

For a time in the seventeenth century, the Eastern Orthodox Church, and in particular the Oecumenical Patriarchate of Constantinople, had been open to Calvinist influence. The Calvinist trend became important with the election to the Patriarchate in 1620 of Cyril Lucaris (1572–1638), who had learned of Protestant doctrines from Lutherans in Poland and from Dutch Calvinists, and whose attempt to spread them in the Orthodox Church received some support from the English and Dutch ambassadors. But the opposition of the Jesuits and the Catholic embassies led to his being deposed more than once, and finally executed.[16]

Of longer duration, and having more lasting effects, were the attempts of Roman Catholic missions to win the eastern Churches to the Roman allegiance. Even after the great schism there had been individuals and groups in the eastern Churches who had wished to restore their communion with Rome, and during the life of the crusading states one eastern Church, that of the Maronites,

---

[15] E. J. W. Gibb, *A History of Ottoman Poetry*, vol. IV (London, 1905); J. Rypka, *History of Iranian Literature* (Dordrecht, 1968), pp. 292ff, 306ff; A. Pagliero and A. Bausani, *Storia della Letteratura persiana* (Milan, 1960), pp. 478ff.

[16] S. Runciman, *The Great Church in Captivity* (Cambridge, 1968), pp. 259ff.

mainly established in the Lebanese coastal range, had accepted papal supremacy as a whole. After the end of the crusading period, however, relations between East and West had grown tenuous: the Roman Church was scarcely present in the eastern Mediterranean, until in 1342 the king of the Two Sicilies acquired from the Mamluk sultan possession of certain holy places in Palestine and handed them over to the papacy, which in turn entrusted the care of them to the Franciscan order. From that time onward, the Franciscan custody of the Holy Land, under the protection of the Spanish king and other Catholic rulers, spread beyond Palestine into Syria, Egypt and elsewhere. At the end of the sixteenth and beginning of the seventeenth century, there began a more active policy, with the establishment in Rome of colleges to educate priests: Maronite (1584), Greek (1577) and the College of the Congregation for the Propagation of the Faith (1621). A little later, some Catholic orders began to work more extensively, under the protection of the kings of France and their ambassadors.[17]

From this time, the number of those in the various eastern Churches who accepted the authority of the pope and Catholic doctrine on disputed points grew; and there grew also a tension between them and others in their communities. This reached its height at the beginning of the eighteenth century, with a struggle for the possession of churches, bishoprics and patriarchates, into which ambassadors, consuls and Ottoman officials were drawn. By the middle of the eighteenth century it had virtually ended with a compromise: 'Uniate' Churches, linked with Rome but preserving their own hierarchies and liturgies, emerged from the body of the eastern Churches. Among the Eastern Orthodox, a regular Uniate patriarchate began in 1730, in the other churches rather later (but they had to wait another century for official recognition by the Ottoman government). In 1736, relations between the Maronite Church and the papacy, which had grown distant, were renewed and precisely defined at the Synod of Mount Lebanon.[18]

The Uniate churches still belonged by language and sentiment to the eastern Churches from which they had emerged, but their inner life was moulded to a great extent by the western Church, its

---

[17] G. Graf, *Geschichte der christlichen arabischen Literatur*, vol. IV (Vatican, 1951), pp. 169ff.

[18] D. Attwater, *The Christian Churches of the East*, 2 vols. (Milwaukee, Wis., 1948–61).

colleges and missionaries. Certain changes in liturgy, law and discipline came about, while organized monasticism on the western model grew up to supplement the older traditions of the solitary hermit – in particular in Lebanon, under the protection of the lords of the mountains (among the Maronites, Lebanese Fathers and Antonians; among the Greek Catholics, Salvatorians and Shwairi Fathers; among the Armenians, the Antonians). Another Armenian Catholic order, that of the Mekhitarists, established itself first in Asia Minor, then in the Morea, and finally on the island of San Lazzaro near Venice. From the new monasteries and the colleges in Rome there sprang a new religious learning, both in Arabic and Armenian, and a new and more self-conscious concern with the history of eastern Christianity, with Catholic theology (the *Summa Theologica* of Saint Thomas Aquinas was translated into Arabic by the Syrian Catholic Patriarch Ishaq ibn Jubair), and with language and literature.[19] Some of what was produced was published in a new form, through the printing press: in Arabic there were a number of small presses in Syria and Lebanon; in Armenian, a press in Istanbul and one at Julfa in the seventeenth century, and, above all, that of the Mekhitarists of Venice.

By the end of the eighteenth century, another movement of ideas can be seen. Members of the merchant families of the cities began to acquire a new kind of education: sons of the Greek and Armenian families of Istanbul went to study in Italy, and in particular at the University of Padua; those from provincial families went to missionary schools or to schools established by the Christian communities themselves, like the Maronite school at ʿAin Waraqa in Lebanon. Apart from their own languages they learned Italian, the lingua franca of the Levant ports. This had a practical use for those engaged in foreign trade or in the employment of local governors, ambassadors or consuls, but it could also be a channel through which there came, not the ideas of Calvin or the Counter Reformation, but those of the Enlightenment. Greek students at the University of Padua and Greek merchants in the wide Greek diaspora in central and western Europe came to know something of classical civilization as European scholars were revealing it, and to identify their own people with it. They also encountered ideas from Voltaire, who is mentioned a hundred times in the Greek literature of the later eighteenth and early

[19] Graf, *Geschichte*, vol. IV, p. 50.

nineteenth centuries. Similarly, a Lebanese Christian writer of the early nineteenth century, Mikha'il Mishaqa, tells us that he and others in Damietta read Volney on the ruins of civilizations, and were troubled about religion.[20]

It would not be correct, however, to think that these new ideas had any effective influence outside the small circle of those who had had an education on the western European model. The Greek Church was opposed both to the study of ancient Greece and to the spread of modern French ideas; its world of thought was that of the Christian fathers and mystics. It was equally opposed to the idea of national independence, and taught acceptance of Ottoman rule, as a divine punishment for sin or a protection against Catholic or Calvinist onslaughts; because of this, from the beginning, Greek nationalism had anticlerical overtones. The thought of the masses was eschatological: the end of Muslim rule would come by some divine intervention.

The Jewish community had not yet begun to be changed by the same kind of influence coming from western Europe. There were, it is true, Jewish merchant communities, from Salonica to Baghdad, which had grown in prosperity and acquired a wider knowledge of the world through the increase of trade in the Mediterranean and in an Indian Ocean now dominated by Europe. The intellectual and spiritual geography of the Jewish world, however, was different from that of Christendom. Ideas of 'emancipation' and 'enlightenment' were only just beginning to spread in certain Jewish communities: in the Marrano communities of the Netherlands, England, the Atlantic coast of France and North America, and in some parts of Germany. But these were still fragile and marginal movements which had not begun to penetrate the Jewish societies of the Mediterranean, Poland or the Ukraine. The eastern Mediterranean had been the cradle of some important movements: in the sixteenth century the thinkers of the school of Safad had codified the law and developed the mystical ideas of the Kabbala; in the seventeenth, the messianic movement of Sabbatai Sevi (1626–76) began in Palestine and Smyrna, and spread throughout a Jewish world already prepared for it by the messianic element in the teaching of the Kabbalists of Safad, and troubled by the great massacres of 1648 in the Ukraine, until it

---

[20] Runciman, *The Great Church*, pp. 208ff, 360ff; C. T. Dimaras, *A History of Modern Greek Literature* (Albany, N.Y., 1972); A. Hourani, *Arabic Thought in the Liberal Age* (London, 1962), p. 139.

was virtually extinguished by his enforced conversion to Islam. In the eighteenth century the creative centres were further north, in Poland and the Ukraine: it was there that the great controversies raged between the Hasidic mysticism formulated by Baal Shem Tob and the legalist opposition of the Gaon of Vilna. In the Ottoman countries, apart from the Rumanian provinces, the second rather than the first was still the dominant trend.[21]

If it was true of eastern Jews and (within limits) of Christians that they still lived in a self-sufficient inherited world of thought, it was even more true of Muslims, whose world of thought revolved around the acquisition, development and transmission, through the medium of one or other of the Islamic languages, of a body of knowledge believed to derive from the revelation of God in the Qur'an and the example of the Prophet Muhammad as recorded in the Tradition. Since the content of revelation was a Book, Muslim society was dominated by the literate to whom had been transmitted the sciences based on it. They can be called, collectively, the *'ulama*; but the use of the term is misleading if it is taken to imply that there was a single class with one culture, outlook and collective interest. It would be safer to think of at least three types of education or training, not necessarily exclusive of each other, but each of them tending to give its own formation to the mind and soul of a Muslim: first, the legal training given in special schools to those who were to enter the legal service of the state; second, the education in the religious sciences given by a wide range of mosques and schools to students who would follow many different vocations, legal, religious, or secular; third, the initiation given within the framework of the orders of mystics into one or other of the paths which would lead, not to *'ilm*, theoretical knowledge of the religious sciences, but to *ma'rifa*, experiential knowledge of God.

All Muslim governments worked formally within the limits of the *shari'a* (religious law) and regarded it as the only law valid, universal and binding on rulers as well as ruled; but the part which the law and its guardians played in the life of states varied from one to another. In Morocco there seems to have been less of a judicial hierarchy than elsewhere, because of the narrow limits within which the government could exercise direct control over the country outside the main cities. At the other extreme, in the regions over which the Ottoman sultan had direct control, the existence of a large, well-organized and relatively effective bureaucracy involved that of a network of judges receiving salaries and *muftis* receiving fees, organized into an official hierarchy and playing an important part in the process of control. In Iran under the Safavis much the same had been true, but by the eighteenth century the disappearance of central control had weakened the official judicial class.

In studying the nature of the official *'ulama* it will be best to take the Ottoman empire as a model, since in this, as in so many other ways, the Ottoman system represented a logical development and formalization of what had existed in earlier states. At least three kinds of specialized training (but all of them having the common basis of a general Islamic education) prepared men for the service of the Ottoman sultan. Those who were to have a political or military role (including, at some periods, princes of the Ottoman family) might receive instruction in the sultan's household, or in that of the grand vizir, in the polite literature which enshrined the human and social ideals that should guide a ruler, and in the arts of war. Those who were to work as bureaucrats in chancery or treasury would be trained under a kind of apprenticeship by senior bureaucrats, to draft and write documents and keep accounts in the correct and traditional forms – forms which persisted through changes of dynasty and the passage of centuries. Those who were to interpret and administer the laws were given a training in Islamic law, and those who were to control the legal system were for the most part trained in the imperial schools of Istanbul. At the top of the hierarchy stood a small number of high posts conferring power and the influence which came from having access to the rulers: the *shaikh al-Islam* or chief *mufti*, the two *kaziaskers* (military judges), and the judges or *mullas* of the great cities. As the hierarchy gradually developed, there grew up a system of specialized schools: first those of Mehmed the Conquerer in Istanbul; then those of the sultans of the late fifteenth century in Istanbul, Edirne and Bursa; and then the great foundations of Sulaiman, Selim II and Murad III in the sixteenth century. Once the *cursus honorum* was fully established, there was a link between each grade in the hierarchy and a corresponding level of attainment in one or other of the imperial schools: no one could have his name inscribed on the register of candidates for the highest posts, unless he had finished his studies at the appropriate level.

In this way there was created an elite of high legal officials between whom and the ruler there was a kind of implicit compact. They could give the ruler two things he needed if his rule was to be stable: on the one hand, recognition as legitimate ruler, given formally in the ceremony of *bay'a* (investiture) and justified in terms of one or other of the theories of authority; on the other, the maintenance of a recognized system of law, through which the fabric of an ordered society could be preserved, and the arbitrary power of officials over subjects be restrained.[22]

In return, the official *'ulama* received power within the limits of their functions, and an influence not easy to define. Examples can be found of their exercising influence over major decisions of the government. More frequent perhaps was the influence in favour of individuals or groups which could be exercised by those who had direct access to the ruler and his ministers. In times of religious conflict or controversy, they could hope to have the backing of the state in order to maintain or spread the interpretation of Islam which they favoured. Thus, when the Safavis became rulers not only of the north-west of Iran but of the great cities, the Shi'ism which they made into the state religion of Iran was not the amalgam of ideas current in Azerbaijan where their power had arisen, but the learned and sober faith of the urban nobility whose help they needed.[23]

The official *'ulama* also received financial benefits, salaries, fees and in some places control of great *waqfs* (religious endowments); the chief *qadi* (judge) of the Moroccan sultans controlled the *waqfs* of Fez; the Safavi *'ulama* controlled that of the shrine at Mashhad. They were able to preserve and transmit their wealth more easily than those directly involved in the exercise of power; they were nearer to being immune from sudden disgrace, confiscation of property and execution. It was because of their possession of power and wealth that the high official *'ulama* had become by the

[22] N. Itzkowitz, *The Ottoman Empire and Islamic Tradition* (New York, 1972), pp. 55ff; R. Repp, 'Some observations on the development of the Ottoman learned hierarchy' in N. Keddie, ed., *Scholars, Saints and Sufis: Muslim, Religious Institutions since 1500*, (Berkeley, Calif., 1972), pp. 17–32; R. Repp, 'The altered nature and role of the ulema' in Naff and Owen, *Studies*, pp. 277–87; E. Burke, 'The Moroccan ulama 1860–1912' in Keddie, *Scholars, Saints and Sufis*, pp. 93–125; N. Keddie, 'The roots of the ulama's power in modern Iran' in Keddie, *Scholars, Saints and Sufis*, pp. 211–29.

[23] J. Aubin, 'Etudes safavides: I Shah Isma'il et les notables de d'Iraq persan', *Journal of the Economic and Social History of the Orient*, 2 (1959), pp. 37–80.

eighteenth century a closed elite immersed in the interests of the world. The high positions tended to be a monopoly in the hands of a small number of families, linked by kinship and marriage with other official elites, and perpetuating themselves through wealth, official influence and privileged access to the imperial schools.

There was, however, a price to be paid for their privileges. To the extent to which they had a monopoly of high judicial posts, they were excluded from others: at least in the Ottoman service, different careers became clearly distinguished from each other, and a member of the official 'ulama would rarely become the chief adviser or minister of a sultan. To some extent, also, they tended to be alienated from the urban society which they helped to control. In some places they may have succeeded in preserving a certain ambiguity of role, acting as intermediaries between the government and the Muslim population of the cities; this may have been so in Morocco, where the judicial hierarchy was drawn from the city population. But in Iran, by the eighteenth century, the general revulsion of the population from the rulers who had tried to fill the vacuum left by the fall of the Safavis seems to have extended to the 'ulama who took service with them.[24] In the Ottoman empire, the higher official elite of 'ulama were very much part of the system of Ottoman control, and were regarded as such. Strict 'ulama outside the system might disapprove of the compromises with the world which judges had to make; students and inferior 'ulama might resent their exclusion from the imperial schools and the offices to which they were the door. In the provincial cities the distance between the official 'ulama and the Muslim population might be greater still: the judges were strangers, sent from the centre for short periods; they were Turks in regions inhabited by other ethnic groups; they were Hanafis while the population might be mainly Shafi'i or Maliki.

There was another price they had to pay, that of administering a law not entirely drawn from the shari'a. Since the 'Abbasid period, the shari'a had been regarded by all Muslim dynasties as the only legal system. But, in fact, there had usually been a duality in the judicial process: the qadi administered Islamic law in respect of those cases which the government allowed to be taken to him, and his decisions were carried out by the civil power, while the ruler or his deputies administered their own justice directly in

[24] H. Algar, *Religion and State in Iran 1785–1906* (Berkeley, Calif., 1969), chapters 1 and 2.

cases affecting public order and security, or in cases of abuse of authority by officials. Like so much else, this practice was formalized by the Ottomans; in their early centuries, the ruler's authority was exercised not by arbitrary act of will, but in accordance with known and written regulations, and breaches of the regulations could be punished by the sultan or his governors. Thus the taxes and dues which financial officials or tax farmers could collect were defined by *kanun* (secular law), which varied from region to region and sought to preserve the local customs of each region, so far as they were compatible with the general policy of the government; jurisdiction in criminal cases was regulated by a criminal code, tending to be uniform throughout the empire, different in some ways from the *shari'a*, and in some ways more severe, and of which the purpose was to ensure that the guilty were punished and the interests of the state preserved. The creation and use of these codes implied a close connection between the official *'ulama* and the civil power: the *qadi*s administered *kanun* as well as *shari'a* law in their courts; the *mufti*s issued *fatwa*s (legal rulings) authorizing those provisions of the *kanun* which were not derived from the *shari'a* although not contrary to it; above them an appeal lay to the sultan or his governors, who dealt in their *divan*s with cases involving the security of the state or petitions against officials in breach of the *kanun*.[25] By the eighteenth century the *kanun* seems to have fallen into disuse, but the subordination of *qadi*s to the civil power continued. A study of the administration of justice in the tributary province of Tunis, under the Husainids in the eighteenth century, has shown that major cases came to the Bey in his *divan*. He himself gave justice in cases involving state security; for others he sat with the chief *qadi*s and *mufti*s; only minor matters went to the *qadi*s sitting by themselves.[26]

It is not difficult, from histories and biographical dictionaries, to construct a picture of the typical member of the Ottoman legal elite: balancing delicately between two kinds of responsibility, to the palace or government, and to the ideal Muslim society enshrined in the teaching of the schools; able to interpret Islamic principles in such a way as to prevent their conflicting with the essential interests of the state; keeping a certain moral distance

---

[25] U. Heyd, *Studies in Old Ottoman Criminal Law* (Oxford, 1973).
[26] R. Brunschvig, 'Justice religieuse et justice laïque dans la Tunisie des Deys et des Beys', *Studia Islamica*, 23 (1965), pp. 27ff.

from those he served, but in the last analysis belonging to a closed corporation linked by kinship, privilege and manners with the ruling elite.

Something of this would be true also of our second group, the *'ulama* in a broader sense, the urban literati, all those who shared in the education dispensed in mosque or *madrasa* (religious school). The imperial *madrasa*s of Istanbul, created to train a certain kind of official, were a special group among a large number of institutions which might train officials but had broader purposes: to perpetuate a tradition of religious thought by producing the scholars and teachers who could carry it on and to maintain the hold of the values of Islamic civilization over the Muslim population of the city, and over that of the countryside so far as the influence of the city could extend.

In Muslim towns of any size there would be, above the schools (*maktab* or *kuttab*) where the rudiments of learning were taught to boys, mosques where public lessons were given by teachers appointed by government or private patron. There might also be one or more *madrasa*s: a more specialized kind of school, as a number of studies by George Makdisi have shown, created by ruler or other patron primarily for the teaching of the sciences of religion, and in particular of *fiqh* (science of jurisprudence), with a building where students could live and teaching be carried on, and an endowment to be used both for the salary of the main teacher and his assistants and for the maintenance of students.[27] Some of the mosques and schools had more than a local influence, and could attract students from far away, to study with a famous teacher and receive his *ijaza*, or permission to teach the book they had read with him. Such were the Qarawiyyin mosque in Fez; the Zaituna in Tunis; the schools of Timbuktu for Muslims of the Niger basin; the Azhar in Cairo for students from North Africa, Syria and the Red Sea area as well as Egypt; the schools of Madina for those drawn to the Hejaz by the pilgrimage from all over the Muslim world; those of the Shi'i holy cities (Najaf, Karbala, Kazimain, Mashhad); and those of the Mogul cities, Lahore and Delhi, which by the eighteenth century were drawing

---

[27] G. Makdisi, 'Muslim institutions of learning in eleventh century Baghdad', *Bulletin of the School of Oriental and African Studies*, 24 (1961), pp. 1–56; 'Madrasa and university in the Middle Ages', *Studia Islamica*, 33 (1970), pp. 255–64; 'Law and traditionalism in the institutions of learning of medieval Islam' in G. E. von Grunebaum, ed., *Theology and Law in Islam* (Wiesbaden, 1971), pp. 75–88; *The Rise of Colleges* (Edinburgh, 1981).

students from a wide area of the Muslim world. (Figures should be treated with caution, but it has been estimated that by the end of the eighteenth century one of these centres, the Azhar in Cairo, had perhaps fifty teachers and 1,000 students.[28])

Apart from the basic sciences of the Arabic language, the indispensable key to an understanding of Islam, the core of what was taught in these mosques and schools consisted of the interpretation of the Qur'an (tafsir), the Tradition (Hadith), law and the 'juridical theology' which underlay it (fiqh and usul al-fiqh). Dialectical theology (kalam) had little place in it, philosophy even less, although it and other rational sciences were still studied outside mosque and madrasa by solitary scholars or in private study groups.

The science of Hadith does not appear to have taken new directions in the eighteenth century, but that of fiqh was broader and livelier. On the one hand, it involved a reference back from the details of law to certain principles and methods about which discussion never ceased. On the other hand, since shari'a is more than law in the European sense, being an attempt to bring all social acts and relations beneath the guidance of general principles derived from Islam, any changes in Muslim society were bound to lead to some attempt at reformulation of it. To take examples from opposite ends of the Muslim world: in Morocco, there had developed before the eighteenth century a special type of legal literature, the handbooks of 'amal, or judicial practice. These were justified by the Maliki precept that opinions formulated and applied by judges, in the light of public interest and necessity, should be preferred to others; they provided a means by which the shari'a could be adjusted to the changing needs of society.[29] In Iran, the century saw a development of the idea of the mujtahid, the scholar qualified by learning and piety to exercise independent judgement in matters of faith and law. Here perhaps we can see a reflection of Iranian history: the collapse of the Safavis left the 'ulama as the only moral leaders of the Iranian Muslims, for no later ruler could claim the kind of authority which

---

[28] J. Heyworth-Dunne, *Introduction to the History of Education in Modern Egypt* (London, 1939), chapter 1.

[29] J. Berque, *Al-Yousi, Problèmes de la culture marocaine au XVIIe siècle* (Paris, 1958); 'Ville et université; aperçu sur l'histoire de l'école de Fès', *Revue Historique de Droit Français et Etranger*, 27 (1949), pp. 64–117; H. Toledano, 'Sijilmasi's Manual of Maghrib 'amal, al-'amal al-mutlaq', *International Journal of Middle East Studies*, 4 (1974), pp. 484–96.

the Safavis had possessed. Since many of them were out of reach of the power of the rulers of Iran, across the Ottoman frontier in the holy cities of Iraq, they could exercise this leadership with a certain freedom. The full theoretical assertion of the authority of the *mujtahid*s was put forward by Aqa Muhammad Baqir Bihbihani, founder of the Usuli school. Opposed by the Akhbaris who asserted that authority lay only with the Imams, the Usulis had become dominant by the second half of the century, even though an Akhbari undercurrent persisted.[30]

Those who went to school in mosque or *madrasa*, and so participated to some degree in the culture maintained and transmitted there, cannot be regarded as forming a single social class. They might have found their place anywhere in that triangle of scholars, merchants and craftsmen who carried on the essential activities of the city. They tended, however, to possess a common attitude to life, society and government. It was essentially an urban attitude, looking with some contempt on the dependent rural hinterland, with some fear on those in the uncontrolled steppe or mountain, thinking of the city as the stronghold of true religion in the face of the forces of religious ignorance. With the government the relations of Muslim city dwellers were complex. There was an ultimate identity of interest, both religious and social, but the city tried to resist too close a control, and to preserve its own latent freedom of action.

At the heart of the urban literati there was a group of local religious 'professionals'. Some of them might take service in the government, even though, in the Ottoman empire at least, they held only minor positions; others had their own bases of power and influence, as teachers, preachers and controllers of *waqf*s. The *'ulama* outside the official elite could have a position of local leadership, particularly in provincial cities where the pressure of the central government was not so present as in a capital city. Linked by culture, kinship and, in some cases, economic interest with the local bourgeoisie, they could at times take a lead in expressing grievances, opposing a governor or filling a vacuum of power during an interregnum. The moral distance which separated *'ulama* from rulers would be more marked with them than

[30] Algar, *Religion and State*, pp. 26ff; A. K. S. Lambton, 'Quis custodiet custodes? Some reflections on the Persian theory of government', *Studia Islamica*, 5 (1956), pp. 125–48, and 6 (1956), pp. 125–46; G. Scarcia, 'Intorno alle controversie tra Ahbari e Usuli presso gli Imamiti di Persia', *Rivista degli Studi Orientali*, 33 (1958), pp. 211–50.

with the official elite. But the Sunni *'ulama* at least were intermediaries rather than independent political leaders; and in the last
resort they were on the side of the rulers, without whom civilized
order could not exist. The Shi'i *mujtahid*s tended to be more distant
from the holders of power.

The widest circle of culture was that which included all those
who participated, at one or another level of understanding, in the
attempt of the Sufis to lead a life of devotion derived from Qur'an
and Hadith and directed towards acquisition of experiential
knowledge of God. Generations of teachers and masters had
gradually evolved the practices and rituals through which this life
of devotion could be sustained: in particular, the *dhikr*, or recollection of God, practised alone or in company, silently or aloud, and
accompanied by movements of the body or rhythmical breathing
which could by repetition help to free the soul from the distract-
ions of the world. Gradually, too, there had evolved a mystical
theology, a description and explanation of the descent of the world
from God through a series of emanations, and the ascent of the
soul, moved by love, through various stages towards knowledge of
God; the multifold imagery through which this vision of the arcs of
descent and ascent could be portrayed was perhaps the most vital
part of the shared culture of eighteenth-century Muslims. In one
or other of the Islamic languages it was still being refined; only a
century earlier, Mulla Sadr al-Din Shirazi (d. 1640) had given a
new formulation in the Persian language to the imagery of light
which was one of the main ways of expression of this theosophy,
and his influence was still widespread in the world of Persian
culture.[31]

It was the general agreement of the Sufis that a guide or teacher
was necessary to initiate the seeker into the path he was to follow,
as he could not find it by his own efforts; the guide would himself
be linked with earlier ones, and it was possible, therefore, to trace
various lines of initiation back through Abu Bakr or 'Ali to the
Prophet Muhammad. A system of devotional practices and
thought, authenticated by one of these lines of transmission,
formed a *tariqa*, an 'order' or 'path'.

In the main tradition of Shi'i Islam the Imams were the
authentic guides, since they had the perpetual mission of teaching

---

[31] F. Rahman, *Islam* (London, 1966), chapters 7 and 8; H. Corbin, *En islam iranien*, vol.
IV (Paris, 1972); M. Molé, *Les mystiques musulmans* (Paris, 1956); A. M. Schimmel,
Mystical Dimensions of Islam (Chapel Hill, N. C., 1975).

the true meaning and practice of Islam. There was, therefore, a certain hostility towards Sufi groups which claimed to have other teachers. There were indeed some Shiʻi *tariqa*s, in particular the Niʻmatullahi, which spread from India to Persia at the end of the eighteenth century; but at much the same time there was a reassertion of pure Imami doctrine by the Shaikhi school, for whom the Imam was present in the heart of the believer as a guide to truth.[32]

In Sunni Islam, too, it was accepted that a seeker after truth might have direct communion with saints of the past, or with the Prophet himself. In general, however, it was believed that the heritage of the past had to be mediated to the seeker, the *murid*, by a living guide, or *murshid*, whom his disciples might regard as the recipient of special graces. When he died the influence of such a 'friend of God' could live on: his intercession with God for the living was believed to be efficacious, and his tomb might become a place of pilgrimage and petition. His pupils in their turn would go into the world, carrying his *tariqa* or modifying it in ways which might be regarded as creating a new one.

The *tariqa*s differed not only in forms of expression and personal loyalties, but in their view of the relationship between exoteric and esoteric knowledge, or, to put it in a more precise way, between obedience to the *shariʻa* and active pursuit of experiential knowledge of God. There was a persistent tension in Sufi thought between the tendency of the mystic to believe he had attained or could attain to a knowledge above that revealed to ordinary men, and the belief of all Muslims that the Qur'an and Hadith contained the commandments of God about how men should worship him and live with each other. Some orders, among those of which the main strength was in the countryside, showed little regard for the *shariʻa*. Those which laid emphasis on it as a stage on the way towards *maʻrifa* taught that mere obedience was not sufficient, and sincerity of intention was necessary. They differed in regard to the place of the *shariʻa* in the life of the believer who had attained to the mystical vision. Some believed that it was a vision of God as the one reality, and the life of human society would henceforth be seen as unreal; others maintained that, once the Sufi had had his momentary glimpse of the reality of God, he should return to the human world in the 'second sobriety',

---

[32] R. Gramlich, *Die schiitischen Dervishorden Persiens*, vol. I (Wiesbaden, 1965).

knowing his own reality as well as that of God, living in conformity with the *shariʿa*, and trying to bring the world under its rule.

In the countryside, a saint and his followers might claim to
belong to one of the great orders of the Muslim world, but the
order itself was less important than the saint, his tomb and the
family which kept it. In regions far from urban *madrasa* or mosque,
one of the functions of the saint was to teach, and his *zawiya* might
offer the only formal education above the elementary teaching of
the *kuttab*. Thus in the Nilotic Sudan, on the expanding frontier of
the Muslim world, the Islamic culture was brought by wandering
Sufis, in whose houses Qurʾanic interpretation and Maliki *fiqh*
were taught to some extent, but the liturgies and practices of a
tariqa and the mystical theology of Ibn ʿArabi even more.[33] But
the rural Sufis were not primarily teachers of ʿ*ilm*. In areas far
from cities and governments, the *shariʿa* was a distant ideal, and
books of *fiqh* could not provide moral guidance or a discipline for
human passions and fantasies; countrymen and women attributed to a living or dead saint their own inherited beliefs and
feelings, and received from him or the guardians of his tomb a
moral guidance which might be far from that of the law books.
Thus the Bektashis in Ottoman Anatolia and Rumelia showed
little concern for the *shariʿa* in their practices, derived their moral
teaching from mystical theology, and justified it in terms of their
spiritual descent from ʿAli.[34]

In the cities, however, there were orders which had the special
favour of the court and the bourgeoisie. Since the fabric of ordered
government and society depended on law, the Sufi guide had
influence only in so far as he was also an ʿ*alim*. His adherents
tended to insert their spiritual lineage into the tradition of ʿ*ilm* and
to emphasize the learning rather than the miracles of their
masters. They were aware of the continuity of their tradition, and
the *tariqa* was therefore something stable and permanent, more
than an individual *murshid* or his family; but for the same reason
adherence to a *tariqa* created only one of the concentric loyalties
which made up what it was to be a Muslim. Among such urban
orders were some of ancient lineage and reputation: Qadiris,
Mawlawis, Suhrawardis, Rifaʿis. The rise of others, however, was
connected with that of the great dynasties of the early modern
period: the Jazulis (a branch of the Shadhilis) with the Sharifian

[33] J. S. Trimingham, *Islam in the Sudan* (London, 1949), pp. 187ff.
[34] J. K. Birge, *The Bektashi Order of Dervishes* (London, 1939).

rulers of Morocco; the Chishtis with the Mogul emperors; and the Khalwatis with the Ottoman sultans from the time of Bayezid II at the end of the fifteenth century. A suborder of the Khalwatis, the Bakris, played a similar role in Egypt, and its shaikhly family had a special position of leadership of the urban population and mediation between it and the Mamluk ruling elite.[35]

Lower down in the social hierarchy of the city, the same or other orders existed, but greater distance from the literate culture and the seat of power tended to change the balance of elements in them. The reverence given to wonder-working saints living or dead was less restrained, the hold of the *dhikr* over the emotions was stronger, and the solidarity of adhering to the same *tariqa* might reinforce that of working in the same craft or living in the same quarter. But the authority of the *shari'a*, of judges who administered it or preachers who expounded it, was strong throughout the city.

The differences between rural and urban *tariqa*s had social and political implications. In the countryside the tomb of the saint or the home of his family could act as a neutral point where different regions or tribal groups met, goods could be bought or sold, alliances made, conflicts be arbitrated, fugitives find asylum and travellers receive hospitality. The saint was the mediator of Islamic values at critical points in the life of rural society, and at times he could be more than that: the focal point around which a rural coalition could crystallize and from which, in some circumstances, a new dynasty might emerge.[36]

In some towns there were great popular shrines which had a rural as well as an urban clientele, and to which the rural visitor or immigrant would gravitate: the tombs of the Imams in the Shi'i holy cities, Sayyidna Husain and Sayyida Zainab in Cairo, Mawlay Idris in Fez. There were also rural shrines which could pull towards them the masses of the cities. At times, therefore, the rural saints, and the kind of Islam for which they stood, could present a challenge to the ruling classes of cities, to the learned class, and to the *tariqa*s which shared their conception of Islam as a framework of laws within which a stable civilization could be maintained. The urban *tariqa*s shared in the characteristic

---

[35] H. A. R. Gibb and H. Bowen, *Islamic Society and the West*, vol. I, part 2 (London, 1957), chapter 13; B. G. Martin, 'A short history of the Khalwati order of dervishes' in Keddie, *Scholars, Saints and Sufis*, pp. 275–305.

[36] E. Gellner, *Saints of the Atlas* (London, 1969).

attitude of the city dweller towards government: acquiescence in the temporal rulers of the world, the keeping of a certain moral distance from them, but the desire to win influence over them so as to keep them on the path of the *shari'a*. The spread in the eighteenth and early nineteenth centuries of *tariqa*s which laid emphasis on the importance of the *shari'a* can, therefore, be seen as one aspect of the reaction of a threatened Islamic urban order.

Such reassertions of the urban literate conception of Islam can be found throughout the Muslim world: to take examples which have been studied in recent years, the extension of the Idrisi, later the Mirghani, order in the Sudan;[37] and that of the Qadiris in Mauritania, where Shaikh Sidiya instilled a stricter adherence to the liturgy and organization of the order, and knowledge also of Maliki *fiqh*, learned by him in Morocco and applied in a rigid and conservative way, without the concessions to rural practice made in Morocco itself through the *'amal* literature.[38]

Two examples of wider importance may be given. In the eastern part of the Muslim world, the *tariqa* which appears to have spread most widely and successfully during the eighteenth century is the Naqshbandiyya in its renewed (*mujaddidi*) form. It first emerged in central Asia as a separate order with its characteristic ritual of the silent *dhikr*, and its emphasis on the importance of combining inward devotion with outward activity aimed at maintaining the rule of the *shari'a*. From there it spread in several directions: eastwards into China, southwards into Iran and northern India, and into the Ottoman empire, where it was known before the end of the fifteenth century. In Iran the order was destroyed by the Safavis, but in India it took root. For a time it had some influence at the court of the Mogul emperors, who used it to oppose the Shi'i ideas spreading from Iran over the countries of Persian culture. (Hence, perhaps, the emphasis laid by Naqshbandis of this period on both lines of their descent, from Abu Bakr and 'Ali; they could claim that they and not the Shi'is were the legitimate heirs of 'Ali.) In the seventeenth century there took place a 'renewal' of the order at the hands of Shaikh Ahmad

---

[37] Trimingham, *Islam in the Sudan*, pp. 228ff.
[38] C. C. Stewart with E. K. Stewart, *Islam and Social Order in Mauritania* (Oxford, 1973); C. C. Stewart, 'A new source on the book market in Morocco in 1830 and Islamic scholarship in West Africa', *Hespéris-Tamuda*, 2 (1970), pp. 209–46; M. Hiskett, 'An Islamic tradition of reform in the western Sudan from the sixteenth to the eighteenth century', *Bulletin of the School of Oriental and African Studies*, 25 (1962), pp. 577–96.

Sirhindi (1564–1624). In his letters to his disciples and in other writings, he reasserted the principles of the order's teaching and in some ways modified them. His followers claimed for him a special spiritual status, as the *qutb*, the pole around which the world revolved on its axis, the heir of the prophets, and the possessor of direct contact with the invisible world.[39]

The teaching of Shaikh Ahmad had much influence on the Indo-Muslim culture of the eighteenth century, its thought and poetry alike. It was carried further by Shah Waliullah of Delhi (1703–62) who, writing in the twilight of Muslim power in India, with Hindu rule reviving in the Mogul provinces, was urgently concerned with a restoration of the *shari'a*: the different schools of law should be unified, for that purpose the Tradition should be studied (his own school was called *dar al-hadith*) and *ijtihad*, the exercise of independent judgement by qualified doctors, be allowed. At the same time, he put forward the idea that there are not separate *tariqa*s, all are parts of a single *tariqa*; and implicit in this was a claim for his own unique spiritual status.[40]

From India the renewed Naqshbandi order spread westward once again. It was carried to the Hejaz by pilgrims, to Iraq and Syria by Mawlana Khalid (d. 1827), a Kurd who went to study in India and brought back with him the same complex of ideas: hostility to Shi'ism, claims to direct contact with the invisible world, insistence on strict observance of the *shari'a*, and the need to win influence with rulers.[41]

A similar role was played in north-west Africa by a new order, the Tijaniyya, founded by Ahmad al-Tijani (1777/8–1815). In his *tariqa*, founded after his return from study in the eastern Muslim world, we can see a claim to special privileges which comes near to being a claim to exclusive possession of the truth; he was regarded by his followers as having had no living teacher and having been

[39] A. Ahmed, *Studies in Islamic Culture in the Indian Environment* (Oxford, 1964), pp. 170ff; M. Mujeeb, *The Indian Muslims* (London, 1967), pp. 243ff; S. M. Ikram, *Muslim Civilization in India* (London, 1964), pp. 166ff; A. M. Schimmel, 'The Sufi ideas of Shaykh Ahmad Sirhindi', *Die Welt des Islams*, 14 (1973), pp. 199–203; H. Algar, 'Some notes on the Naqshbandi tariqat in Bosnia', *Die Welt des Islams*, 13 (1971), pp. 168–203; 'Bibliographical notes on the Naqshbandi tariqat' in G. F. Hourani, ed., *Essays on Islamic Philosophy and Science* (Albany, N.Y., 1975), pp. 254–9; Y. Friedmann, *Shaykh Ahmad Sirhindi* (Montreal, 1971).
[40] A. Bausani, 'Note su Shah Waliullah di Delhi', *Annali, Instituto Universitario Orientale di Napoli*, 10 (1960), pp. 93–147.
[41] A. Hourani, 'Sufism and modern Islam: Mawlana Khalid and the Naqshbandi order' in A. Hourani, *The Emergence of the Modern Middle East* (London, 1981), pp. 75–89.

initiated into the truth through direct contact with the spirit of the Prophet; his followers were discouraged from making visits to other saints, living or dead. There was also an emphasis on obedience to the *shari'a* which made his order an ally of those forces which wished to extend urban control over the countryside: for a time he was favoured by Mawlay Sulaiman of Morocco and settled in Fez, but his order did not take such deep root there as in Algeria.[42]

All these were movements which took place within the framework of the practice and thought of the Sufi orders, but another movement of the eighteenth century broke out of that framework and indeed threatened to destroy it. Muhammad ibn 'Abd al-Wahhab (1703–87) came from Najd, where the fragile settled society and Muslim learning of small market-towns were always threatened by the forces and customs of the nomadic society of the steppe. The bases of his opposition to the religious ignorance of his time and place came from the Hanbali tradition of his own family, reinforced by studies in Madina and elsewhere: a tradition which combined theological reserve with a willingness to exercise independent judgement, *ijtihad*, in matters of practice so as to bring all human acts within the sphere of the *shari'a*. What is new, however, is a rejection of the Sufi way which appears to go beyond earlier Hanbali thinkers. God has communicated His will to men through the Qur'an and the Prophet alone; He should only be worshipped in ways He himself has commanded in the Qur'an; speculation about His nature should not be carried beyond the 'agnosticisme prudent' of the Hanbali *kalam*;[43] the Prophet is the best of men, able to intercede with God, but not the Primal Light existing before the world was created; neither he nor any other teacher can stand between the individual believer and God, neither he nor any other created being, whether living or dead, should be associated with God in worship.

Once more we find the convictions of a reformer intent on restoring the authority of the *shari'a*, and the interests of a ruler wishing to extend his control over an unsettled countryside, in harmony with each other. The alliance of Muhammad ibn 'Abd al-Wahhab with the Sa'udi dynasty led to an attempt to establish a state based on the *shari'a* over an expanding area in Arabia and

[42] J. M. Abun-Nasr, *The Tijaniyya* (London, 1965), chapters 2 and 3.
[43] H. Laoust, *Essai sur les doctrines sociales et politiques de Taki-d-Din Ahmad b. Taimiya* (Cairo, 1939), pp. 506ff; G. Makdisi, 'The Hanibali school and Sufism', *Humaniora Islamica*, 2 (1974), pp. 61–72.

beyond, to the destruction of the tombs of saints, an attack on the Shi'i holy places, and a refusal to accept the authority of the Ottoman sultans, whom the Wahhabis regarded as the protectors of a false interpretation of Islam. Implicit in such acts was a certain view of the nature and unity of the Islamic community: that not all those who called themselves Muslims were really so, and correctness of belief and strict observance were essential parts of the definition of what it was to be Muslim.

This view, however, was not yet able to shake, outside the Arabian peninsula, an older conception of the community as something broadly comprehensive, widely tolerant, and unified at more than one level: by a single law which should provide the norm of human action in the world; by common concern for a spiritual life modelled on the example of the Prophet and those most closely associated with him; by the various lines of physical or spiritual descent through which scholars and Sufis alike legitimized their beliefs and practices; and by the pilgrimage, the symbolic act of unity.

8

BUSTANI'S ENCYCLOPAEDIA

Le Nahda manifesta une poussée d'adaptation des intellectuels syriens
à l'Europe. Ils remirent en honneur les ancestrales facultés de poly-
glossie caractéristiques de la région, et sublimèrent en littérature,
encyclopédisme, pédagogie, journalisme leur succès de transmission et
de courtage. Chemin faisant, ils entendaient bien entrer, et leurs
communautés derrière eux, dans l'histoire arabe par la grand porte.

Jacques Berque, *Arabies*[1]

IN 1875 the editor of *al-Jinan*, a periodical appearing in Beirut,
announced his intention of publishing an encyclopaedia. Butrus
al-Bustani was already well known to the Arabic-reading public
in Syria and Egypt, and to the foreign community of Beirut, as
teacher, translator and scholar, and not unknown to the learned
world in Europe, but there may well have been some doubt
whether he, or anyone else, could succeed in the task, difficult in
all circumstances, of compiling and publishing a work on this
scale. In 1876, however, the first volume was finished, and
appeared under the title *Da'irat al-ma'arif*, with the French subtitle
Encyclopédie arabe. Five more volumes followed quickly between
then and 1882. Volume VII, published in 1883, carried the
announcement of Bustani's death. His son Salim, who had been
his assistant from the beginning, was to carry on as editor, but his
death too was announced in the eighth volume, which appeared in
1884. After that the pace grew slower. Two younger sons of
Bustani, Nasib and Najib, helped by another member of the
family, Sulaiman, were able to publish volume IX in 1887. Then,
after a long delay, volume X came out in 1898 and volume XI in
1900; they were published not in Beirut but in Cairo, and printed

---

[1] Revised edn (Paris, 1980), p. 133.

on the press of the well-known periodical *al-Hilal*. The eleventh volume was the last to appear; it carried the encyclopaedia down to the letter ʿ*ain*, the eighteenth out of the twenty-eight consonants of the Arabic language. The last article was that on the Ottoman dynasty, and this was perhaps appropriate; it was the increasing difficulty of publishing freely in the domains of the Sultan Abdülhamid, as well as financial problems, which had led to the long delay, and the transfer of the enterprise from Beirut to Cairo.

The encyclopaedia attracted attention from the beginning, and not only in the Arab countries; the first three volumes were reviewed by the orientalist H. L. Fleischer in the *Zeitschrift der Deutschen Morgenländischen Gesellschaft* in 1880.[2] It remains until now the most complete work of its kind in Arabic. Its readership extended beyond the Arab countries to others where Arabic was well known; its articles on Islamic history were appreciated by Iranians with a traditional religious education.[3]

How could an encyclopaedia of this kind and scope have been published as early as the 1870s in Arabic, and in a moderate-sized provincial town of the Ottoman empire? Encyclopaedias of the modern type had appeared in England, France and Germany from the eighteenth century onwards, but they were only beginning to be published in other countries by the middle of the nineteenth. *Daʾirat al-maʿarif* is not much younger than the first proper Russian encyclopaedia,[4] and its first volume came out thirteen years earlier than that of the first Turkish encyclopaedia, a smaller and more limited work, the *Qamus al-aʿlam* of Şemseddin Sami Fraşeri.[5]

Various kinds of answer can be given to this question, all interrelated with each other. The first lies in the nature of Beirut during that period: one of the ports which grew as European sea-borne trade with the outer world expanded, connected by regular steamboat services with ports of the Mediterranean basin and Atlantic seaboard, the home of consulates, religious missions and schools, and a class of merchants both indigenous and foreign importing European manufactured goods. Not only goods were exchanged. Steamships brought books and newspapers from Europe and America; the telegraph, which reached Beirut in the

[2] 34 (1880), pp. 579–82.   [3] Information from Dr Hossein Modarressi.
[4] R. L. Collison, 'Encyclopaedia', *Encyclopaedia Britannica*, 15th edn (Chicago, 1979), Macropaedia, vol. VI, pp. 779–99.
[5] Samy Bey Fraschery (Şemseddin Sami Fraşeri), *Qamus al-aʿlam; dictionnaire universel d'histoire et de géographie*, 6 vols. (Istanbul, 1889–98).

1860s, made the news of the world known within hours; consuls, merchants, missionaries and teachers were channels through which knowledge could flow and exemplars of a new way of life.

In his review of the encyclopaedia, Fleischer called Beirut the principal market-place (*Hauptemporium*) of Syria, and quoted the words of Goethe:

Orient und Occident
Sind nicht mehr zu trennen.[6]

To carry on the business of the market, and bring Orient and Occident together, intermediaries were needed, and Lebanese Christians were well suited to this task, as Greeks and Armenians were elsewhere in the Ottoman empire. Members of the Maronite and other Uniate Churches, in particular, had long been accustomed to dealing with Europeans as priests, merchants, employees of consuls or trading companies, and some of them were acquainted with Latin and Italian through mission schools and Roman seminaries. They had now begun to learn French or English at the new mission schools, and found new scope for work as teachers, translators and consular officials. By the 1860s and 1870s their field of activity was widening. They were not only explaining their own language and society to foreigners; as teachers and journalists, they were beginning to explain the new world of Europe and America to the growing number of those who could read Arabic.

Of this group of intermediaries, Butrus al-Bustani was both an example and a leader.[7] Born in a Maronite family of southern Lebanon, he studied at the Maronite school at ʿAin Waraqa, and there learned Latin, Italian and Syriac as well as Arabic. His first contact with the English-speaking world came in 1840, when British forces landed at Beirut as part of the campaign to oblige Muhammad ʿAli to abandon Syria. Soon afterwards he began to work for the American Protestant missionaries in Beirut, as teacher in their schools, private tutor in Arabic, translator and collaborator in their publications; they taught him English, and

---

[6] *Zeitschrift der Deutschen Morgenländischen Gesellschaft*, p. 579.
[7] *Daʾirat al-maʿarif* (Beirut, 1883), vol. VII, pp. 589–608; J. Zaidan, *Tarajim mashahir al-sharq*, vol. II, 2nd edn (Cairo, 1911), pp. 25–32; both these based on *al-Muqtataf*, vol. VIII (1883–4), pp. 1–7. Among more recent studies: A. L. Tibawi, 'The American missionaries in Beirut and Butrus al-Bustani' in A. Hourani, ed., *Saint Antony's Papers 16: Middle Eastern Affairs*, vol. III (London, 1963), pp. 137–82; B. Abu Manneh, 'The Christians between Ottomanism and Syrian nationalism: the ideas of Butrus al-Bustani', *International Journal of Middle East Studies*, 11 (1980), pp. 287–304.

he became a Protestant. For some years he helped the missionaries with their new translation of the Bible, and for this purpose studied Greek and Hebrew. At a certain point he seems to have moved away from the tutelage of the missionaries. He was dragoman of the United States consulate for a time, and opened a school with a significant title, *al-Madrasa al-wataniyya* (the National School); it was to be a school for all denominations, with the purpose of teaching love of the 'fatherland' and knowledge of the Arabic language.

Then came the period of his large scholarly enterprises: a new Arabic dictionary, *Muhit al-muhit*, and a cultural periodical, *al-Jinan*.[8] Periodicals and newspapers of this kind were a new phenomenon; they answered the need of the literate public for useful and edifying reading-matter, and did so in a new way, by issues appearing at regular intervals for subscribers. The encyclopaedia, which also came out in periodical parts sent to subscribers, and aimed at giving a systematic survey of knowledge, was in a sense an extension of the periodical.

Surrounded by sons, pupils and collaborators, Bustani became the centre of what may be called the first modern intelligentsia of the Arab world: a socially mobile group dedicated to the discussion and spread of ideas, skilled in the arts of verbal communication, and prepared to question what existed and had been accepted. The disavowal of the Maronite Church and acceptance of Protestantism had been the first step in this direction: in a society based upon religious allegiance, to become a Protestant was to go as far as possible towards an assertion of the right to follow the lead of one's own mind and conscience.[9] The sense of loyalty to teachers and colleagues was to remain strong in this group. It was made stronger by the memory of certain episodes. One such was a famous incident at the American college in Beirut, when the professor of natural sciences, giving the Commencement Address for 1882, spoke in favour of the ideas of Darwin and was compelled to leave the college.[10] Some of the other teachers, led by the famous medical missionary Cornelius Van Dyck, resigned in

---

[8] *Muhit al-muhit*, 2 vols. (Beirut, 1869–70); *al-Jinan* (1870–85).

[9] J. Fontaine, *Le désaveu chez les écrivains libanais chrétiens de 1825 à 1940* (thèse de doctorat de troisième cycle, Paris, 1970), pp. 172–6.

[10] Among several studies: N. Farag, 'The Lewis affair and the fortunes of *al-Muqtataf*', *Middle Eastern Studies*, 8 (1972), pp. 72–83; D. M. Leavitt, 'Darwinism in the Arab world: the Lewis affair at the Syrian Protestant College', *Muslim World*, 71 (1981), pp. 85–98. See also J. Zaidan's autobiography: English trans., T. Philipp, *Gurgi Zaidan, His Life and Thought* (Beirut, 1979), pp. 128–206.

protest. This was the occasion of the first appearance in Arabic of
that familiar device of the intelligentsia, the collective letter of
protest; leading personalities of Damascus, led by the mufti,
Mahmud Hamza, and the Amir ʿAbd al-Qadir, sent Dr Van Dyck
a letter of appreciation.[11] Another such episode was the death of
Butrus al-Bustani in 1883; sixty years later, someone who had
been present at his funeral was able vividly to remember the
manifestations of grief, the tears of Van Dyck and the eloquence of
Adib Ishaq.[12]

However much they wished to be independent, the new writers
needed patrons. Bustani's dictionary had been noticed with
favour by the Ottoman government, and for the encyclopaedia he
turned to two high Ottoman officials; they promised help, but
were unable to give it until the first part should have appeared. He
turned then to the Khedive Ismaʿil, who responded promptly,
recognizing the value of a work which supported his own efforts to
bring Egypt into the new world being created by Europe.[13] He
offered to take a thousand copies, and financial help came later
from members of his entourage, his son Tawfiq and his minister
Riaz.[14] The introductions to the volumes paid tribute to this help,
but also carried loyal references to the Sultan Murad V and his
successor Abdülhamid II.[15]

No work of reference is entirely neutral. A dictionary can be a
literary manifesto, and an encyclopaedia, claiming to include all
that is necessary or useful to know, must have its principles of
selection and arrangement. This need, and the problems it raised,
were recognized by the great compilers of the eighteenth century.
The preface to the first edition of the *Encyclopaedia Britannica* stated
the problems clearly. While 'the method of conveying knowledge
by alphabetical arrangement' is obviously useful, it carries with it
a danger: the 'method of dealing out the sciences in fragments,
according to the various technical terms common to each, [is] a
method repugnant to the very idea of science, which is a connected series of conclusions deducted from self-evident or previously
discovered principles'. These principles need to be 'laid before

[11] Text in *al-Muqtataf*, 19 (1985), p. 888.
[12] F. Hawrani (Hourani), 'al-Muʿallim Butrus al-Bustani', *al-Mustamiʿ al-ʿarabi*, 4
    (1943), pp. 10–12.
[13] *Daʾirat al-maʿarif*, vol. I (Beirut, 1876), pp. 2–3. See also Amin Sami, *Taqwim al-Nil
    wa ʿasr Ismaʿil Basha*, part 3, vol. III (Cairo, 1936), pp. 1217, 1404. I owe this
    reference and other suggestions to the kindness of Dr Butrus Abu Manneh.
[14] *Daʾirat al-maʿarif*, vol. IV (Beirut, 1880), p. i.
[15] Ibid., vol. I, p. 4; vol. IV, p. 1.

[the reader] in one uninterrupted chain', and the chain must be complete: 'the sciences ought to be exhibited entire, or they are exhibited to little purpose'.[16]

Makers of encyclopaedias, therefore, felt the need to give a general view of the system of sciences in their relations with each other. The elaborate introductions to their works are among the most permanently valuable parts of them: Diderot's *discours préliminaire* to the great *Encyclopédie*, with its system of sciences based upon an epistemology, a distinction between the functions of memory, reason and imagination;[17] and, fifty years later, Coleridge's *Treatise on Method*, in which an attempt is made to exhibit the relationships between the sciences by showing how they arise from the act of mind which imposes its own order on what is knowable.[18]

In the light of such schemes, most encyclopaedias tried to maintain a balance between long general articles in which a whole field was surveyed and shorter ones dealing with limited subjects. Difficulties could arise, however: some kinds of subject which could not easily be related to general principles might be excluded. In the first edition of the *Encyclopédie*, information about history and biography is given mainly in articles on geography, which could be related to general principles; there is no separate entry for Shakespeare, but he is treated in the article on Stratford, his native town.[19]

The introduction to *Da'irat al-ma'arif* does not contain so elaborate a portrait of the sciences, but it gives some hints of its intentions. It begins with what may now seem to be commonplaces, but were at that time guiding ideas of social and cultural change: the needs of nations vary from one time and place to another; a nation cannot meet the demands of the new age without knowledge, the basis of economic and social progress and intellectual and moral well-being; the 'people of the Arabic language' (*ahl al-lugha al-'arabiyya*), being neighbours of the civilized countries, have become aware of their need for knowledge. The encyclopaedia is intended to meet these needs, and to do so in

---

[16] *Encyclopaedia Britannica: or a New and Complete Dictionary of Arts and Sciences*, 1st London edn, vol. I (1773), preface, p. v.

[17] *Encyclopédie ou dictionnaire raisonné des sciences, des arts et des métiers*, vol. I (Paris, 1751), *discours préliminaire*, pp. i–xlv.

[18] *General Introduction to the Encyclopaedia Metropolitana; or, a Preliminary Treatise on Method*, 3rd edn, in prospectus to 2nd edn of the encyclopaedia (London, 1849).

[19] *Encyclopédie*, vol. XV (Paris, 1765), pp. 541–4.

a way which will avoid factionalism (*al-ibtiʿad ʿan al-tahazzub*) and be acceptable to all religious communities.[20] The introduction also contains an explanation of 'the method of conveying knowledge by alphabetical arrangement'. This was less familiar to readers of Arabic than it had become in Europe. The medieval compendia of knowledge, such as that of Ibn Qutaiba, had been arranged by subject. Dictionaries had after a time begun to be arranged according to the first consonants, not of all words but of their roots. Biographical dictionaries such as that of Yaqut were arranged according to the first consonants of names, and these were the closest models for Bustani to follow; his first intention had, in fact, been to compile a biographical dictionary.

What was the knowledge which the 'people of the Arabic language' needed to acquire? The main emphasis of *Da'irat al-maʿarif* is upon three kinds of subject: modern science and technology, the history of Europe, and Arab history and literature. Articles on the first two ranges of subjects are for the most part translated, summarized or adapted from those in works written in English or French. This was inevitable in a work produced so quickly, and written for the most part by five members of the Bustani family, although an occasional article is attributed to another author. (The illustrations which appear at the end of each volume from the fourth onwards were also supplied from abroad, by the American firm of Appleton and Company,[21] although in the first three volumes illustrations in the text had been provided by a local artist, Mikha'il Farah.) As Fleischer pointed out in his review, the choice of subjects for biographies is sometimes odd, as if in this field the compilers had gone beyond the limits of their knowledge.[22] Whether original or not, these articles are written in that expository prose, clear and simple even if not beautiful, which Bustani and his group used in order to express the ideas and knowledge of the modern world in a manner comprehensible to all who could read.[23]

Even in these parts of *Da'irat al-maʿarif* there are surprises. That the telegraph should be described is only to be expected, since it had become familiar, but it is perhaps surprising to find the

---

[20] *Da'irat al-maʿarif*, vol. I, p. 2.
[21] Ibid., vol. IV, p. i; H. H. Jessup, *Fifty-three Years in Syria*, 2 vols. (New York, 1910), p. 485.
[22] *Zeitschrift der Deutschen Morgenländischen Gesellschaft*, p. 582.
[23] Anis al-Maqdisi, *al-Funun al-adabiyya wa aʿlamuha fi'l-nahda al-ʿarabiyya al-haditha* (Beirut, 1963), pp. 183–222.

telephone described in volume VI, published in 1882, when Bell's first patent had only been issued in 1876, and the first commercial telephone exchange established in the United States in 1879.[24]

The numerous articles devoted to Greek history, literature and mythology also appear to reveal a clear decision about what it was important to know. This may not seem unusual, in view of the close connection between the Greek and Arabic scientific traditions, but in fact the articles go beyond the range of knowledge available to Arab writers of an earlier age. Themistocles, Thucydides, Theseus, Theodosius, Theophrastus and Theocritus follow each other in quick succession: only one of the six would have been familiar to a medieval Muslim.[25] Homer is given an article and a portrait.[26] He had never yet been translated into Arabic, but one of the editors, Sulaiman al-Bustani, was to translate the *Iliad* a few years later;[27] a path was opened which was to lead, some generations later, to the familiar use of Greek myths as symbols in Arabic poetry.[28]

The articles on science and technology were probably those which most readers wanted. In the introductions to volumes III and IV, the editors had to apologize for the fact that the order of consonants in Arabic had made it necessary to devote most of the first two volumes to Arabic names beginning with Ibn and Abu.[29] For the modern reader, however, the entries on the Arabic and Islamic subjects are more interesting. Based to a great extent on Arabic sources, including unpublished manuscripts, they express judgements and preferences which do not necessarily reflect those of the European scholarship of the day. Those on Arabic poets, illustrated with plentiful quotations, might have been expected from writers in a milieu where the Arabic poetic heritage was being discovered and appraised anew, but the fullness of the articles on Islamic history and thought are perhaps unexpected; there are for example, five pages on Abu Bakr[30] (*Da'irat al-ma'arif* never reached the point when it would have dealt with Muhammad). The interest in Ibn Khaldun, expressed in more than one article, was becoming common to European, Arab and Turkish

---

[24] *Da'irat al-ma'arif*, vol. VI (Beirut, 1882), p. 201.   [25] Ibid., pp. 331f.

[26] Ibid., vol. IV, pp. 691–3.

[27] *Iliyadhat Humirus* (Cairo, 1904).

[28] S. K. Jayyusi, *Trends and Movements in Modern Arabic Poetry*, 2 vols. (Leiden, 1977), in particular vol. II, p. 720n.

[29] *Da'irat al-ma'arif*, vol. II (Beirut, 1877), p. ix; vol. III (Beirut, 1878), p. i.

[30] Ibid., vol. II, pp. 37–41.

writers of the period, but other articles show a judgement which European scholars might not have shared at that time. The one on al-Hallaj[31] is fuller than that which a European compilation of the kind would have given him before Massignon's researches; even in 1913, the *Encyclopaedia of Islam* gave him one page only, although Massignon's work was known and he himself was asked to write it.[32]

The articles on Hamza and al-Hakim bi-amr Allah[33] are long, and the reason for this must lie in the special interest which a Lebanese writer or reader would have in the origins of the Druze religion. Other articles on local history are equally full: those on cities (Beirut, Damascus, Aleppo, Baghdad), and those on local families, which continue the tradition of Lebanese history-writing, to which Bustani had already contributed when he helped in the publication of Tannus Shidyaq's *Akhbar al-a'yan fi Jabal Lubnan.*[34]

For the historian, perhaps the most significant articles are those on certain general ideas. They display a characteristic feature of the Arabic writing of their period, the attempt to find a link between ideas coming from the modern West and those familiar to the Arab Muslim tradition. The article on history (*ta'rikh*) begins with the Greeks, from Herodotus onwards, sketches the development of European historiography, and then proceeds to a survey of Ibn Khaldun's ideas about 'the art of history'.[35] That on truth (*haqq*) begins with definitions taken from al-Taftazani and al-Jurjani, and then gives the views of modern philosophers.[36] Some of the articles in the early volumes reflect the comparative freedom and optimism of the age of the Ottoman constitution. 'Government' (*hukuma*) published in 1883, states the different types of regime as Aristotle defined them (his *Politics* had not been part of the classical Islamic tradition); it claims that no ancient kingdoms had the freedom and equality which exist in modern civilized states, where government is based upon a constitution (*qanun asasi*) and a parliament (*majlis al-nuwwab*).[37]

The article on Europe calls it 'the smallest continent except

31 Ibid., vol. VII, pp. 150–4.
32 'al-Halladj', *Encyclopaedia of Islam*, 1st edn, vol. II (Leiden, 1913), pp. 239–40.
33 'Hamza', *Da'irat al-ma'arif*, vol. VII, pp. 177–214; 'Hakim bi amrihi', ibid., vol. VI, pp. 650–9.
34 Beirut, 1859.   35 *Da'irat al-ma'arif*, vol. VI, pp. 9–20.
36 Ibid., vol. VII, pp. 120–2.
37 Ibid., pp. 132–3.

one, but the most important in the history of civilization'.[38] This is
the profession of faith of the encyclopaedia. It is an attempt to
bring the whole of European civilization into the Arabic language,
and by so doing to take the 'people of the Arabic language' and
their inherited culture into the new world created by modern
Europe. Arab and Muslim history becomes a part of world
history, and not even a privileged part, but one to be thought and
written about in the same way as anything else, and judged by the
same criteria, freedom (*hurriyya*), and civilization (*tamaddun*).[39]

Thus the encyclopaedia symbolizes an opening of the Arabic
language to the modern world, and an opening of the modern
world's culture to Arabic and Islamic themes. It is also an
opening in a third sense. For the Bustanis, Arabic belongs equally
to all those who use it, and so does what is expressed in it. For the
first time, perhaps, Arabic-speaking Christians are writing about
Islamic themes in the same tone of voice as about others. *Da'irat
al-ma'arif* marked a stage in the process by which they tried to
appropriate Muslim history and culture as their own and 'entrer
... dans l'histoire arabe par la grande porte'.[40]

---

[38] 'Urubba', ibid., vol. IV, pp. 606–20.
[39] 'Hurriyya', ibid., vol. VII, pp. 2–4; 'Tamaddun', ibid., vol. VI, pp. 213–5.
[40] Berque, *Arabies*, p. 133.

9

SULAIMAN AL-BUSTANI AND THE *ILIAD*

IN a famous study of contemporary Arabic literature, published in 1928, H. A. R. Gibb remarked that the social and literary flowering of Lebanon in the last decades of the nineteenth century 'still awaits a historian'.[1] In the half century or so since he wrote, something has been done to fill the gap, but certain important figures have still not received what is due to them, and there are unanswered questions about the origins and nature of the movement. One matter which has aroused controversy is that of the extent to which it sprang from forces inside the Lebanese and Syrian community, or was the product of the work of schools founded by western missionaries, in particular French Jesuits and American Protestants. In his *Arab Awakening*, George Antonius laid emphasis upon the role of the Americans: 'The intellectual effervescence which marked the first stirrings of the Arab revival owes most to their labours.'[2] A. L. Tibawi, however, believed that to say this was to exaggerate: the influence of the missionaries upon the cultural movement was more limited than Antonius stated, and, in so far as it existed, it was a by-product of activities directed to other ends.[3] His arguments were cogent and valid up to a point, but we should not ignore the influence which a small group of serious and well-educated men must have had in the society of a town growing rapidly, and opening to the outside world, such as was Beirut in the later nineteenth century. This influence was not confined to the graduates of the American schools but spread beyond them, to many of those who worked or had contact with the schools, consulates and trading houses of

---

[1] 'Studies in contemporary Arabic literature' in H. A. R. Gibb, *Studies on the Civilization of Islam* (London, 1962), p. 305.

[2] *The Arab Awakening* (London, 1938), p. 43.

[3] *American Interests in Syria 1800–1901* (Oxford, 1966).

Beirut. To write about one of them may, therefore, be an appropriate tribute to Malcolm Kerr, and to the University with which he was so closely linked.

It is generally agreed that one of the central figures of the Lebanese *Nahda*, the renaissance of culture, was Butrus al-Bustani (1819–83), teacher, journalist and encyclopaedist. Much has been written about him, and deservedly so, and in what is written some reference is usually made to those members of his family whom he inspired and who worked with him. One of them deserves more than a passing mention. Already in 1928 Gibb could say of Sulaiman al-Bustani that he was 'the outstanding representative of the Christian Syrian community in the last decades of the century, with all its eager, many-sided activities and restless wanderings'.[4]

The Maronite Christian family of Bustani had its origin in the district of Bsharri in northern Lebanon. Some members of it are said to have moved to the small town of Dair al-Qamar in the Shuf district during the sixteenth century, and from there they spread to other towns and villages of the southern half of Lebanon.[5] It was in the village of Bkashtin in Shuf that Sulaiman was born in 1856, one of four brothers all of whom made their mark in the life of Lebanon and the Lebanese diaspora. He received his first instruction in Arabic from his uncle 'Abdallah, formerly Maronite archbishop of Tyre and Sidon, and then at the age of seven was sent to the National School (*al-Madrasa al-wataniyya*) newly founded by his kinsman Butrus in Beirut.[6] He remained there for eight years, from 1863 to 1871, and this period was decisive for the formation of his mind. The curriculum of the school included English and French as well as Arabic and Turkish, and he later recorded the influence upon him of the English poetry he read, and in particular a kind of poetry scarcely familiar to Arab readers, narrative and epic; he memorized part of Milton's *Paradise Lost* and Scott's *Lady of the Lake*.[7] He must have been affected

[4] 'Contemporary Arabic Literature' in *Studies*, p. 250.
[5] For Bustani's ancestry and life, see: F. A. Bustani, 'Sulaiman al-Bustani', *al-Mashriq*, 23 (1925), pp. 778–91, 824–43, 908–26; M. Sawaya, *Sulaiman al-Bustani wa Iliyadhat Humirus* (Beirut, n.d.); J. Hashim, *Sulaiman al-Bustani wa'l-Iliyadha* (Beirut, 1960); J. Abdel-Nour, 'al-Bustani', *Encyclopaedia of Islam*, 2nd edn, suppls. 3–4 (Leiden, 1981), pp. 161–2; C. Brockelmann, *Geschichte der Arabischen Litteratur*, suppl. 3 (Leiden, 1942), pp. 348–52.
[6] A. L. Tibawi, 'The American Missionaries in Beirut and Butrus al-Bustani' in A. Hourani, ed., *Saint Antony's Papers 16: Middle Eastern Studies*, vol. III (London, 1963), 171–2.
[7] Hashim, *Sulaiman al-Bustani*, p. 14.

too by the political and social ideas of Butrus: the idea of a Syrian community in which Muslims and Christians lived in amity within a reformed Ottoman empire, and that of an Arabic culture open to the new world. Echoes of such ideas were to appear in his own writings a generation later.

After leaving school Sulaiman worked for a few years in Beirut, teaching, writing for the various periodicals which Butrus founded, and working as dragoman at the consulate of the United States. In 1876 he went to Iraq, first to Basra and then Baghdad. He worked for a time in a trading company which exported dates, and seems also to have held posts in the local Ottoman government. He may now have become aware of the reforms in the administration and economy of the province introduced by Midhat Pasha when he was governor a few years earlier; this too was an influence which was to last, and to be reflected in later writings of his. In this period he married the daughter of a local Chaldaean Catholic, but, according to his biographers, the marriage was not successful.[8]

It was perhaps his work in the date trade, mingled with a certain intellectual curiosity, which led him in these years to undertake some journeys, unusual for a man of his time and place, in the Arabian peninsula. He is said to have visited Najd, Hadramawt and Yemen, and his observations on the life of the Arabian nomads were recorded later, in a series of articles in al-Muqtataf in 1887–8;[9] his description of Beduin society shows a curiosity unusual in men of the towns and mountain villages of the Mediterranean littoral, and can perhaps be explained by the interest in classical Arabic poetry which was typical of the *Nahda*.

By 1885 he was back in Beirut, helping to write and edit the first Arabic encyclopaedia, *Da'irat al-ma'arif*, begun by Butrus al-Bustani and continued after his death in 1883 by his son Salim, and then, after Salim died in 1884, by two other sons, Nasib and Najib, with help from Sulaiman.[10] Some more years of wandering followed – in India, Iran and Iraq once more – and then seven years (1891–8) spent mainly in Istanbul; during this period he was appointed Ottoman commissioner at the great exhibition, the World's Columbian Exposition, held in Chicago in 1893.

He seems to have spent the ten years from 1898 to 1908 mainly

---

[8] Sawaya, *Sulaiman al-Bustani*, p. 18.
[9] 'al-Badu', *al-Muqtataf*, 12 (1887–8), pp. 141–7, 202–7, 270–4.
[10] *Da'irat al-ma'arif*, 11 vols. (Beirut/Cairo, 1876–1900).

in Cairo. Little information is available about his work and life during this period, but his main preoccupation was revealed when, in 1904, the Hilal Press, founded in Cairo by another Lebanese man of letters, Jurji Zaidan, published his translation of the *Iliad*, the fruit of many years of work, begun, as he tells us, in 1887, and pursued in the midst of travel and work, 'in the mountains, on the decks of ships, and in railway carriages'.[11]

This was the first translation of the *Iliad*, and indeed of any of the poetry of the ancient Greeks, into Arabic. The later classical tradition which the Arabs inherited was one in which the literature of ancient Greece was not so familiar as it had been. The works of Greek philosophy which were translated during the 'Abbasid period carried occasional references to Homer and other poets, and their names were therefore known, but a statement of al-Jahiz expresses what may have been the common attitude towards the translation of poetry, as being both unnecessary and impossible:

Only the Arabs and people who speak Arabic have a correct understanding of poetry. Poems do not lend themselves to translation and ought not to be translated. When they are translated, their structure is rent; the meter is no longer correct; poetic beauty disappears and nothing worthy of admiration remains in the poems.[12]

One of the main characteristics of the *Nahda* was a widening of awareness. As early as 1859, Butrus al-Bustani, in a lecture on Arabic literature and culture, had pointed out that the strength and independence of the Arabic poetic tradition had prevented it acquiring or borrowing anything from Homer, Virgil or others of the ancients; in the present age, the Arabic language could only be raised from its low state if, among much else, there were translations from foreign languages.[13] The fourth volume of his encyclopaedia, published in 1880, contains a fairly long and well-informed article about Homer, presumably drawn from American or European works of reference; it gives the generally accepted version of the life of Homer, summarizes the story of the *Iliad* and *Odyssey*, and shows knowledge of the discussions about authorship, method of composition and transmission, and his-

---

[11] *Iliyadhat Humirus* (Cairo, 1904), p. 72.
[12] Quoted in F. Rosenthal, *The Classical Heritage in Islam* (London, 1965), p. 18. For Arab knowledge and use of Greek poetic theory, see, W. Heinrichs, *Arabische Dichtung und Griechische Poetik* (Beirut, 1969).
[13] *Khutba fi adab al-'arab* (Beirut, 1859), pp. 15f.

torical authenticity which were current in the classical scholarship of modern Europe.[14] It may have been this article which gave
strength to the interest in narrative poetry which had been
aroused in Sulaiman by his early reading of *Paradise Lost*, and gave
direction to the desire to revive the Arabic language and its
culture which he had acquired in the school of Butrus al-Bustani.

The translation is a book of a kind which had never appeared in
Arabic before: a handsome, well-produced volume of 1,260 pages,
with an introduction, a running commentary, indexes and illustrations in the text. The introduction of 200 pages is perhaps the
part which will have the greatest interest for a modern reader. Its
aim is to introduce Homer and the *Iliad* to a reading public which
was scarcely aware of them. The traditional version of the poet's
life is given, in a form which perhaps would not have been
acceptable to most Homeric scholars of the late nineteenth
century. For the most part Bustani follows the biography attributed to Herodotus; he expresses some doubts about it, but thinks
it more worthy of credence than later versions. He does, however,
show a general knowledge of the Homeric scholarship of the
century, of the 'Homeric question' as it had been posed by
scholars from the time of the *Prolegomena* of F. A. Wolf (1759–
1824). Was the poem the work of a single man called Homer? Was
it written by him, or composed, memorized and transmitted
orally? How far could its narrative be regarded as preserving
genuine historical events? Bustani's response to such questions on
the whole is a conservative one. He believes that the *Iliad* is the
work of a single poet; the unity between its different parts, and the
consistency in the characterization of the main personalities, seem
to him to prove this. He finds no difficulty in the theory that it was
recited, and gives examples from his own Arabian travels of tribal
poets memorizing long poems. (He was writing, of course, long
before the work of Milman Parry and Albert Lord threw new light
on the ways in which oral narrative poetry was composed and
transmitted.[15]) He does not think it necessary to accept that the
narrative is historically authentic.[16]

Of more lasting interest is Bustani's discussion of the problems
of translating the poem. He begins by asking why it had not been
translated earlier. Homer was known by name to Arab writers of
the classical period; he refers to Ibn Abi Usaibi'a, al-Biruni and

[14] *Da'irat al-ma'arif*, vol. IV (Beirut, 1880), pp. 691–3.
[15] A. B. Lord, *The Singer of Tales* (New York, 1971).
[16] *Iliyadhat Humirus*, pp. 9f.

Ibn Khaldun, who had some knowledge of Greek poets by way of Plato and Aristotle. If he was not translated, there were, Bustani suggests, three kinds of reason. Those who translated works of Greek philosophy and science in the 'Abbasid period were for the most part not Arabs, and did not know Arabic well enough to translate poetry, and Arabic poets did not know Greek. Incentive and patronage were lacking; the 'Abbasid Caliphs who patronized the translators wanted works of medicine and philosophy, not literature, and most later dynasties were not great patrons of learning and culture. Equally important, however, was a reason of another kind: the strangeness of the Homeric world, and in particular Homer's description of the life of the gods. This had posed a problem for Christians, but for Muslims the problem was even graver: the multiplicity of the Homeric gods, and their modes of behaviour, could not be reconciled with the tenets of their faith.[17]

Times had changed, however, and Bustani believed that there was now a pressing need to give Homer to the Arabic reader. Homer was a very great poet, and had had a deep influence on the whole of European poetry. Poets had ransacked his work freely and openly; Bustani gives examples from Virgil, Tasso, Milton and Voltaire (all quoted in their original languages).[18] To translate him would help that revival and expansion of the Arabic language, in order to make it adequate to all the needs of modern life, which was one of the main purposes of the *Nahda*.

It was for this reason that he decided to translate the *Iliad*. He tells us that he began by trying to translate it from English and French, but soon came up against the inconsistencies of the various renderings. He had to go back to the original; his first teacher of ancient Greek was a French Jesuit in Cairo, and later, when he lived in Istanbul, he received help from Greeks living there.[19] Acquiring a sufficient knowledge of Greek was only the first of his problems, however. More fundamental were the problems posed by the differences between the European and Arabic poetic traditions. There were no epic or lengthy narrative poems in classical Arabic (although they existed in the vernacular tradition), and the conventions of Arabic literature made it difficult to write narrative poetry. The norm was the *qasida* or ode, with a single metre and a single rhyme running through it from beginning to end; blank verse was unknown. The poem was built up by a skilful juxtaposition of lines or couplets. Each line tended to be a separate unit of meaning; the poem as a whole might have

[17] Ibid., pp. 63f.   [18] Ibid., pp. 181f.   [19] Ibid., pp. 70–2.

a structural unity, but it was difficult to carry on a narrative from one line to another.[20] Bustani's solution to this problem was not without ingenuity. He divided the *Iliad* into shorter units – an episode or a speech – preserved the unity of metre and rhyme within each unit, and chose for each of them the metre and form which seemed appropriate to it.

The strangeness of the Homeric world to readers of Arabic also created difficulties. The names of Homer's protagonists sounded strange in Arabic; Bustani was not always successful in devising forms which would not seem too discordant. The physical world of Homer's heroes, and still more of his gods, was alien; how to convey to the reader that gods ate and drank, and how could 'nectar' and 'ambrosia' be translated? Manners, customs and moral ideals would not be easily recognizable. It was for this reason that the translation could not be published by itself. The commentary, which runs from page to page, gives parallels to Homer's images and descriptions drawn from Arabic poetry; Bustani says that he read the works of 200 poets for this purpose. The introduction was no less necessary. Part of it contains a history and description of Arabic poetry in its various phases. The conclusion is drawn that, if Homer's poetry is to be understood, it should be seen as the Greek equivalent of the poetry of the *Jahiliyya*; the world which Homer described was analogous to that of Arabia before the coming of Islam.[21]

There was another range of problems, those which confront all translators of poetry. Should the translation be literal, or should it try to recreate the poem in another language and poetic tradition? Bustani had thought about this and come to clear conclusions. His translation should take away nothing and add nothing (although he did in fact eliminate some repetition of epithets); and it should render the poem into real Arabic, so that 'when the reader reads it, he is reading Arabic and not a foreign language'.[22]

Like all methods of translating poetry, this one has its dangers, and those who have written about Bustani's *Iliad* believe that he did not completely avoid them. In her important work on modern Arabic poetry, Salma Jayyusi says that Bustani was 'too much under the influence of the Arabic poetic spirit', and was therefore

---

[20] M. M. Badawi, review of M. Zwettler, 'The oral tradition of classical Arabic poetry', *Journal of Semitic Studies*, 25 (1980), pp. 285–6; J. Maisami, 'Arabic and Persian concepts of poetic form', *Proceedings of the International Comparative Literature Association, 10th Congress* (New York, 1982), pp. 146–9.

[21] Bustani, *Iliyadhat Humirus*, pp. 167f.   [22] Ibid., pp. 95–6.

unable fully to absorb and express the spirit of the original.[23] In a careful and sympathetic analysis of the translation of book 6, Andras Hamori comes to a similar conclusion. The translation, he tells us, is

a mirror of the Arabic tradition opening up to foreign works, although not yet relinquishing its own conventions ... Bustani used the received idiom in places where it flawed certain aspects of the Homeric narrative ... He failed his Homer in precision and economy; he could not hold on to the power that issues from austerity or the exact coupling of situation and emotion ... It is an example of unpreparedness: not of linguistic or philological unpreparedness, where homework could be done and scholars consulted, but of a more fundamental kind for which he cannot be reproached and which he could not remedy.[24]

This is perhaps not very different from what Bentley told Pope: 'It is a pretty poem, Mr Pope, but you must not call it Homer.'[25] Pope was a great poet, and no one has said that of Bustani, but he might have argued that he was trying to do what Pope had done: his purpose, like Pope's, was that of 'inventing an idiom that could mediate effectively between disparate worlds'.[26] This expression is that of the latest biographer of Pope, who goes on to suggest that 'every historical period ... reformulates the great poetry of the past partly by its own conceptions of that greatness and that past as well as by its own views of what constitutes poetry and the art of translation'.[27] Bustani could at least have claimed that he had given his readers a Homer they could understand and appreciate, a poet who wrote in language they considered appropriate to a great theme. A reader of our time might find the language stilted and artificial, but at least he might give Bustani credit – as Salma Jayyusi does – for having initiated that 'opening up to foreign works' which has enabled Arabic poets of today to draw images and symbols from the myths and legends of the whole world.[28]

The publication of Bustani's *Iliad* was received with much applause. A dinner was given for him in June 1904 at Shepheard's Hotel in Cairo. This seems to have been a unique occasion, bringing together the most important writers of the day, both Egyptians and Lebanese living in Egypt: the poets Ahmad

---

[23] *Trends and Movements in Modern Arabic Poetry*, 2 vols. (Leiden, 1977), vol. I, p. 66.
[24] 'Reality and convention in book six of Bustani's *Iliad*', *Journal of Semitic Studies*, 23 (1978), pp. 95–101.
[25] M. Mack, *Alexander Pope: A Life* (New Haven, Conn., 1985), p. 348.
[26] Ibid., p. 269.
[27] Ibid., p. 348. [28] *Trends*, vol. II, p. 721.

Shawqi, Hafiz Ibrahim and Khalil Mutran, the scholar Ibrahim al-Yaziji, the journalists Faris Nimr, Ya'qub Sarruf, Jurji Zaidan and Jibra'il Taqla, and two future Prime Ministers, Sa'd Zaghlul and 'Abd al-Khaliq Sarwat. Muhammad 'Abduh could not be present but sent a message. His support of something which opened the minds of Arab readers to the culture of Europe is not difficult to understand, but it is more surprising to find that Rashid Rida, the editor of al-Manar and stern custodian of the inherited values of the religion of Islam, is reported to have been present and to have made a speech.[29] Long articles appeared in leading Arabic periodicals, al-Muqtataf in Cairo and al-Mashriq in Beirut,[30] and some European orientalists expressed their appreciation. In a long and thoughtful review, the Laudian Professor of Arabic at Oxford, D. S. Margoliouth, pointed out the difficulties which Bustani had faced, and praised him for his thorough command of the Arabic language and the excellence of his versification, although he found the translation sometimes too free.[31] The German Arabist Martin Hartmann called the translation

a masterly work which deserves the highest praise, and a monument of unwearying application combined with high intelligence, remarkable knowledge and distinguished poetic craftsmanship.[32]

Four years later, in 1908, Bustani's life was suddenly transformed by a public event, the Ottoman revolution which ended the autocratic rule of Sultan Abdülhamid II and restored the constitution. His experiences during his years of residence in Istanbul had made him an opponent of the autocracy, and he must have had contacts with the constitutionalist opposition, in Istanbul or Cairo. Almost immediately after the revolution he published a book which shows his sympathy with the ideas of the Committee of Union and Progress. In a letter a few years later, he told his correspondent that the book was written in three weeks and printed in about a month, so as to be ready for distribution to members of the Chamber which was about to be elected:

The optimism which prevails in it was not only judged indispensable for the encouragement of a new constitutional regime struggling for the regeneration of a quasi-condemned empire, but this was and still is the sincere conviction

---

[29] al-Muqtataf, 29 (1904), pp. 610–18; Hashim, Sulaiman al-Bustani, p. 143.
[30] al-Muqtataf, 29 (1904), pp. 497–510; al-Mashriq, 7 (1904), pp. 780–1, 865–71, 911–19, 1118–26, 1138–43.
[31] Journal of the Royal Asiatic Society (1905), pp. 417–23.
[32] Der Islamische Orient: vol. III, Unpolitische Briefe aus der Türkei (Leipzig, 1910), p. 236.

of the author, provided that the right ways of administering the country were followed.[33]

The book, therefore, has something of the nature of an extended political pamphlet.

'Ibra wa dhikra contains both a criticism of the past and a plan of action for the future.[34] The critique of the absolute rule of Abdülhamid gains strength from the way in which it is expressed. The mistakes and excesses are not seen in the perspective of an imaginary utopia, or of an unreal contrast with western Europe: they are contrasted with the achievements of the reign of Sultan Abdülaziz (1861–76), when the Ottoman empire had seemed to be on the right path of reform, and a young, high-minded and well-educated Lebanese Christian could hope to serve his people by serving the state. The example which Bustani holds up is that of Midhat Pasha, who had been Grand Vizir briefly in 1876–7, and had finally been killed by Abdülhamid's officials in prison in al-Ta'if; the book is dedicated to his memory. Beyond the age of Abdülaziz, the book looks back to the age of Ottoman greatness as Bustani imagines it: an age of religious tolerance and of local autonomy in the mountain districts.

The criticism covers the whole range of life in society. All Ottomans, including the highest officials of the government, have gone in fear, spied upon and denounced by secret agents. There has been no freedom of association or publication; all books have had to be submitted to censorship by the Council of Education. Official schools have been subject to severe control; foreign schools have been a little freer, but their defect is that they have created 'a division in our minds'.[35] What is perhaps most harmful is the spirit of fanaticism (*ta'assub*) which has been rampant, and has been encouraged for political and personal profit. Bustani has in mind the Armenian massacres which he had himself witnessed in Istanbul in the 1890s, and also the civil war and massacres of 1860 in the Lebanon of his childhood: before 1841, he points out, there had been political factions in Lebanon, but from 1841 onwards political divisions had become religious ones.[36]

If we look for the causes of all this, he suggests, we should find it

---

[33] Letter to T. W. Arnold, 10 June 1913. I must thank Dr B. Abu Manneh for drawing my attention to this letter, and for a number of helpful suggestions and criticisms.

[34] *'Ibra wa dhikra; aw al-dawla al 'uthmaniyya qabl al-dustur wa ba'duahu* (A Lesson and a Memory: or The Ottoman State Before the Constitution and After It) (Cairo, 1904; reprinted Beirut, 1978). References are to the original edition.

[35] Ibid., p. 38. [36] Ibid., pp. 90f.

first of all in the tyranny, caprice and uncertainty of unrestrained absolute rule. He does not mention Sultan Abdülhamid by name. The sultan was still on the throne, and, in the first moment of euphoria after the revolution, it was possible to believe that a sultan shorn of his powers would co-operate with the new constitutional government; the explicit criticism is therefore not of him but of his entourage, the courtiers of the *Mabayn*.

There was, in Bustani's view, a more fundamental cause of the ills from which the empire suffered, and that was the absence of unity between the different groups of which it was composed. No attempt had been made by the Ottoman sultans to draw Muslims and non-Muslims, Turks and non-Turks, into a single community, and there had been two omissions of particular importance: non-Muslims had not been conscripted into the army to serve alongside Muslims, and knowledge of the Turkish language had not been spread.[37] As a consequence, there had been no sense of unity to check and balance the sense of solidarity of more limited groups, whether religious or ethnic (*jinsi*); in the absence of an overriding sense of unity, particular loyalties, reinforced by ignorance and prejudice, had led naturally to fanaticism and all its consequences.

Bustani is dealing in fact with the basic problem which had faced those who tried to change the nature of the Ottoman state in the nineteenth century. If the empire was to survive in the modern world, it could no longer be a group of disparate communities held together by armed force and obedience to a ruling family; it needed a unity of consciousness which would create an active moral link between rulers and ruled. It might have been expected that Bustani, with his care for the revival of the Arabic language, would have been touched by the ideas of the Arab decentralizers or separatists, but there is no sign of this; he may have believed that an Arab or Syrian state would face the same kind of problem as the empire, but be less able to resolve it because it would have less freedom of action.

His remedy is that of the Committee of Union and Progress (CUP) during its first period of power, before the internal tensions of its ideology moved it in the direction of Turkish nationalism. The basic principle is that there is an Ottoman nation: 'Thank God, we have not ceased to be a living people.'[38] Between the different groups which compose the nation, there is a need for

[37] Ibid., p. 98.   [38] Ibid., p. 197.

'solidarity and cooperation', and for mutual toleration. Bustani asserts that Christians and Jews have had more liberty in the Ottoman empire than in Europe.[39] There is a certain exaggeration in this, but it is not difficult to understand what he means: he is thinking of the freedom of Christian villages in the mountains, and the wide powers of the religious communities. At the same time, he does not believe, however, that the empire should become something different from what it has always been: the Muslim element is the strongest pillar of the Ottoman *umma*, and the Turks have always been its defenders and the possessors of power in it.

How could unity and co-operation be achieved? Some chapters of the book deal with the political system, in a way which does not show great originality: the Chamber of Deputies should not obstruct the government in carrying out reforms, the members of the Chamber should not act simply as representatives of local interests.[40] Of greater interest are the chapters on economic development, in which the lessons learnt during his years in Iraq can be seen.[41] The empire needs modern industry, and this demands better communications, an Ottoman merchant navy, and above all public confidence; Ottoman citizens do not have the confidence to invest in Ottoman companies. Agriculture must be extended, and this will need better security, schemes of irrigation and better communications, and above all greater care for the welfare of the cultivators. Here an unusual note is struck, and a reader may become aware that Bustani is not a member of the Ottoman urban elite, and his own roots lie in the countryside. The Ottoman lands are full of potential cultivators, but they need help if they are to become producers. There are immigrants from elsewhere: the refugees from the lost provinces of the empire, Bosnians, Cretans and Circassians, need help in settlement; another group of immigrants, those in Palestine, have their own organizations and facilities, and do not need help. (There is no sign in the book of concern about the implications of Zionist immigration, although a few years later Bustani is said to have opposed the sale of certain lands in Palestine to Jewish interests.) In the vast areas of Iraq the beduin should be persuaded to become farmers. Some of them are already used to cultivation, and all they need is a good system of tax-collection and elementary education. Others have never farmed, and they will need

[39] Ibid., p. 20.   [40] Ibid., p. 193.   [41] Ibid., pp. 138f.

special inducements to settle on the land: training, and exemption from taxation for an initial period.

When elections took place for the first Ottoman parliament after the revolution, Bustani was chosen as one of the two deputies for Beirut; he stood as one of the candidates of the CUP, and *al-Hilal* states that his election was unanimous, and praises him for his truthfulness, lack of exaggeration and freedom from envy.[42] For the next few years he stood near the centre of Ottoman politics, not possessing the kind of support which would give him real political weight, but by all accounts greatly respected. In his annual report for 1908, the British Ambassador calls him 'a man of considerable learning and breadth of view ... His rendering of the Odyssey [sic] is reported to be exceptionally good'.[43] He was an active member of the Chamber, becoming its vice-president as well as chairman of several committees: he was a member of the mission to the courts of Europe which announced the succession of Sultan Mehmed V in 1909. He was later appointed as a member of the Senate, and at the end of 1913, after the CUP *coup d'état*, became Minister for Commerce, Agriculture, Forests and Mines in the government headed by Said Halim Pasha but in fact dominated by the 'triumvirate' of Enver, Talaat and Jemal.

In this ministry, Bustani did not belong to the inner ring of those who made the great decisions, but he appears to have taken an active interest in the affairs of his department and to have initiated several measures of reform. He was concerned about the financial position of the empire, and discussed with the Ambassador of the United States, Henry Morgenthau, the possibility of an American loan. Morgenthau called him one of the most popularly respected members of the Ministry.[44]

As a minister, he was involved in the agonizing discussions about the Ottoman attitude towards the European war which broke out in August 1914. There were three main groups among the ministers: those who believed that the empire should enter the war on the side of Germany, those who were prepared to go some way towards helping Germany but were not willing to enter the war, at least until the situation became clearer, and those who supported a policy of strict neutrality, on the grounds that the

---

[42] *al-Hilal*, 17 (1908–9), pp. 177f.
[43] G. P. Gooch and H. W. V. Temperley, eds., *British Documents on the Origins of the War 1898–1914*, vol. V (1928), p. 279.
[44] *Ambassador Morgenthau's Story* (London, 1918), pp. 37, 121.

empire could not survive another conflict after the Balkan and Italian wars. Bustani belonged to the third group, along with the Grand Vizir and the Minister of Finance, Djavid. The decision was not made by the full ministry, however, but by the small inner group, and in particular by Enver. When the decision came, and the empire entered the war, Bustani resigned, together with some of those who thought like him.

There is little more to tell of his life. He spent the years of the war in Switzerland. He may have been involved in abortive schemes for the Ottoman empire to make a separate peace; he was ill and spent some time in hospital: his eyesight was beginning to fail. When the war ended he went to Egypt, and a little later to the United States at the invitation of Lebanese emigrants there. He was received with honour by the Lebanese literati of New York – Nu'ima, Jibran, Abu Madi – but his health continued to decline, and he died in America in 1925.

His body was brought back to Beirut and buried in Lebanon, where he had not lived much since his youth, but for which he had the longing typical of the emigrant and wanderer.[45] His death and burial were the occasion for numerous obituary articles which disclose, beneath the conventional words of praise, the lineaments of his personality: a modest, unworldly, deeply cultivated man.[46] He would probably have wished to be remembered for his translation of the *Iliad*, and the tribute which might have pleased him most is that which Andras Hamori paid him half a century later: the translation

remains a monument to an adventurous mind, and to a literary man whom it would have been a pleasure to know.[47]

---

[45] Hashim, *Sulaiman al-Bustani*, p. 161.
[46] *al-Muqtataf*, 67 (1925), pp. 241–7; Bustani, 'Sulaiman al-Bustani', pp. 829f.
[47] Hamori, 'Reality and convention', p. 101.

INDEX